SO-BAE-526

The Maritime Dimension

The Maritime Dimension

Edited by
R. P. BARSTON
Department of Politics, University of Lancaster
and
PATRICIA BIRNIE
Faculty of Law, Edinburgh University

London
GEORGE ALLEN & UNWIN
Boston   Sydney

JX
4411
M27

First published in 1980

This book is copyright under the Berne Convention. All rights
are reserved. Apart from any fair dealing for the purpose of
private study, research, criticism or review, as permitted under
the Copyright Act, 1956, no part of this publication may be
reproduced, stored in a retrieval system, or transmitted, in any
form or by any means, electronic, electrical, chemical, mechanical, optical, photocopying, recording or otherwise, without the
prior permission of the copyright owner. Enquiries should be
sent to the publishers at the undermentioned address:

GEORGE ALLEN & UNWIN LTD
40 Museum Street, London WC1A 1LU

© George Allen & Unwin (Publishers) Ltd. 1980

British Library Cataloguing in Publication Data

The maritime dimension.
  1. Maritime law   2. International relations
I. Barston, Ronald Peter   II. Birnie, Patricia
320.1′2′09162   JX4411   80-40751

ISBN 0-04-341015-4
ISBN 0-04-341016-2 Pbk

Set in 10 on 11 point Times by Servis Filmsetting, Manchester
and printed in Great Britain by
Lowe & Brydone Ltd, Thetford, Norfolk

3 3001 00664 8751

Contents

322856

Acknowledgements

A number of people have directly and indirectly contributed to the preparation of this book. Not all are mentioned here but our thanks nevertheless go to them. Officials in several national administrations and international organisations were generous of their time, and though often hard pressed, were willing to give interviews and discuss issues. In particular our thanks go to officials in IMCO, FAO, and UNCLOS Secretariat in Geneva and the UN Information Centre in London, who speedily provided documents and gave helpful advice. The Greenwich Forum has organised valuable meetings which have drawn scholars and officials from a wide variety of areas. A research grant from the University of Lancaster enabled work to be carried out in Geneva. *Trawling Times* – the journal of the British Fishing Federation – was a valuable source of information and comment on British as well as international fisheries questions, until it very regrettably ceased publication in mid 1979.

Brian Taylor of NERC has given considerable support over a number of years. Professor Olav Knudsen (University of Oslo) also gave a considerable amount of his time, whilst visiting professor at Lancaster, to discuss his research work on multilateral maritime conferences. Finally our thanks go to Annette Stoddart, Sue Unsworth and Pat Demery who typed parts of the manuscript.

Notes on Contributors

RONALD P. BARSTON is lecturer in international relations in the department of politics at the University of Lancaster. He is also director of the Foreign Service Training Programme. He was educated at the University College of Wales, Aberystwyth (department of international politics). From 1974 to 1976 he was seconded to the Foreign and Commonwealth Office. His publications include *The Other Powers* (London: Allen & Unwin, 1973).

PATRICIA BIRNIE is an honours graduate in jurisprudence of Oxford University, and is also a barrister (Gray's Inn). She has taught public international law at Edinburgh University since 1966. Her special interest is the law of the sea and she has published widely in this field. She recently acted as a specialist adviser on the legal aspects of fisheries and oil pollution to the Department of Trade Sub-Committee of the House of Commons Select Committee on Expenditure. She is on the editorial board of *Marine Policy* and a member of the Advisory Committee on Oil Pollution of the Sea (ACOPS) Legal and Policy Committee.

DR PAUL DRIVER is director of the Lancashire and Western Sea Fisheries Joint Committee, the body responsible for inshore fisheries management and pollution control on the west coast of Britain between Barrow-in-Furness and Cardigan. His main interest is in shellfish fisheries and he has published widely on this as well as other fisheries subjects. His work with the Sea Fisheries Committee has been concerned with general fisheries management problems, some examples of which are described in 'Fishery problems of Morecambe Bay' in E. Nelson-Smith and E. M. Bridges (eds), *Problems of a Small Estuary* (Swansea: Institute of Marine Studies, 1977).

DR VICTOR PRESCOTT was educated at King's College, Durham University, and obtained his doctorate from the University of London. After spending five years as a lecturer in geography at University College, Ibadan, Nigeria, he went to the department of geography in the University of Melbourne in 1961 and is currently a reader in geography. He has written seven books on political geography in general and international land and maritime boundaries in particular, and has shared the authorship of four others which include studies of Antarctica, *Last of lands – Antarctica*, and *Australia's Continental Shelf*.

DR PETER ODELL graduated in geography from the University of Birmingham and after service with the RAF worked for the Shell International Petroleum Company in its economic division in London. He has taught at the London School of Economics and in 1968 was appointed to the chair in economic geography at the Netherlands School of Economics, now part of the Erasmus University, Rotterdam, where he is also director of the Economic Geography Institute. He has published widely on energy and resource questions, including *Oil and World Power*, *The Optimal Development of the North Seas Oilfields* (with K. E. Rosing) and *The Pressures of Oil* (with L. Vallenilla).

CHRISTOPHER HAYMAN has been involved with the shipping industry for eight years. After reading history at Oxford he spent some time in general journalism and broadcasting in Canada before joining *Seatrade* magazine in the UK. He was editor of *Seatrade* from 1973 to 1978. He is now publisher and managing director of *Seatrade* and other magazines in the City Press group, including the recently relaunched *Transport* magazine.

PETER NAILOR is professor of history, and head of the department of history and international affairs at the Royal Naval College, Greenwich. He was formerly professor of politics at the University of Lancaster and has held visiting chairs and fellowships at Carleton University, Ottawa and the Australian National University. His publications include articles and monographs on Western European security issues, strategic concepts and British defence interests, and naval administration.

Introduction

R. P. BARSTON AND P. W. BIRNIE

Throughout history man has used and been involved with the sea. It is only comparatively recently, however, within the last twenty years or so, that maritime issues – arising out of the use, exploration and exploitation of the sea and its resources – have come to have much greater importance in international relations.[1] Today, a wide variety of events such as maritime boundary disputes, fisheries conflicts, major oil tanker accidents and sessions of the Law of the Sea Conference regularly feature in the international press and are accorded importance on the foreign policy agendas of growing number of states. Less publicised, but still an important part of the maritime dimension, are bilateral and multilateral issues such as the establishment of rules and standards for controlling pollution, vessel designs and the routing of ships in congested or vulnerable sea areas. Whilst many of these issues are handled at a technical level they can from time to time become highly politicised when linked with other policy areas.

THE CHANGING IMPORTANCE OF MARITIME ISSUES

There are four general reasons for the increased importance of maritime questions in international relations since the early 1960s. In the first place, the growing number of fisheries disputes from the late 1950s onwards reflected greater world fishing effort and the corresponding dissatisfaction felt by coastal states with the ineffectiveness of international fisheries organisations at establishing acceptable catch limits and conservation regulations. By the mid 1960s world fish production had in fact more than doubled to 67 million metric tons, of which an ever-growing percentage was being used for animal protein and industrial requirements. Increased catches during this period were made possible by rapid advances in marine acoustic technology, net design and the gradual replacement of ageing prewar vessels. The development too of large mobile factory fleets, particularly by the Soviet Union and Japan, operating at considerable distances from home bases and able to stay away for several months, exacerbated the problem of overfishing and made international regulation more difficult. Additionally, a number of countries bordering on the North Sea began to switch their fishing effort in the 1950s to the distant water ground off Iceland and the Barents Sea as the North Sea became less profitable.

In response to these and other pressures Iceland became the first of the Scandinavian states to challenge the traditional fisheries limits by declaring a 50 mile limit in July 1971, which was implemented in September 1972 and subsequently extended to 200 nautical miles. The resultant bitter conflict with the United Kingdom – the third of the Anglo-Icelandic Cod Wars since 1945 – had serious implications for the management of fisheries in the North Atlantic, as well as being, in the shorter term at least, a divisive issue within NATO.[2]

The Icelandic action, along with that of Canada, which the previous year had established a 100 nautical mile Arctic waters pollution zone, served as a catalyst on the law of the sea debate over maritime limits. Iceland too had now joined the minority group of mostly Latin American states claiming 200 nautical mile limits – a decision the European states in particular could not ignore. For the United Kingdom, the loss of access to the Icelandic waters meant that fisheries questions would remain high on the central agenda of British foreign policy and, for the EEC, a subject of acute controversy.

A second reason for the increased inportance of maritime issues lies in the impact of marine technology on scientific research and exploration, which we have already briefly referred to in the fisheries context. In the offshore context, technological advances during the early 1960s made possible the exploration and exploitation of oil, gas and other resources in commercial quantities, considerably beyond previously known limits. The prospect of rich offshore resources has forced states to show a growing interest in and stake competing claims to areas of ocean which previously might have been the subject of little economic or scientific interest. As a result an additional range of boundary disputes – in such areas as the Aegean, the South China Sea and off the Falkland Islands – has been added to international relations during a period of political and legal uncertainty.

Marine environmental issues, thirdly, have within the last two decades come to receive considerable attention. In one respect the change is illustrated by a comparison of the current texts of the Law of the Sea Conferences with those of the 1958–60 sessions, which contained virtually no provisions of the preservation and protection of the marine environment. Since the 1960 Geneva Conference the number of international marine environmental conventions has steadily grown to cover such aspects as land-based sources of pollution (Paris Convention, 1974), dumping (Oslo, 1972) and pollution from ships (IMCO, 1954, 1973).[3] The gap, nevertheless, between the purposes of such conventions and international practice remains wide as is most clearly illustrated through the continuing large-scale oil pollution from vessels. A succession of tanker accidents since the *Torrey Canyon*, and blow out incidents such as Ekofisk in the North Sea and Ixtoc in the Gulf of Mexico, has served to dramatise the environmental issues at stake. It has also highlighted the related problems of poorly enforced conventions and the technical difficulties in dealing with large oil spills, as well as human error. A fourth reason for the changed importance of maritime issues lies in the increasing military uses of the ocean.[4] For the major naval powers, the development of submarine launched ballistic missiles has meant an enhanced interest in strategic sea routes, long-range operations and the acquisition of naval intelligence. At the Law of the Sea Conference these factors have been at least one of the main sets of considerations shaping the approach of the major naval powers to such questions as access through straits for civil and military vessels and the freedom to conduct marine scientific research. Conventional naval power has since the 1970s become more important as a means of establishing claims to and monitoring maritime boundaries, as well as in minor power conflict. Apart from these tasks, naval forces have been used most strikingly by the Soviet Union to project Soviet power through the acquisition of bases, port visits and demonstrating support for client states.

THE MANAGEMENT OF INTERNATIONAL MARITIME QUESTIONS

Traditionally maritime questions have been handled by states and private interests on an *ad hoc* basis via bilateral international agreements on specialised issues. Prior to 1945 the lack of international institutions dealing with maritime questions reflected this preference as well as the corresponding unwillingness of states – the chief of which were European – to accept the need for a global organisation to formulate legal rules and standards. Indeed, one of the few international institutions to exist before 1945 was the International Council for the Exploration of the Sea (ICES), set up in 1902 to encourage and co-ordinate scientific investigation of the eastern North Atlantic, including the waters off Greenland and Iceland. Before 1945 maritime politics were managed by, and were very much the preserve of, the major European maritime powers and the United States.

The postwar period has seen, as we have suggested, three, at times conflicting, management trends – the continued extension of national jurisdiction beyond the three mile limit (either unilaterally or by international agreement), the gradual emergence of regional institutions, supplemented, thirdly, by the work of the UN, through its agencies (for example, FAO, UNESCO, IMCO),[5] periodic conferences and codification of legal practice. Regional co-operation has largely taken place in the fisheries and pollution sector, through for example the North East Atlantic Fisheries Commission (NEAFC), the European Fisheries Convention and environmental conventions such as Barcelona and Paris, as states increasingly recognised and accepted the need for some form of international regulation. However, regional intergovernmental fisheries organisations have achieved only modest results, in the main because individual member states have been unwilling to transfer to the Commissions sufficient political power. Frequently, too, scientific advice had been institutionally located *outside* the Commissions, as in the case of NEAFC. Other problems, such as different national legal systems and resource requirements, have also limited progress in fisheries management, as well as in other sectors such as the control of marine pollution. The overall result has been to make the handling of *distributional* questions (for example, catch quotas) much more politicised – an annual exercise in fisheries haggling – which is subject to complex trade-offs with other policy areas. In fact, the variety of trade-off issues, along with the problem of the number of actors in the bargaining process (not all of which may be party to a regional co-ordinating organisation), has inevitably led to protracted decision-making and the frequent shelving of problems. The protracted negotiations of, for example, the European Community on the revised Common Fisheries Policy have underlined the dual difficulty of reaching agreement with non-member states such as Norway and the Soviet Union, when internal consensus on the overall form the Community's fisheries regime should take has not been achieved. As a result two Community members, the United Kingdom and Ireland, have taken unilateral action to control their fisheries resources on conservation grounds.

A further constraint on European regional co-operation has been the postwar East–West political division. With the easing of the German problem in the early 1970s, along with progress in United States–Soviet *détente*, a number of East–West agreements were made possible. For example, following the recognition of the German Democratic Republic, the Baltic riparian states met in Gdansk in June 1973 to conclude the so-called Gdansk Convention on fishing and conservation in the Gulf of Finland, Bothnia and the Baltic.[6] By contrast, in the previous year, the Soviet Union and Eastern bloc withdrew from the 1972 Stockholm Environment Conference because the German Democratic Republic was not invited, although the Federal Republic had been as a member of the World Health Organisation.

INTERNATIONAL ORGANISATION

Within the UN framework the approach to managing international maritime questions has similarly been on a specialised and piecemeal basis with, for example, the International Oceanographic Commission (IOC) located within UNESCO and fisheries handled by the Food and Agriculture Organisation. A UN agency dealing with international shipping problems (the Inter-Governmental Maritime Consultative Organisation – IMCO) was not operative until 1958. The overall lack of co-ordination has necessarily resulted in duplication of effort and limited strategic planning. In November 1967, an important initiative aimed at restructuring the UN system was taken by Malta's then ambassador to the UN, Arvid Pardo.[7] In his address to the General Assembly on 1 November, Ambassador Pardo pointed to the need for a coherent international policy to develop seabed resources beyond the limits of national jurisdiction. The Maltese initiative served to trigger the process of developing a more integrated approach to promoting new law and institutions, and in the following month the General Assembly created an *ad hoc* committee of thirty-five states to consider seabed issues and make recommendations to the Assembly. In 1970 the General Assembly extended the competence of the Seabed Committee to cover a much broader range of law of the sea questions. The trend towards a more integrated UN approach, in part influenced by increasing international concern over ecological issues, was continued in 1972 with the hosting in fashionable Stockholm of the 113-nation Environment Conference. The Law of the Sea Conference met in New York for the first time in 1973, instructed by the General Assembly to consider the problem of ocean space as a whole and produce one comprehensive treaty on all law of the sea issues. At this session, which was devoted to procedural questions, the important principle was established that the conference would proceed on the basis of consensus rather than formal voting. The first substantive session was held in Caracas in 1974.

INTERNATIONAL OCEAN ORDER AND THE COMMON HERITAGE OF MANKIND

The discussions and negotiations at UNCLOS since 1974 have revealed widely differing conceptions of the form of maritime regime for coastal jurisdiction in the exclusive economic zone (EEZ), the outer limit of the continental shelf, high seas and the rights of a new group of claimants – the landlocked and geographically disadvantaged states. However, the problem which proved the most intractable was the issue of the seabed regime beyond the outer limit of national jurisdiction. For Ambassador Pardo and many others, the seabed resources beyond the economic zone were regarded as 'a common heritage of mankind'. It can be argued that the concept of a 'common heritage' attempts to reverse the traditional high seas concept of free and uncontrolled access to seabed resources; according to this view these resources should not be reserved for the few but access should be regulated and the benefits distributed, especially to the poorer members of the international community. As Ambassador Pardo put it in a November 1967 address to the UN: 'in the light of technological developments . . . will [the seabed] be exploited under national auspices and for the benefit of mankind?' Three years after Pardo's proposal the concept of the common heritage was incorporated in the United Nations Declaration of Principles Governing the Seabed, and became, nominally at least, accepted by most member states of the international community. The concept also become incorporated in the wider demands of the Third World, intensified by the energy crisis, for a New International Economic Order put forward at the sixth and seventh Special Sessions of the General Assembly.[8] Others, such as the United States, accept the general concept that the international community, particularly the poorer members, should benefit from the resources of the deep seabed area, but argue nevertheless that this should not be at the cost of unduly restricting access to seabed resources.

Since becoming part of the broader issue areas of the international economy such as trade, commodity price regulation and technology transfer, the seabed issue became increasingly more emotive and less easy to isolate and deal with in a self-contained manner; the conflict over the issue in effect served to highlight the gap between the advanced industrialised states and Third World countries. Moreover, continued delay in reaching a generally acceptable outcome on the seabed issue posed for UNCLOS the classic problem that one issue area might be used to reopen the previously 'negotiated' package on other regimes.

A number of aspects of the major regime proposals discussed at UNCLOS have been copied into state practice, with some national variations. The continued absence, however, of an overall regime for the sea which has wide acceptance, means that maritime issues such as coastal state powers and the extent of the territorial sea will continue to be important sources of conflict and instability in the international system.

FUTURE DEVELOPMENTS

Apart from the question of legal uncertainty, a number of contemporary developments in three main areas – security, threats to the marine environment and the search for resources – will also make it likely that maritime issues remain significant sources of international tension. As we have already noted, the increased use of the sea for a wide variety of foreign policy and security purposes will place an enhanced requirement on maritime derived intelligence, marine scientific research and the capability to deploy in order to deter, weaken or defeat other actors. Thus issues connected with access, for example, through territorial seas and straits, seabed installations, acoustic detection and the acquisition of maritime 'territory', will come to feature frequently in interstate disputes. In the second area – the marine environment – the growth of a network of heavily used main and feeder tanker routes to supply the oil requirements of the major industrialised states and other users has made a number of traditional strategic routes, such as the Malacca Straits and the English Channel, vulnerable to shipping accidents and pollution, as well as several new areas, such as those in the Caribbean.

Also in the field of shipping, the growing trend of dumping industrial waste at sea, and transporting waste by-products, such as spent nuclear fuel, to receiving states for reprocessing, is likely to become a source of controversy as transnational environmental groups and bordering coastal states seek to limit the practice. Finally, there are those problems which are likely to stem from what might be called the quest for maritime 'territory', as states show renewed interest in establishing claims to unoccupied or sparsely populated islands in order to acquire possible resources. Recent technological developments in, for example, offshore installation design, artificial islands, ocean data acquisition systems and sensing of the earth's resources by satellite, are beginning to extend significantly the range of civil and military exploration and inquiry. These developments, along with those referred to above, will no doubt generate new, and at times critical, issue areas for the maritime dimension of international relations as the sea is explored and used within and beyond the limits of technology.

NOTES AND REFERENCES

1 A good introduction to the geology, marine life and resources of the oceans is contained in a clear and well-illustrated volume, *The Atlas of the Oceans* (London: Beazley, 1977).

2 For an analysis of the conflict see R. P. Barston and Hjalmar W. Hannesson, 'The Anglo Icelandic fisheries dispute' *International Relations* (London: David Davies Institute, vol. IV, no. 6, November 1974), pp. 559–84.

3 See Geoffrey Marston, 'International conventions on ship-based pollution', *Journal of World Trade Law*, vol. 10, no. 4 (July–August 1976), pp. 389–93.

4 See *Adelphi Paper* 122 (1976). The text of the 1971 Seabed Arms Control Treaty is contained in *Arms Control and Disarmament Agreements 1959–72* (United States Arms Control and Disarmament Agency, June 1972).

5 The Brookings Institution study *Regimes for the Ocean, Outer Space and Weather* (1977) provides a useful survey of the main international institutions concerned with maritime issues.

6 See Bo Johnson, 'The Baltic Conventions', *International and Comparative Law Quarterly*, vol. 25 (1976), pp. 1–13.

7 The collected papers of Arvid Pardo can be found in IOI Occasional Papers. No. 3. *The Common Heritage* (Malta: University of Malta Press, 1975).

8 For the linkage between the New International Economic Order and UNCLOS see Karl P. Sauvant and Hajo Hasenflug (eds), *The New International Economic Order* (London: Wilton House Publications, 1977), pp. 178–89.

Chapter 1

The Law of the Sea Before and After UNCLOS I and UNCLOS II

P. W. BIRNIE

INTRODUCTION

The United Nations convened its first Conference on the Law of the Sea (hereafter referred to as UNCLOS I) at Geneva in 1958 and its second (UNCLOS II) in 1960. The preparation for, organisation and results of these conferences were vastly different from those of the present UN Conference on the subject (UNCLOS III). The problems facing the present conference are more complex for a variety of reasons than those facing the international community as it was constituted in the 1950s, but before we examine these differences and the outcome of the first two conferences, we must first look at the basic concepts of the law of the sea that prevailed immediately preceding these conferences, and their historical development. These concepts are the key to understanding the difficulties faced by all three conferences in arriving at global and uniform solutions to law of the sea issues.

THE LAW OF THE SEA PRECEDING THE GENEVA CONFERENCES OF 1958 AND 1960

The freedom of the seas
It has been said that 'the history of the modern international law of the sea can perhaps be best understood by perceiving it as a continual conflict between two opposing, yet complementary, fundamental principles – territorial sovereignty and the freedom of the seas'.[1] Since early times states have seen it to be in their interests to assert national sovereignty in a protective belt of sea adjoining their coasts, known as the territorial sea, but to exercise freedom for all their maritime operations in the area of sea beyond this limit known as the high seas, since in the sixteenth century this furthered the development of the great trade routes to the East Indies being opened up by the exploring seafarers of the day, who came from a few powerful states. There has,

however, always been some uncertainty concerning the jurisdictional content and nature of these doctrines and therefore a lack of uniformity concerning the precise extent of the territorial sea; states disagreed about the basepoints from which the territorial sea should be measured, the distance from the shore at which its outer limit should be fixed, the rights of foreign vessels to pass through the territorial sea as long as their passage is innocent, and the identity of the freedoms which all states can exercise upon the high seas. Traditionally these freedoms have included the freedom to fish and to navigate but, following the industrial revolution and the advances in technology that it brought about, which affected not only the kind of vessels used but also the uses of the sea itself, many states began to use the sea for a variety of purposes which were not so generally acceptable to the growing community of states as had been the earlier uses. Even the traditional freedoms of fishing and navigation were eventually called into question as technological advances intensified, to the extent that the capacity of the sea's resources to sustain such unrestricted freedom of use began to be called into question. Even before the contemporary challenges to the doctrine, however, history had witnessed earlier onslaughts upon it since it is essentially a political doctrine supported by states when it advantages them, rejected when it does not.

The limits of the territorial sea

Although many states, and for a period, most states, limited themselves to a territorial sea of three miles (a limit conveniently identified with either a marine league or the distance of a cannon shot in the sixteenth and seventeenth centuries), Britain amongst others asserted the right in the seventeenth century to enclose much larger areas, at one point including the Western Approaches, the English Channel and the whole of the North Sea up to the north of Norway, in order to protect fisheries. Other states protested against such extravagant claims which harmed their trading interests. The great doctrinal battle between John Selden in Britain, who argued in favour of the *mare clausum* (closed sea), and Hugo Grotius., who supported the *mare liberum* (free sea), which favoured the Dutch trade with the East Indies, is well known. It was resolved in the seventeenth century in favour of the latter doctrine and thereafter for about 350 years the doctrine of a narrow territorial sea and wide areas of high seas beyond prevailed. At various times Scandinavian and Mediterranean states have also made extensive claims but in the period immediately preceding the 1958 Geneva Conference the freedom of the seas had become a well-established doctrine; the UK firmly adhered to it, as did the United States after gaining its independence, and the USSR which, although continuing to claim a 12 mile territorial sea, as had the Tsarist regime, insisted on maximum freedom beyond. The doctrine of freedom in fact worked well when there were only a few powerful states exercising a limited number of freedoms – to fish and to navigate mainly – and the vessels and techniques they used for the purposes were relatively unsophisticated; the maritime interests of the most powerful states concerned generally converged at that period. The doctrine again began to be attacked, however, when all these factors began to change. Some changes occurred in the early twentieth century but it was the technological advances made possible by military inventions during the Second World War, coupled with the wider international forum provided by the institution of the United Nations in 1945 and the accelerated progress of many formerly dependent peoples to independent statehood, that made a review of the existing law of the sea an urgent necessity, both in order to codify and to develop it. A conference on the law of the sea had been held by the League of Nations which rejected a proposed functional jurisdiction beyond three miles.

The limits of the territorial sea
The League concentrated most of its attention on draft articles on the above questions. Even here it failed to agree by the necessary two-thirds majority to adopt a three mile limit or zone beyond. Agreement was difficult though the conference was attended by only about forty states (the United Nations' first conference was attended by eighty-two; the UNCLOS III has 150 states participating representing a much wider variety of interests). The League Conference failed to reach agreement not only because, even at that date, several states maintained limits of 6 to 12 miles, but because it was attempting to develop new international law. The League's failures were compounded by the failures of UNCLOS I and II also to resolve them: not only did these two UN Conferences do little to change the existing legal order, or impose uniformity; they added, as we shall see, several new issues to the historical problems of freedom of fishing, navigation and territorial limits described above. States in fact continued to use freedom 'as an ideological tool'[2] when the national interest required it. After the Second World War, however, new states began to emerge which did not see the maintenance of traditional high seas freedoms as being in their interest; they began to develop new ideological implements in order to shape the law of the sea more to their advantage.

Changes following the Second World War
By 1945 several states, in the light of the wartime technological advances which were now being applied to peacetime uses of the sea, and *inter alia* enabling the exploitation of the seabed, considered that the time was ripe for the assertion of new doctrines. The two major proclamations that were to do so much to change the fundamental doctrines were issued within two years of each other. The first was promulgated in 1945 when the United States issued a proclamation on the continental shelf.

This US decision originated primarily from consideration given in 1943 to postwar problems of securing unimpeded access to an augmented supply of natural resources.[3] The continental shelf not only represented a storehouse of such resources, but was also the breeding ground for fish and vital to national defence since it presented a hiding place for submarines. After internal argument (the US economic departments were at that time pursuing a policy of free global access to resources) concerning the legal propriety of these actions, national interest overrode questions of international law. In any case the extension of national jurisdiction could be defended as 'natural' on the basis of the contiguity and propinquity of these areas, a view later approved by the World Court.

The Fisheries Conservation Proclamation was more controversial. The UK strongly favoured preservation of the freedom of fishing and was therefore at that very date seeking to establish international management for North-west and North-east Atlantic fisheries by means of multilateral agreements and Commissions. The UK initially favoured negotiation of reciprocal bilateral agreements for exploitation of the submarine areas.

It has recently been concluded that the US proclamations, which in the event provoked no official protests, were a manifestation of 'economic nationalism' inspired by wartime panic about failure of natural resources, a panic rooted in the US national history of the 'moving ever open frontier which offers new resources for exploitation once those of the present have been exhausted'[4] and which has led the US to pioneer conservation. The US action, however subsequently presented, was 'undoubtedly directed to find a way of breaking the freedom and commonality of the seas',[5] without, of course, damaging other US interests in fisheries and navigation. That it was not possible to contain the action by jurisprudential niceties is confirmed by the subsequent actions of west coast South American states and others.

The Truman Proclamation on the continental shelf 1945
President Truman announced that:

> The Government of the United States regards the natural resources of the continental shelf beneath the high seas but contiguous to the coasts of the United States as appertaining to the United States, subject to its jurisdiction and control.[6]

President Truman officially justified the doctrine by reference to the urgent need to conserve the resources and to develop and use them prudently which required the co-operation and protection of the coastal state, and the fact that the shelf may be regarded as an extension of the land mass of that state and 'naturally appurtenant to it'. Finally he propounded that the coastal state needed to keep close watch over activities off its shores for self-protection.

The proclamation did not establish any clearly defined legal limit to these continental shelf rights; it referred only to the criterion of the 'contiguity' of the shelf. It was, however, accompanied by the second proclamation concerning the conservation of fisheries which declared the interest of the United States in improving the jurisdictional basis for conserving the fisheries contiguous to its coasts. No limit was set on this interest and it was not proposed that in areas where other states' nationals also fished the United States would attempt to legislate unilaterally, merely that in such areas 'zones may be established by agreement between the United States and such other states and joint regulations and control will be put into effect'. It was more in the nature of an expression of support for further conservation treaties concerning fisheries than an assertion of jurisdiction since at that date the US adhered to only three such treaties – the Whaling Convention, the Bering Fur Seal Treaty and the Pacific Halibut Convention. The US intended to declare fishery conservation zones off its coast and would expect further agreements to follow with foreign states participating in the fishery. The US would have no powers to compel such states to participate as the areas concerned were high seas which the Truman Proclamation was careful to preserve as such. The two United States proclamations were therefore quite different in juridical content and effect from those of Chile and other Latin American states which followed them.

Latin American claims to a 200 mile patrimonial sea
In 1947 Chile became the first country to assert national sovereignty over a zone of 200 miles from its coasts and offshore islands including jurisdiction over the resources of its continental shelf and the water column above.[7] The prime reason for this move was the protection of the Chilean whaling industry though the separation of the claim to the continental shelf from the 200 miles of superjacent waters was based on the precedent of the Truman Proclamation. The reason for the choice of a limit of 200 miles appears to have been that Chilean legal advisers were insistent that a precedent should be found to which to relate the new claim and that the Chileans mistakenly thought that the 1939 Declaration of Panama, which had established a somewhat ineffective 300 to 500 mile 'neutral' security zone at the initiative of the US on the outbreak of the Second World War, provided an appropriate one. As one commentator remarks, 'the distance finally adopted could as easily have been 50 or 300 miles as 200 miles'[8] and in fact the whaling industry had only sought a 50 mile protective zone, in order to preserve the Chilean whaling fleet from the increasing operations of foreign factory ships off its coasts, a threat which had not existed during the Second

World War when the whaling industry had virtually ceased. Postwar shortages of oil and fats resulted, however, in the relaxation of the restrictions on whaling operations which had been imposed by the states which adhered to the 1930 Convention and its subsequent protocols. In 1946 the whaling states negotiated a new International Convention for the Regulation of Whaling which established a Commission and imposed a quota for Antarctic catches and some restriction of land stations. Chile signed this convention[9] but because the other members of the Commission refused to relax the restrictions on land stations which Chile found too onerous for her needs, she never ratified it.

Chile proclaimed its 200 mile zone on 23 June 1947; her neighbours, Peru and Ecuador, which had expressed support, followed suit in August 1947 and February 1951 respectively, although for slightly different reasons and in somewhat different language which more accurately expressed their different national interests. Peru and Ecuador were not so interested in protecting their whaling industry since they did not have Antarctic waters and their own fishermen kept largely within a 25 mile belt. They did, however, want to protect their tuna fisheries from the growing American fleets, and Peru in particular wanted to develop its fishmeal industry based on the anchoveta. None the less, both Chile and Peru were careful to tie the language of their declarations to the alleged precedent of the Truman Proclamation, including therein the continental shelf as well as the superjacent waters. The 200 mile zone which has become so much a key part of the UNCLOS III negotiations was thus born from 'the concerns of a weak whaling industry to protect its exclusive access to a resource and the mistaken interpretation of a 1939 security declaration and zone'.[10]

Preparations for UNCLOS I

These two major innovations made urgent a reappraisal of the law of the sea. The newly established United Nations which had been equipped with an International Law Commission (ILC), instituted by statute for the specific purpose of 'the promotion of the progressive development of international law and its codification',[11] decided in 1950 to convene a Conference on the Law of the Sea and instructed the ILC to prepare draft treaty articles on various subjects. The ILC, which it must be stressed consists of twenty-five members of 'recognized competence in international law', spent the next seven years carefully preparing articles, circulating them to member states and reviewing them in the light of comments received, and by the time UNCLOS I finally met in Geneva in 1958 it had before it well-polished legal texts on which, after debate, it could proceed to vote – a very different process from that used by UNCLOS III. Although there were important political implications in many proposed articles, the political committees of the UN were not brought into the drafting stages. As a result some proposals failed to gain acceptance by the necessary two-thirds majority, and vital provisions had to be omitted as we shall see. Moreover the UN in its first two UNCLOSs evinced no more enthusiasm for a comprehensive approach to the issues than had the League. Although, unlike the League, UNCLOS I did debate and adopt treaties on four subjects, the treaties were not correlated and in fact established four separate regimes. They did, however, contain a number of important new developments of the law, as well as clarifying and codifying other aspects. Let us look now at these four treaties[12] which provided the framework of the law for the next decade even though they were not widely ratified by the international community.

THE GENEVA CONVENTION ON THE TERRITORIAL SEA AND CONTIGUOUS ZONE

It is important to note that this convention, in spite of its title, did not, for lack of agreement, set any outer limit on the territorial sea, although it did introduce important innovations, as well as codifying existing customary law.

The convention, which by January 1977 had been ratified by forty-five of 157 existing states, confirmed in its first article that 'the sovereignty of a State extends, beyond its land territory and its internal waters, to a belt of sea adjacent to its coast, described as the territorial sea', that this sovereignty extends to the airspace above it (an important point since every extension of the territorial sea thus automatically extends the coastal state's control over the air, which is not the case with extensions of merely functional zones which retain their status as high seas), and to the seabed below it. The convention adds, however, that this sovereignty is subject not only to the other articles of the convention but to 'other rules of international law' which it does not specify.

The right of innocent passage

The most well known of these, which is also laid down in the convention, is the customary rule that vessels of all states, whether coastal or not, shall enjoy a right of innocent passage through the territorial sea. The convention lays down, in article 14(4), subject to certain conditions and exceptions, that the coastal state must not hamper innocent passage and affirms the customary criteria that 'passage is innocent so long as it is not prejudicial to the peace, good order or security of the coastal state'. These criteria are not further defined; it has been left to state practice to interpret this doctrine and until recently the interpretation has been narrow, so that a passage was not regarded as losing its innocence merely if it resulted in pollution, or threatened it. The advent of supertankers and the growth in their tonnage following the closure of the Suez Canal in 1956 and the introduction of liquid natural gas carriers

(LNG) and oil/bulk/ore carriers (OBO) led some coastal states along whose coasts these vessels pass to reject this doctrine and to propose that passage of vessels which posed an environmental threat should be regarded as non-innocent, should require the prior consent of coastal states concerned and should take place only subject to regulations laid down by them. The same view is taken by many states concerning the right of innocent passage of military vessels which the major naval states insist is part of customary law but which some coastal states insist requires their consent. The convention omits any reference to this disputed right but does require that submarines navigate on the surface and show their flag. This means that if the territorial sea is extended, areas of high seas in which submarines have hitherto exercised a freedom of hidden passage become subject to this rule.

Passage through international straits
Surface passage creates particular problems where the area of high seas concerned is within a narrow strait. If a strait is less than 24 miles across and if the bordering state or states extend their territorial sea to 12 miles the strait is effectively closed to high seas passage. The coastal state is empowered by article 16(1) to 'take the necessary steps' (which are not defined) to prevent non-innocent passage, but article 16(4) does not allow it to suspend, as it can in the other parts of the territorial sea, innocent passage 'through straits used for international navigation' between parts of the high seas or between them and a foreign territorial sea.

Foreign vessels in innocent passage are subject to the criminal jurisdiction of the coastal state only if *inter alia* 'the crime's consequences extend to it or disturb its peace or the good order of its territorial sea' (article 19), but they are, under article 17, required to comply with the laws and regulations of the coastal state, especially those relating to transport and regulation, although customarily the coastal state does not interfere with the discipline of the vessel, its crewing, construction or design, except in so far as has been agreed by means of international conventions. Such conventions are generally negotiated through two relevant international organisations – the International Labour Organisation (ILO) and the Inter-Governmental Maritime Consultative Organisation (IMCO).

The baselines of the territorial sea
As well as defining the content of the jurisdictional rights over the territorial sea the convention lays down the rules for the baselines from which, whatever its distance, it is to be measured. This is important because the further the baselines are placed from the coast the greater the area of sea under coastal state sovereignty since the outer limit is also extended. This convention incorporated the decision of the International Court of Justice in the Anglo-Norwegian Fisheries Case 1952

that baselines do not always have to follow the natural coastline (although it is normal to use the low-water mark along the coast) but that, exceptionally, where the coastline is deeply indented and cut into, or if there is a fringe of islands along it and very close to it, the method of straight baselines can be used, joining appropriate points and taking account in particular cases of the economic interests special to the region. Harbour works and low-tide elevations can also be used as basepoints. The territorial sea of islands, other than those so close to the coast that they come within the above rule, is measured by the same principles. Article 10 defines an 'island' only as 'a naturally formed area of land, surrounded by water, which is above water at high tide'; there is thus *per se* no bar to using uninhabited rocklets which meet this criterion as a basepoint for the territorial sea. Since, as we shall see, the continental shelf rights of the coastal state, as well as contiguous and functional zones, are also measured from these baselines, this convention, and the customs it codified, offer the possibility of very wide extensions of coastal state jurisdiction. States were quick, following UNCLOS I, to take advantage of them.

The contiguous zone
The convention legitimated the new zone rejected by the 1930 League Conference and allowed the coastal state in a zone contiguous to its territorial sea but limited to a distance of 12 miles from its baselines to exercise the control necessary to prevent and punish infringements of its customs, fiscal, immigration or sanitary regulations within its territory or territorial sea. It is important to note that the zone remains high seas, subject to the customary freedoms, apart from this restriction. In addition, although the convention set no limit for the territorial sea, as the above zone is contiguous to it, by implication the territorial sea at that date could not exceed 12 miles though it could be any distance within that figure. The contentious nature of this outer limit contributed to such international conflicts as the Gulf of Tonkin incident (which led to escalation of the war in Vietnam) and the arrests of the USS *Pueblo* and the *Mayaguez*.

For the first time a new kind of jurisdictional belt gained international approval, a significant advance in international law, which paved the way for other functional zones although the contiguous zone was so limited in distance and jurisdiction content that it in no way implied international approval of the extensive South American claims.

THE HIGH SEAS CONVENTION

This convention was the most widely ratified of the four conventions, having by January 1977 received fifty-six ratifications. This is the only one of the four conventions which specifically states that its objective is to codify the law, a misleading statement as in some respects the convention progressively develops the law and parts of the other three conventions are also codifying. The high seas are defined in article 1 as 'all parts of the sea that are not included in the territorial sea or in the internal waters of a State'. They may not be subjected to state sovereignty. On them all states, including the landlocked who should have free access, exercise not only the four freedoms: fishing, freedom to lay submarine cables and pipelines and freedom of overflight, but 'others which are recognized by international law' (article 2). This lack of specific definition has led, as technology advances and industrialisation spreads and intensifies, to considerable dispute concerning the identity of the unnamed freedoms. Do they include freedom to conduct scientific research, to dispose of wastes at sea by dumping or discharge, to conduct weapon testing or military manoeuvres? The answers are unclear but whatever the freedoms they must 'be exercised by all States with reasonable regard to the interests of other States in the exercise of their freedoms'. There is no definition of 'reasonableness' but it at least requires that the seas should not, for example, be used for waste disposal to such an extent that fishing and navigation by others is impaired or the seas become polluted.

Flags of convenience
Every state, even the landlocked, has the right to sail ships under its flag on the high seas. Ships must fly a flag but because the convention permits registering states alone to fix the conditions for grant of their nationality, for registration of ships in their territory and for the right to fly their flag, there is no uniformity of conditions or standards between registering states. The convention insists in article 4 that ships have the nationality of their flag state but article 6 requires no more than that there should be a genuine link, which it does not define, between the state and its flag. There is in practice an open-ended choice of links – the owners, the captain, the crew, the shipbuilders, and so on. The ship is subject to the exclusive jurisdiction of the flag state on the high seas, which jurisdiction that state 'must effectively exercise'. The only exceptions are those provided for in this convention, for example, over slave and pirate ships, and by other international conventions such as the IMCO Intervention Convention of 1969. Warships and state ships used only on government non-commercial service have complete immunity from the jurisdiction of states other than the flag state. Thus was the so-called system of 'flags of convenience' codified since a state can register vessels whose owners are not its own nationals and with which it may have very remote connections. It is thus difficult for such states, even if they are anxious to do so (and not all are so concerned), effectively to exercise their jurisdiction over their vessels, which may never return to their state of registration.

Rendering assistance in distress

The recent plight of the Vietnamese 'boat people' has given particular significance to the convention's provision in article 12(1) that every state *shall require* the masters of its flag ships, unless it endangers their ship, crew or passengers, 'to render assistance to any person found at sea in danger of being lost' and 'to proceed with all possible speed to the rescue of persons in distress if informed of their need of assistance' in so far as such action may reasonably be expected of them.

Prevention of pollution

Although the High Seas Convention deals with this problem only in very general terms it provided the framework within which a large number of international and regional treaties and national laws for prevention of pollution from a number of sources have been developed. Article 24 demands that every state draw up regulations to prevent pollution of the seas by the discharge of oil from ships or pipelines or resulting from the exploration and exploitation of the seabed and its subsoil, taking account of existing treaty provisions on the subject. The High Seas Convention could not require that *all* states become party to such treaties because of the established customary rule that treaties cannot bind third party states. The vague requirement merely to 'take account' (a familiar term in maritime treaties) leaves even party states complete discretion concerning the extent to which they do this.

These and other difficulties are discussed in more detail in Chapter 5. Article 25 relating to radioactive waste is equally unspecific. It requires every state to take measures to prevent pollution of the seas from dumping of such substances, 'taking account' of any standards and regulations which may be formulated by 'the competent international organisations'. States party to the High Seas Convention are not *obliged* to incorporate the regulations of such bodies as the International Atomic Energy Agency, and states not party to the High Seas Convention are not covered by the requirement even to take account of them. Article 25 also requires that all states co-operate with the competent international organisations in taking measures for the prevention of pollution of the seas or air space above, from activities with radioactive materials 'or other harmful agents'. As the latter phrase is not defined there is scope for argument concerning the meaning of harmful, the proof of harm and the identity of agents which fall within this category once its scope is agreed, as well as the meaning of pollution.

Hot pursuit

It is not possible in the confines of this chapter to detail all the provisions of the High Seas Convention but mention must finally be made of the codification in article 23 of the right of hot pursuit, a well-established customary doctrine. If a coastal state has good reason to believe that a ship has violated its laws it can pursue the offending vessel on to the high seas as long as the pursuit is commenced while the foreign ship, or one of its boats, is within the coastal state's internal waters, territorial sea or the newly approved contiguous zone, though only for violation of regulations related to that zone. Here the High Seas Convention was developing the law even though it purported to be codifying it. The pursuit can continue on to the high seas only if it is not interrupted. The right of hot pursuit is a useful weapon both for enforcement of laws regulating fisheries and prevention of pollution. It has become even more important with the modern assertions of 200 mile fisheries zones and proposals for EEZs (exclusive economic zones) within which coastal states might control other activities.

THE CONVENTION ON FISHING AND CONSERVATION OF THE LIVING RESOURCES OF THE SEA [13]

This was the least widely ratified of the four Geneva Conventions, having received only thirty-five ratifications by January 1977, and it did not make any provision for fishery limits. It evaded this question by concerning itself only with conservation of fisheries on the high seas and recognising, in article 6, that 'a coastal State has a special interest in the maintenance of the productivity of the living resources in any area of the high seas adjacent to its territorial sea' without referring to any limit for the latter. In recognising this interest of the coastal state in fisheries outside its national jurisdiction it opened the way to fisheries zones but as the Territorial Sea Convention also did not set a limit for that belt, coastal states were able, under these two conventions, only to claim exclusive rights to exploit and conserve fisheries within the territorial sea; at the very most this could not exceed 12 miles as explained above, and in many cases states limited themselves to 3 miles, as does the UK. Beyond that limit freedom of fishing existed in 1958 under the High Seas Convention. The international community was, however, well aware that overfishing of several species was taking place and that conservation of fisheries was necessary even on the high seas if freedom of access was not to be a freedom to deplete. This convention recognised 'that the nature of the problems involved in the conservation of the living resources of the high seas is such that there is a clear necessity that they be solved, whenever possible, on the basis of international co-operation through the concerted action of all the states concerned'. This, however, is a pious preambular hope, not a binding obligation, since, as already remarked, sovereign states cannot be forced to participate in treaties. The first article of this convention therefore had to concede that all states have the right for their nationals to engage in fishing on the high seas, subject only to their treaty obligations (if any), coastal states' interests 'as provided for in this Convention' (to which a majority of coastal states including the Soviet Union and Japan never became party) and the convention's provisions on conservation.

The convention at least, however, specifically imposed on states the *duty* (which can now also be said to have become part of customary law) to adopt, or to co-operate with other states in adopting, conservation measures for their nationals as may be necessary to achieve the form of conservation described above.

The convention attempted to protect the coastal state's recognised interest by requiring, in article 6(3), that a state whose nationals are engaged in fishing in any area of the high seas adjacent to the territorial sea of another state shall, at the request of that coastal state, 'enter into negotiations' of the kind described in the preceding paragraph. If negotiations do not lead to an agreement within six months any coastal state can adopt unilateral measures of conservation appropriate to any stock of fish or other marine resources in any areas of the high seas adjacent to its territorial sea, as long as the measures are urgently needed in the light of existing knowledge of the fishery, are based on scientific findings and do not discriminate in form or in fact against foreign fishermen.

This provision went too far for some states, which regarded it as an infringement of sovereignty, and not far enough for others, such as the Latin American states, which had already declared 200 mile zones. Because it was not widely ratified, the convention failed to solve the problem of overfishing. Although it may have had some effect in that there were a number of new Fishery Commissions established following this convention, for the reasons outlined in Chapter 2 they too failed to halt the decline of many species. Co-operative regulation of fishing whilst the doctrine of freedom of fishing prevailed was not successful, since states were reluctant to surrender any of their sovereign rights to international Fishery Commissions.

UNCLOS II: TERRITORIAL SEA AND FISHERIES LIMITS[14]

An attempt was made in 1960 at a second UNCLOS to reach agreement on the limits of coastal states' exclusive control of fisheries exploitation and conservation on the basis of a formula which provided for a territorial sea of 6 miles plus an additional 6 mile fisheries zone. This conference too failed to reach agreement, partly because of the problem of phasing out the so-called 'historic rights' of states which had habitually fished in the 3–12 mile zone and partly because some states, like Iceland, wanted a 12 mile territorial sea, and others, like some South American states, held out for their existing 200 mile zones. Thereafter states adopted national solutions to the limits problem although in some areas regional conventions were negotiated, such as the 1964 European Fisheries Agreement, which adapted the above formula for fishery zone purposes, allowing participants to assert exclusive fishery rights in a 6 mile zone and preferential rights in an additional outer 6 mile belt in which other states could continue to fish on the basis of rights recognised in the agreement and negotiated with the coastal state. The agreement carefully avoided using the term 'historic rights' as their existence is disputed in international law. This agreement has recently been overtaken by the declaration of 200 mile fishery zones by most of its parties and the subjection of such of these extended zones as appertain to states party to the Treaty of Rome to the EEC's Common Fisheries Policy, some features of which are, however, likely to be based on the historical framework of the European Agreement. It should be noted that from 1964 to 1976 the UK claimed only three belts: it retained a 3 mile territorial sea, a 6 mile exclusive fisheries zone and an outer 6 mile fisheries zone in which states party to the European Agreement which had fished there for a long time could continue to do so by agreement.

THE CONTINENTAL SHELF CONVENTION[15]

The outer boundary
This convention had received fifty-four ratifications by January 1977, although it was the most innovatory and, arguably, the most important of all the Geneva Conventions since it enabled not only the exploitation of continental shelf resources throughout the world, including the North Sea, but also the considerable expansion of the limits of coastal state jurisdiction over them because of its open-ended *legal* definition of the shelf. It is therefore worth quoting its first article in full, viz.:

> For the purposes of these Articles the term 'continental shelf' is used as referring (a) to the seabed and subsoil of the submarine areas adjacent to the coast but outside the area of the territorial sea, to a depth of 200 metres or, beyond that limit, to where the depth of the superjacent waters admits of the exploitation of the natural resources of the said areas; (b) to the seabed and subsoil of similar submarine areas adjacent to the coasts of islands.

This definition gives the coastal state the certainty of rights to the depth mentioned but beyond 200 metres rights depend on the availability of technology not just to explore but to exploit the seabed. There does not *prima facie* appear to be any distance limit to this right once the technical ability is there. However, it is generally agreed that the title of the convention and its reference to the 'adjacency' of the areas in question does impose an ultimate limit. It is still not clear, however, where this should be drawn. In 1969 the ICJ (International Court of Justice) in the North Sea Continental Shelf cases,[16] in an *obiter dictum*, acknowledged that the coastal state had an 'inherent right' to explore and exploit the natural resources of its continental shelf because it is a 'natural prolongation of its land territory into and under the sea'. The court confirmed the convention's statement that it is not necessary to constitute the right by proclamation: it exists *ipso facto* and *ipso jure* by virtue of the fact stated. Although the Continental Shelf Convention tied its definition to exploitability the ICJ's statement appears to relate the outer limit to tests of 'naturalness' or natural features of geology, geography, geophysics or even geomorphology. This has encouraged many states, as we see in Chapter 3, to assert that the outer limit should be drawn not at the outer edge of the geographical continental plateau but somewhere on the outer margin.

The question of the outer limit of the continental shelf is now one of the most contentious in international law and has divided states at UNCLOS III because of its economic implications. When the concession of continental shelf rights to islands is related to the definition of island in the Territorial Sea Convention even more problems arise since *prima facie* such rights could be delimited from baselines taken from uninhabited islets such as Rockall. There is not sufficient space in this work to discuss the complexities of the problems involved but they are both serious and delicate and contribute greatly to the political difficulties of reaching agreement on a package treaty at UNCLOS III.

The nature of continental shelf rights
The convention does not give the coastal state sovereignty over the shelf but 'sovereign rights to explore and exploit it'. It must therefore extract oil, for example, before it can assert ownership rights over it; as no other state can enter another state's shelf for that purpose, however, the right is an exclusive one. It extends not only to the mineral resources such as oil and gas but also to all natural resources, living and non-living, including the so-called 'sedentary species', defined in article 2(4) as 'living organisms . . . which, at the harvestable stage, either are immobile on or under the seabed or are unable to move except in constant physical contact with the seabed and subsoil'. This definition is not one readily recognised by scientists and leads to such legal niceties as categorising crabs as coming within the terms of the convention and lobsters as being outside. It has therefore given rise to such international disputes as the French–Brazilian Lobster War and the USSR–Argentinian King Crab dispute, though the problem is to a large extent now removed since such species are found mainly within the new 200 mile fisheries zones.

The legal status of the waters above the continental shelf
One point on which the convention was very clear (article 3) was that the superjacent waters retained the legal status of high seas and that the status of the air space above was not affected. This made the convention

unacceptable to states which had declared 200 mile patrimonial seas but was regarded as essential by states which wanted to preserve the rights of their distant water fishermen to fish off the coasts of other states, for example, the USSR, Japan, the UK, the USA.

Jurisdiction over the shelf
A key article, upon which all coastal states, even those not ratifying the convention, have built their national continental shelf regimes, is article 5 which gives the coastal state the right to construct and operate installations and other devices on its shelf as necessary for its exploration and exploitation, and to establish 500 metre safety zones round them. These zones retain the status of high seas, however. The article places the installations under the jurisdiction of the coastal state, specifically denying them the status of islands so that they cannot be used as basepoints for other zones. Continental shelf activities must not result in 'any unjustifiable interference' with navigation, fishing or the conservation of the living resources of the sea, or interference ('unjustifiable' is omitted here) with 'fundamental oceanographic or other scientific research carried out with the intention of open publication'. As none of these phrases is defined there are many loose ends in this provision and states have since 1958, through their national laws and practices, sometimes harmonised through regional organisations such as ICES or treaties or bilateral agreements, been working out their own interpretation of these requirements. Some interference with traditional and treaty freedoms is unavoidable; the question is what is reasonable and therefore unlikely to provoke protest from other users. In addition to pipeline provisions in Article 4, a further inroad on high seas freedom was introduced in respect of marine research related to and taking place on the shelf. This requires the consent of the coastal state, though it is not allowed to withhold it if the research relates only to physical or biological characteristics of the shelf and if certain criteria are met.

Delimitation of opposite and adjacent continental shelf sectors
The rules laid down in article 6 bind only the states party to the convention but it appears that in the light of the decisions in the North Sea cases, as interpreted recently by the 1977–8 Arbitral Tribunal in the UK–French Delimitation of the Continental Shelf in the English Channel and the South-Western Approaches, they may not differ substantially in practice from the customary law concerning the application of equitable principles. Article 6 provides, in the case of adjacent shelves of *adjacent* states, for the use of a line of equidistance (the equidistance of which from each sector is determined by cartographic techniques) failing agreement between the parties on another method of delimitation and in the absence of special circumstances (not defined but

related in practice to such factors as islands, troughs and other special peculiarities of the coastline or shelf) which might justify another line as being more equitable. In the case of adjacent shelves of *opposite* states the rule is similar but the line is a median line, related to the basepoints of the territorial sea. There can be many legal niceties and complexities involved in the application of the convention as evidenced by the cases referred to but in general, where coasts or seabed or both are not irregular, the equidistance line is most often used, because it effects the most equitable solution, as the ICJ and the Arbitral Tribunal concerned pointed out. Some writers consider that the rules laid down in article 6 in fact codified the customary law, since 'special circumstances' allows deviation from equidistance when it produces inequitable results in the light of these circumstances.[17] Delimitation gives rise to many disputes because of the uncertainty concerning the applicable rules and principles, but the UK–French arbitration does much to clarify the law and pave the way for further negotiations and arbitrations.

CONCLUSION

It will readily be seen that although the Geneva Conventions clarified or codified a number of points, they also left a number of problems unresolved and even created new problems because, in order to effect the compromises necessary to reach agreement on a convention which would be sufficiently widely accepted to be effective, the states concerned either left many definitions open ended or used vague and ambiguous terminology which left states room for further interpretation and development in their national interest. Many of the new states joining the international community after 1958 were poor and developing, including a large number of landlocked states. Most of these did not find that the regime of loosely regulated freedom laid down in the Geneva Conventions, especially the freedoms of navigation and fishing, met their interests as technologically deprived states. Nor did they approve the extensive and specifically unlimited rights over continental shelves conceded to coastal states. They therefore did not adhere to the conventions on gaining independence. Even without this lack of enthusiasm on the part of both new states and many existing states the gaps and ambiguities of the conventions soon gave rise to disagreement.

The failures of successive conferences to place a clearly fixed limit on the territorial sea and continental shelf and to establish the concept of a limited fishery zone, encouraged unilateral assertions of extended and comprehensive jurisdiction and led, *inter alia*, to the so-called 'Cod Wars' between the UK and Iceland and the UK–French delimitation dispute. By 1973 seventy-two states claimed jurisdiction exceeding 3 miles; fifty-nine coastal states claimed jurisdiction over 12 miles or more (a 33 per cent increase from 1960). Thirteen claimed over 12 miles including seven fishery or other zones of 200 miles. Canada in 1970 asserted a unique 100 mile pollution control zone in her Arctic waters which was strongly protested by the USA and others. The law was formed during this period by three processes and their interactions – international treaties, unilateral declarations and decisions of international courts. The ambiguous Geneva provisions concerning conservation, rights in international straits, the definition of innocent passage, prevention of pollution, in conjunction with the gaps mentioned, further encouraged the demand for greater coastal state control as industry and technology quickly progressed in the next decade. The Geneva Conventions' most notable omission was perhaps any reference to or provision for the areas of seabed beneath the high seas beyond the continental shelf. It was not long before the new members of the world community called attention to this and the need to develop new laws since the existing institutions, such as the largely ineffective Fisheries Commissions, were either regional or species specific, or if international, like IMCO, specialised to a narrow field, such as vessel safety. The present decade has therefore seen a proliferation of regional and other treaties and Commissions which now generate their own problems, as will be seen in Chapter 9.

NOTES AND REFERENCES

D. Bowett, *Law of the Sea* (Manchester: Manchester University Press, 1967) gives a fluent and succinct analysis of UNCLOS I and II and makes the best starting-point for study of the 1958 Geneva Conventions especially for non-lawyers. C. J. Colombos, *International Law of the Sea* 6th edn (London: Longman, 1967) gives a more detailed but concise account of all aspects of the law of the sea and its history but is now somewhat out of date. Myers S. McDougal *et al.*, *The Public Order of the Oceans* (New Haven, Conn.: Yale University Press, 1962) adopt an idiosyncratic theoretical approach to the development of the law of the sea but this is an important work which directed much subsequent analysis of claims and counter-claims to maritime rights as a source of new laws. S. Oda in *International Control of Sea Resources* (Leyden: Sijthoff, 1963) looks at the new conventions from the illuminating angle of the struggle for national control of resources. An interesting regional study of a semi-enclosed sea is made in M. Sibthorp (ed.), *North Sea: Challenge and Opportunity* (London: Europa, 1975); Chapter IV gives a good account of the application of the Geneva Convention regime to that area and other chapters explore its multifarious uses, and the potential conflicts. The individual 1958 Conventions are dealt with specifically in some works. For example, the Geneva Convention on Fisheries and Conservation of the Living Resources of the Sea is exhaustively examined by D. M. Johnston in *The International Law of Fisheries* (New Haven, Conn.: Yale University Press, 1965), a work giving a wealth of interesting background on this convention and others. A Koers in *The International Regulation of Marine Fisheries* (London: Fishing News (Books), 1976) also summarises and analyses briefly the Geneva Fisheries Convention and the constituent treaties of Fisheries Commissions at that date. F. T. Christy and A. Scott, *The Common Wealth in Ocean Fisheries* (Baltimore: Resources of the Future, Johns Hopkins Press, 1965) though out of date is still the most readable work making the case for a more international approach to fisheries management following the Geneva Convention's failure to do this. The Continental Shelf Convention is dealt with exhaustively by E. D. Brown in *The Legal Regime of Hydrospace* (London: Stevens, 1971).

26 *Maritime Dimension*

He gives a detailed legal history of the convention and analyses its subsequent application, including the North Sea Continental Shelf case, as well as making proposals for the future regime of the seabed. He also covers the law concerning marine pollution from vessels at that date. Latin American 200 mile zones are defended skilfully by G. Amador in *The Exploitation and Conservation of the Resources of the Sea* (Leyden: Sijthoff, 1963). This is a thorough, if partisan, explanation of the Latin American position. A very useful general reference work for law of the sea studies is R. Churchill *et al.* (eds), *New Directions in the Law of the Sea* (New York: Oceana and British Institute of International Law, 1973). Volume III contains the collected papers of the conference of that title, which cover all aspects of the legal regime of the sea existing at that date, before the opening of UNCLOS III. See especially E. D. Brown, 'Maritime zones: a survey of claims', for the details of zonal limits in 1973, and A. Koers, 'Freedom of fishing in decline: a case for the N.E. Atlantic'. The papers are written by an internationally representative selection of lawyers concerned in the subject; Vols I–X include selected LOS documents including the Geneva Conventions and declarations of fisheries and other zones, and most important documents affecting the law of the sea to 1979.

1   E. D. Brown, 'Maritime zones: a survey of claims', in R. Churchill *et. al.* (eds), *New Directions in the Law of the Sea*, Vol. III (New York: Oceana, 1973), p. 157; H. Waldock, 'International law and the new maritime claims', *International Relations*, Vol. 5 (April 1965), pp. 163–94.
2   Brown, op. cit., p. 158.
3   D. C. Watt, 'First steps in the enclosure of the oceans', *Marine Policy*, Vol. 3, no. 3 (July 1979), pp. 211–24.
4   ibid., p. 224.
5   ibid., p. 224.
6   Presidential Proclamation no. 2667, 28 September 1945.
7   Anne Hollick, 'The origins of 200 mile offshore zones', *American Journal of International Law*, Vol. 71, no. 3 (July 1977), pp. 494–500; see n. 3, p. 494 for a description of other alleged origins of the zone.
8   ibid., p. 495.
9   International Whaling Commission, *First Report of the Commission* (London, 1950), p. 2 and p. 3, paras 3, 4 and 7.
10 Hollick, op. cit., p. 500.
11 I. Brownlie, ed. *Basic Documents in International Law* (Oxford: 1969).
12 The four conventions are included in Brownlie, op. cit., pp. 70–97 and in UN Doc. A/CONF. 13/L.52–L.55; and MISC no. 15 (1958), Cmnd 584. For general information on the four conventions see the bibliography and A. H. Dean, 'Geneva Conference on the Law of the Sea: what was accomplished?', *American Journal of International Law*, Vol. 52 (1958), p. 610. The UK ratified all four conventions.
13 D. M. Johnston, *The International Law of Fisheries* (New Haven and London: Yale University Press, 1965), especially ch. 9, pp. 358–430.
14 D. Bowett, 'Second United Nations Conference on the Law of the Sea', *International and Comparative Law Quarterly*, vol. 9 (1960), pp. 415–35; A. H. Dean, ' The Second Geneva Conference on the Law of the Sea; the fight for freedom of the seas', *American Journal of International Law*, Vol. 54 (1960), pp. 751–9.
15 Joyce Gutteridge, 'The 1958 Geneva Convention on the Continental Shelf', *British Yearbook of International Law*, Vol. XXV (1959), p. 102; Marjorie Whiteman, 'Conference on the Law of the Sea: the continental shelf', *American Journal of International Law*, Vol. 52 (1958), p. 629.
16 'North Sea Continental Shelf cases 1969', *ICJ Report* (1969), p. 1. For a good analysis see Brown, op. cit., pp. 41–70.
17 See Brown, op. cit., pp. 61–2.

Chapter 2

International Fisheries

PAUL A. DRIVER

THE SIZE OF THE RESOURCE

Distribution of world fish catch
The distribution of fish stocks is related to the abundance of the small
invertebrate animals, or zooplankton, on which many species feed,
either directly or indirectly. The concentration of zooplankton is, in
turn, dependent on the abundance of microscopic plants, or phytoplankton, upon which most members of the zooplankton graze. As with
other plants, the production of phytoplankton varies seasonally. It also
varies geographically, the distribution being largely determined by the
availability of chemical plant nutrients in the water.[1] The areas of high
production fall into three groups: (1) upwellings and divergencies off the
sub-tropical western coasts of the continents (Peru, California, north-
west and south-west Africa) and along the Equator, where cold, nutrient
rich waters rise to the surface; (2) the temperate and sub-Arctic waters
of the Southern Ocean, North Atlantic and North Pacific; (3) shallow
continental shelf waters. The distribution of fish low in the food chain,
like the Peruvian anchoveta, will coincide exactly with these areas,
whilst species higher in the food chain like the roaming tunas will be
more loosely related to the areas of high production. Table 2.1 shows the
present distribution of landings of different types of fish (not including
whales) throughout the world.[2]

Development of Fisheries
Until the Second World War there was a slow but steady development of
fisheries, brought about by gradual mechanisation and improvement of
the methods of catching, processing and transportation of fish. Since the
war this type of modernisation has proceeded in the developing
countries and has increased their fish supplies. In Thailand, for example,
following the introduction of 'otter' trawling in 1961, catches increased
from 78,000 tonnes in 1962 to 337,000 in 1965.[3] In the developed
countries, too, technical improvements of fishing vessels has continued
with the introduction of sophisticated electronic fish-finding and
navigational equipment, automated gear-handling and high capacity
freezing equipment, all of which have brought about a significant

Table 2.1 1976 World Fish Landings (thousands of tonnes)

	Flounders, halibuts, soles	Cods, hakes, haddocks	Redfishes, basses, congers	Jacks, mullets, sauries	Herrings, sardines, anchovies	Tunas, bonitos, billfish	Mackerels, snoeks, cutlass fish	Sharks, rays, ratfish	Miscellaneous marine fishes	Shads, eels, salmon, trout, sturgeon, etc.	Crustaceans (crabs, prawns, lobsters, etc.)	Molluscs (squids, clams, oysters, etc.)	Total
North-west Atlantic	233	859	240	383	623	9	242	30	29	23	132	624	3,427
North-east Atlantic	314	4,346	1,204	3,402	1,945	43	848	90	293	34	152	512	13,183
West-central Atlantic	4	0	179	47	706	55	3	12	90	<1	220	242	1,558
East-central Atlantic	16	99	321	589	1,417	268	187	35	339	17	25	245	3,558
Mediterranean/Black Sea	10	39	100	93	638	24	15	14	137	50	28	114	1,262
South-west Atlantic	2	221	268	73	235	23	3	20	219	0	108	18	1,190
South-east Atlantic	2	819	94	685	996	24	76	2	101	0	23	5	2,827
West Indian Ocean	11	7	339	102	65	183	115	98	300	19	248	23	1,510
East Indian Ocean	2	<1	128	55	146	78	74	44	545	15	77	10	1,174
North-west Pacific	301	4,057	1,211	658	1,802	386	1,436	98	4,160	245	266	1,599	16,219
North-east Pacific	199	1,434	186	<1	121	18	0	3	31	198	185	32	2,407
West-central Pacific	21	<1	576	816	405	537	282	51	1,864	133	389	298	5,372
East-central Pacific	4	5	29	25	620	477	15	17	115	2	85	27	1,408
South-west Pacific	2	96	52	47	<1	58	15	6	41	0	6	57	380
South-east Pacific	1	134	23	405	4,769	27	43	11	86	0	66	47	5,612
Total	1,123	12,116	4,950	7,389	15,089	2,209	3,340	533	8,350	737	2,014	3,854	61,704

Source: FAO Yearbook of Fisheries Statistics (figures rounded to nearest 1,000 tonnes), Vol. 42.

increase in fishing effort and fish landings.

However, since 1945 two developments in particular have been responsible for the growth of the world fish catch, which on average has been increasing by 7 per cent per year, or doubling every ten years. First, there has been industrial fishing: the use of mid water trawls and purse seines to capture large shoals of small pelagic fish which are reduced to fishmeal for use as fertiliser and animal feedstuff, especially in the broiler chicken industry. Industrial fishing in the North-east Atlantic began in the 1950s with the Norwegian and Danish North Sea fishery for immature herring, at that time a cheap and abundant fish. By 1968 most herring stocks in the North-east Atlantic had been severely reduced and the seiners had to turn to other species like mackerel, sprats, sand eels and horse mackerel to supply the meal factories. The Norwegian mackerel catch, for example, increased from 20,000 tonnes in 1963 to a peak of 870,000 tonnes in 1967.[4] It is interesting that as catches of the traditional edible species are reduced by overfishing and closure of distant water fishing grounds, some of these industrial species like the mackerel and even the horse mackerel are slowly becoming accepted for human consumption. Other examples of stocks exploited for fishmeal are the British Columbian herring, the pilchards off South and south-west Africa, Alaskan pollack, Atlantic capelin, menhaden off the east coast of the USA, and, the most famous example, the Peruvian anchoveta. Landings in this fishery roughly doubled each year between 1955 (60,000 tonnes) and 1961 (5 million tonnes). This rate of increase eventually slowed down, but between 1967 and 1972 the fishery yielded about 10 million tonnes of anchovy per year for reduction to meal, over 17 per cent of the total world catch of all marine fish. At the time of writing industrial fish make up about 28 per cent of the world catch of all species.

The other major contribution to the growth of world fish catches has been the development of long-range fishing. Examples are the self-contained fleets of catching, processing, supply and transport vessels used by the USSR and other Eastern bloc countries, and the large individual freezer-stern-trawlers of 5,000 tonnes and more used by the Japanese and Koreans which can work throughout the Pacific catching and processing over 100 tonnes of fish per day each.

Many of the areas of high productivity mentioned earlier in this chapter are adjacent to countries which have low populations, poor lines of communication between the coast and the interior, and national diets containing little or no fish, that is, where there is hardly any demand for fish. (In many cases these countries are also ill equipped to harvest the local fish resources.) The greatest demand for fish, fish products and whale products is in those countries with either intensive agriculture, high populations or population densities, traditional fish-eating habits or a combination of these, that is, Europe, North America, Japan and other Far Eastern countries. The developments of industrial fishing and distant water fishing have therefore essentially been the development of lines of transportation between areas of high productivity and areas of high demand. The political and economic consequences of such a situation will be further developed at the end of this chapter.

Future Development of Fisheries
The most recent reliable estimate of the potential world catch of familiar types of marine fish is around 100 million tonnes per annum,[5] excluding the product of fish farms, and catches of unfamiliar species such as krill and oceanic squids, of which more later. Table 2.2 shows the world distribution of this potential catch, and the present state of exploitation in each area. The world catch of marine fish in 1976 was something

Table 2.2 *Potential and Present Yield of Conventional Marine Fish Stocks (million tonnes)*

	Potential[a]	1976[b]
North-west Atlantic	6·5	3·4
North-east Atlantic	13·5	13·2
West-central Atlantic	5·8	1·6
East-central Atlantic	3·5	3·6
Mediterranean/Black Sea	1·2	1·3
South-west Atlantic	7·4	1·2
South-east Atlantic	4·3	2·8
West Indian Ocean	8·9	1·5
East Indian Ocean	5·4	1·2
North-west Pacific	5·4	16·2[c]
North-east Pacific	4·8	2·4
West-central Pacific	16·7	5·4
East-central Pacific	6·1	1·4
South-west Pacific	2·0	0.4
South-east Pacific	12·6	5·6
Total	104·1	61·7

Notes: a Not including molluscs, for which production is dependent on scale of cultivation.
b Including all species shown in Table 2.1.
c Catches probably include some from potential considered under West-central Pacific.

Sources: FAO Yearbook of Fisheries Statistics, Vol. 42; J. A. Gulland, *Fish Resources of the Oceans* (London: Fishing News (Books), 1972).

around 62 million tonnes which, given the logarithmic rate of increase in annual world catch described earlier, means that attainment of the maximum might be expected in the mid 1980s. However, there is reason to believe that this rate of expansion might not continue and that the maximum might not be reached. When any fish stock is first exploited its stock size is decreased and the catch per unit of fishing effort falls over a period of time. Until now, continuing increases in world catch have been possible in spite of this because, year by year, previously unexploited or under-exploited stocks have come under exploitation anew. Now there are few remaining unexploited stocks and already species previously unattractive because they were expensive to exploit, of low value or difficult to process, like the blue whiting, are being utilised. This means that it will not be possible to balance falling catches per unit effort of old stocks by diversion to new stocks for very much longer. Increases in world catch of familiar types of fish will then only be effected by the more rational exploitation of presently exploited stocks. The actual maximum catch is therefore dependent on the effective future management of world fisheries, which is discussed at the end of this chapter. As previously mentioned, in the late 1960s the Peruvian anchoveta fishery was yielding over 17 per cent of the world fish catch. When landings fell from around 10 million tonnes per annum to less than 2 million tonnes in 1973, due to a combination of overfishing and 'el Nino' (changes in the Peru current), the total world fish catch continued to climb. In future the collapse of such an important fishery will have a much more dramatic impact on world supplies of fish and fish products.

There is another reason why the 100 million tonnes potential yield of 'conventional' fish might not be realised. Many of the well-known and productive fisheries, particularly those in temperate and northern waters, are demersal fisheries for mixed fish, that is, several species are caught with the same gear and on the same grounds. For reasons which will be explained later, it is not possible to obtain the maximum yield of each species within a mixed trawl fishery even with a good system of fisheries management. It is also likely that valuable species like sole will be over-exploited, whilst species which are of low value or more dispersed on the grounds, like dabs, will be under-exploited. A maximum figure of 80 per cent[6] of the potential has been put on the practicable harvest from such fisheries.

Once all the stocks of conventional fish are being fished, more unconventional groups will start to be utilised. These are little used at present either because there is little consumer demand for them, or because they are difficult or expensive to catch or process. Increases in the world population, which is expected to double between 1970 and 2000, will increase the demand for such fish in three ways: (1) simply by the increase in number of fish eaters, (2) by the reduction in area of agricultural land and (3) by the increased demand for fish protein extracts for human and animal consumption that these factors will bring about. World consumption of fish, estimated to be 10 kg per capita in 1960, is consequently expected to rise to 16 kg per capita in 2000.[7] The technological problems that will need to be overcome are involved in the catching of distant, deep or diffuse fish stocks, and in the processing of fish which contain a high proportion of bone or shell, or which have poorly textured flesh. In many cases the product will be some kind of paste, or a liquid or powdered fish protein extract.

An example of these unconventional stocks is the cephalopod molluscs or squids. These are already exploited off those coasts where they are traditionally part of the diet, that is, Japan and the Mediterranean countries where about 2 million tonnes per annum are taken. However, the potential sustainable world catch of all cephalopods from all continental shelves is estimated to be 8–12 million tonnes per annum. There are also large oceanic squid stocks whose size is imprecisely known, but if included, would increase the figure by between 8 and 60 times.[8] Again, the mesopelagic fish, small oceanic fish like the lantern fish which are particularly abundant in the upwelling areas, could potentially provide an annual harvest of over 100 million tonnes.

At each step in the food chain, there is a loss of organic material estimated to be 80–90 per cent.[9] Thus 1 kg of phytoplankton will yield 100 gm of herbivorous zooplankton which will in turn provide 10 gm of first-rank carnivore and 1 gm of second-rank carnivore. It is therefore obvious that the lower the level in the food chain that man exploits the living resources of the sea the greater will be the potential total catch. Some of the plentiful pelagic fish are first-rank carnivores but many of the most popular demersal fish like cod are second- or third-rank carnivores. To harvest phytoplankton would mean effectively filtering the sea, which could not be cost effective in the near future. However, it is becoming technologically feasible to harvest some of the larger zooplankton, for example, *Euphausia superba*, the 'krill' of the Southern Ocean, which at times occurs in dense swarms, and upon which the baleen whales feed. Of course, reduced catches of the present commercial species of fish could result from exploitation of the zooplankton upon which they depend. However, whale stocks already having been reduced to low levels by fishing, the utilisation of krill is a logical step to take. The annual production of Antarctic krill is estimated to be well over 100 million tonnes, and the potential yield to be around 50 million tonnes,[10] although at this stage margins of error must be fairly wide. Recent West German and Polish krill expeditions have experienced catch rates of tens of tons per hour by experimental mid water trawling and it is estimated that several hundred tons per day could be taken aboard each vessel. It is therefore expected that once the technological problems of processing have been ironed out catches of krill will be far and away in excess of the few thousand tons presently taken by the Japanese for their high-price, speciality market.

Together, these unconventional species could, within a decade, provide quantities of fish as great or even greater than the present landings of traditional species; the world catch of all species is expected to reach 130 million tonnes in 2000. However, the catching and processing of new species will require far more energy than conventional species, and it remains to be seen whether these new developments will be economically as well as technically viable. A further question is who will exploit these huge resources? Those nations with experience of distant water fishing will obviously be the ones technologically able to fish them. However, the ownership of such stocks is now very much open to question, particularly in the Antarctic where the rights of states with a traditional interest in the area[11] are being challenged by the developing countries[12] who feel that the resources of Antarctica should be shared by the world community.

Further supplies of fish will be produced by marine fish farming, a topic which is outside the scope of this chapter.[13] However, the importance of fish farming should be put into perspective. Already, world production of farmed freshwater and marine fish and shellfish is around 6 million tonnes (half of it in China), having doubled in five years. The majority of this is still low-value, herbivorous fish like milk fish or tilapia, grown on an artisanal basis in shallow lagoons in the tropics, where high water temperatures encourage rapid growth of both fish and their food. Unfortunately, in the higher latitudes marine lagoons are less common and naturally warm sea water is not available. Other methods of marine fish farming are often capital or labour intensive and there are few popular fish that can be cheaply fed on algae or other plant material. Further expansion of marine fish farming will therefore be very much controlled by economics and will be seen in two fields: firstly, in the extensive culture of animals low in the food chain, like oysters and mussels, which are conveniently sessile, and which are filter feeders and therefore require no artificial food; secondly, in the intensive culture of confined mobile animals which are high in the food chain and therefore expensive to feed, but which are considered delicacies and are consequently of high value, for example, salmon and turbot. Therefore, whilst marine fish farming will undoubtedly expand, it will certainly not provide a substitute for, or even an equal to, fish supplies from wild stocks. In the UK, for example, utilisation of all potential marine fish farming sites and all suitable supplies of waste heat could produce 58,000 tonnes of fish per annum, that is, only 5 per cent of the present total UK consumption of fish by weight.[14] World production of all farmed fish is not expected to exceed 20 million tonnes per annum by 2000.

THE BIOLOGICAL BASIS OF THE RESOURCE

Fishing
The regulation of marine fisheries might easily be seen as the division of a finite cake between participants and indeed national negotiating teams often appear to take this view. However, it is in fact the tool used for the

management of a living and growing resource. To appreciate the logic and importance of management measures it is necessary to understand the nature of this renewable resource.

How is it that fish can be taken from the sea, apparently *ad infinitum*? First, advantage is taken of growth. All the fish in a stock are growing, so that if fish are taken from the stock before they die from the natural causes of disease, parasitism or predation, then the production of flesh during the lifetime of those fish is taken for the fishery, rather than being returned to the ecosystem. It is also possible that growth may be density dependent in some species, so that removal of fish from the stock will create increased growth in the remainder, presumably because of reduced competition for food.[15]

Secondly, any fish stock has an inherent reproductive over-capacity. This has adaptive value in that it allows a stock to expand into vacant environment and allows it to recover from any natural depletion of its numbers. There is, then, an excess of eggs, larvae or juveniles available to join the adult stock. The mortality of these pre-recruit stages is partially density dependent, due to the effects of competition for food and space, predation, or both. For a stock that is in equilibrium with the carrying capacity of its environment, this density-dependent mortality produces a relationship between recruitment and stock size such that a fall in stock size will result in an increase in recruitment, whilst an increase in stock size will result in decreased recruitment, as demonstrated by the curves in figure 2.1. This is a combination of negative and positive feedback systems which leads to stability of stock size. When the stock size is reduced by fishing, recruitment will increase, and if fishing continues at a fixed rate the stock will eventually stabilise at a smaller size, with the fishery taking advantage of the surplus reproduction and producing a *sustainable yield*. The annual catch will then be equal to the absolute growth or natural increase of the stock at its new size.

Overfishing

At low rates of fishing a high proportion of potential yield is lost from the fishery by natural mortality, a situation which may be termed *underfishing*. At high rates of fishing mortality due to fishing predominates and a high proportion of fish are taken from the stock before they have contributed significantly to its biomass. This results in the yield from the fishery being lower than its potential, a situation which may be termed *growth over fishing*.[16] An example of this was 'the small plaice problem' in the southern North Sea, one of the first problems to be considered by the International Council for the Exploration of the Sea in the early 1900s.

Reference to the recruitment curves in Figure 2.1 indicates that a reduction of stock by fishing will only result in an increase in recruitment

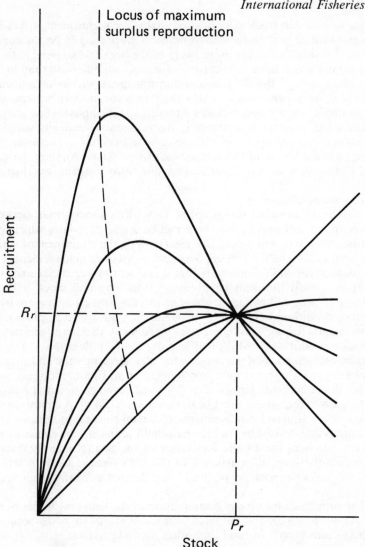

Figure 2.1 *Graph of Locus of Maximum Surplus Reproduction*

A family of theoretical curves showing different degrees of dependence of recruitment on stock size (from D. H. Cushing (1975) after W. E. Ricker, 'Handbook of computations for biological statistics of fish populations', *Bulletin of the Fisheries Research Board of Canada*, Vol. 119 (1958). A curve for cod would be like the steeply domed curve, whilst that for herring would be rather flat; flatfish would fall between the two. The point where the curves cut the bisector is the replacement level of stock and reproduction, that is, the point at which a stock will stabilise.

down to a certain stock size. Beyond that point recruitment will fall, a situation which may be termed *recruitment overfishing*.[17] As the curves show, this situation is far more likely in the herring-like pelagic fishes (clupeoids) which have little capacity for stock stabilisation than in the cod-like demersal fishes (gadoids) and flat fishes which have a huge potential for recruitment. It is also likely to occur in marine mammals, for example, whales, and in elasmobranch (cartilaginous) fishes, such as skate, which produce few offspring. Recruitment is naturally variable, which makes recruitment overfishing difficult to confirm. However, it is likely that the failure of the North Sea 'Downs' (East Anglian) herring and Californian sardine fisheries were due to recruitment overfishing.

Management Objectives
It will be obvious in the simplest view of a fishery that between underfishing and overfishing there will be a rate of fishing which will produce the *maximum sustainable yield* (MSY), the attainment of which has been held to be the general objective of fisheries management. The problem of the MSY concept is that it is essentially artificial since the maximum yield that can be obtained from any real stock without altering its size will change from year to year with changing environmental conditions. A further problem is that without protracted experimental fishing at different rates it is difficult to determine whether a stock is producing its MSY, a little above it, or a little below.[18] It must also be recognised that the reasons for management vary and may be aimed at providing maximum employment or maximum economic gain rather than maximum yield of fish. They may even be aimed at a short-term gain rather than the usual sustained yield.[19] A more useful objective of fisheries management which takes these questions into account is that devised by the International Technical Conference on the Conservation of the Living Resources of the Sea (Rome, 1955) and subsequently adopted in article 2 of the 1958 Geneva Convention on Fishing and Conservation of the Living Resources of the High Seas:

> The principal objective of conservation of the living resources of the seas is to obtain the *optimum sustainable yield* so as to secure a maximum supply of food and other marine products.

This more pragmatic and flexible approach can take account of such considerations as the fact that at a point below the MSY the 'law of diminishing returns' may make it uneconomic to fish right up to the MSY. However, MSY remains a useful biological, or rather mathematical, concept upon which further objectives may be developed.

Fisheries Research
In order to take sound management measures that will satisfy the chosen

objective it is necessary to carry out research on the fish stock. The study of fish population dynamics is a science in itself which cannot be adequately treated in a summary such as this,[20] but some brief notes on the methods used will help to put the subject into perspective.

The earliest methods were the descriptive or surplus production methods. Here catch (equilibrium yield) is plotted against stock (biomass) to give a parabolic relationship in which maximum sustainable yield will be obtained at half the maximum or virgin stock. A similar relationship will exist between catch and fishing effort. Unlike other methods, the surplus production model can be applied to mixed fisheries. However, the difficulty with such models is that, as outlined above, many years of historical data at different levels of fishing effort are required. With so much fishing power now available a fishery can be decimated before such information has been accumulated.

The more recently developed dynamic pool or analytical methods can be applied with greater speed. Here, fish-tagging experiments and records of catch per unit effort are used to determine fishing mortality, stock size and stock density, and market sampling of fish is used to produce weight, length and age distribution of the fish population, from which the growth rate and total mortality rate can be estimated. From such information it is possible to construct curves showing yield per recruit as a function of fishing mortality for a given age at first capture, or as a function of age at first capture for a fixed level of fishing mortality. The two curves can be combined to produce a yield isopleth which can be used to determine the management measures needed to produce maximum sustainable yield per recruit.[21] A further refinement would be to determine the stock recruitment relationship and combine this with yield per recruit analysis.

It should not be assumed from the comments above that research on a fish stock will always provide exact formulae for the management of its fishery.[22] In many cases vital information is lacking or is difficult or time-consuming to obtain, and here educated guesswork by the biologists in framing management proposals is, perhaps, preferable to waiting until the information is available. The stock size of a fish species depends upon a web of interaction between the species, its environment, its competitors, its predators and diseases and its food.[23] Fluctuations in these ecological factors will result in natural variations in reproduction, growth and mortality which cannot possibly be predicted by the described methods of population study. The study of fish population dynamics must therefore be considered as an attempt at estimating the effect of fishing on fish stocks which are also affected by many other factors.

MANAGEMENT OF THE RESOURCE

Measures
The management measures that can be taken to optimise yield are based on the population dynamics of the stock and are therefore the same in national or international management. Individual fish species will have special management requirements, for example, in order to protect young fish it may be necessary to close nursery grounds to fishing, to introduce closed seasons, or to ban industrial fishing for low-value industrial fish like pout, sand eels or sprats, where the by-catch of young consumption fish like haddock or herring is unacceptably high. However, as will have been deduced from the foregoing section, the two general methods of management are to control the age or size at first capture and to limit the total fishing effort. This would seem to be a relatively simple matter but it is by no means so.

For species like lobsters that are taken in pots, size at first capture can be controlled by escape gaps in the gear or by legal minimum sizes for the landed fish. However, in the commonest methods of fishing, those using some form of net, control of size at first capture is attempted by setting a legal minimum mesh size so that the young fish can escape through the meshes. This could be a satisfactory measure in fisheries for pelagic fish which swim in single species shoals. Ironically, in these species it is not usually necessary to control age at first capture since growth is very slow after the first few years and growth does not therefore need to be conserved. With these species control of stock size (that is, control of fishing effort) is needed to maintain recruitment. Most demersal fish, on the other hand, are liable to growth overfishing, and growth does need to be conserved. However, many demersal fisheries are for mixed species and it will be obvious that for each species the age at first capture which will give optimum yield will be different. The result is a mesh size compromise, one of the many which have to be made in managing a mixed fishery. The difference in shape between the sole and the ray is an indication of the difficulty that exists in trying to find such a compromise and it is likely that the value of the individual species will eventually be the deciding factor.

As a further attempt to regulate age at first capture of individual species in mixed fisheries, minimum sizes for taking the fish are set for each species. The value of these will depend upon the viability of discarded fish, which in the case of fish with gas-filled 'swim bladders' (most bony fish except the flatfishes) is not great because as the fish is drawn to the surface and external water pressure is suddenly reduced, the bladder explodes. Such measures do, however, ensure that boats avoid areas where the percentage of young fish on the ground is high.

From an economic point of view effort is best controlled by limitation on entry to the fishery by licensing since this allows individual units to operate at a high level of economic efficiency. This cannot, however, take account of the effect of increases in individual effort so the amount of gear per boat may also need to be regulated. However, effort can still be increased. For example, in the Western Australian rock lobster fishery the number of boats was fixed by licence in 1963 and the expected increase in amount of gear per boat was forestalled by making a gear allowance of three pots per foot of boat length, with a maximum of 200 pots per boat. The average size of boats then started increasing and in 1965 boat length was also limited. There were, however, still increases in total effort by more frequent lifting of pots, better reef location and longer fishing trips.[24] It is now estimated that 75 per cent of the fishable stock is taken in each fishing season.

To control total effort effectively without using very complex legislation it is, therefore, usually necessary to introduce a limit on catch for each species, particularly in an international fishery. This has the advantage of being easy to alter annually or more frequently in pelagic fisheries, depending on the latest estimates of recruitment. The disadvantage is that it can again result in uneconomic fishing since the participants will tend to over-capitalise in order to take as large a share of the total allowable catch (TAC) in as short a time as possible.[25] The TAC can then be divided up into quotas for nations, regions, individual boats or even individual fishermen.

A framework of management measures is usually built up over a period of time and, whilst economic fishing may not be one of the management objectives, unless licensing is introduced as a new fishery starts, over-capitalisation is almost inevitable. Over-capitalisation has become a feature of many European fishing fleets, both the small boat inshore fleets and the distant water fleets deprived of grounds since the introduction of national 200 mile fishing limits. Legislation has therefore been put forward by the EEC to introduce laying up subsidies, early retirement pensions and retraining schemes for fishermen to remedy the situation. In South Australia, a recent report has suggested the establishment of a vessel 'buy back' scheme, financed by fishing licence fees, as a means of reducing over-capitalisation in the rock lobster fishery.[26] Where possible, limitation on entry to the fishery before such measures become necessary would be preferable from an economic and social point of view.

International Management of Fisheries
Fisheries are managed internationally by some twenty-two international Commissions[27] which have been established over the years since the International Fisheries Commission (for Pacific halibut) was first formed in 1924. Five of these Commissions are subsidiary bodies of FAO (Food and Agricultural Organisation of the UN) and the rest were established by various international conventions. The Commissions fall

into two groups, the species Commissions which are concerned with one species or a group of related species, for example, the Inter American Tropical Tuna Commission, and the regional Commissions which deal with all or the most important fished species within a defined region, for example, the Indian Ocean Fisheries Commission. These Commissions have had various degrees of success in achieving their aims which, whilst differently expressed, are generally to conserve the fish stocks within their jurisdiction. Examination of a few case histories will give an indication of the problems involved.

Species Commissions. The International Pacific Halibut Commission (IPHC) has been one of the most successful in conserving its fish stock (*Hippoglossus stenolepis*).[28] The Commission was formed by Canada and the United States when construction of the transcontinental railway system resulted in such an expansion of the longline fishery that halibut catches and stock fell dramatically. The Commission's own scientific staff, pioneers in their field, developed a descriptive model of the fishery which related catch to fishing effort and in 1930 regulations were introduced to control effort by closed seasons. Abundance and catch then increased steadily until 1960, during which time further regulations were introduced. (Landings have fallen since 1960 due possibly to adverse environmental conditions and certainly to trawling by-catch of halibut. Time-area trawl closures agreed by Canada, USA, USSR and Japan in 1976 should reduce the latter considerably.) The most recent (1953) Halibut Convention defines MSY as the Commission's objective but, unfortunately, does not give the Commission authority to limit entry or to allocate the catch. Improved catches up until 1960 and more recent improvements in the price of halibut have therefore led to increased entry into the fishery and over-capitalisation which has been further exacerbated by the resulting need for shorter open seasons (presently around 100 days per annum). The very constitution of the Commission has, then, prevented biological conservation from being accompanied by economic conservation.

The International Whaling Commission (IWC)[29] is perhaps the antithesis of the IPHC in terms of its record of stock conservation. During the major part of its life since it was established by the Convention for the Regulation of Whaling in 1946, the IWC has acted more like a trade association than a management body. Indeed, the various international whaling agreements of the 1930s, out of which the 1946 Convention was born, were concerned as much with bringing economic stability to the whaling industry in an atmosphere of over-supply of whale oil (over 3·6 million barrels were produced in the 1930/1 season) and falling prices as with halting the decline in abundance of Antarctic whales. Even the method of TAC regulation used until 1972, a limit on the number of Blue Whale Units (BWU) (1 blue whale = 2 fin whales $= 2\frac{1}{2}$ humpbacks $= 6$ sei whales) taken, was based on oil yield of the whales, rather than the population dynamics of the individual species. For years the member states of the Commission (now including Argentina, Australia, Canada, Chile, Denmark, France, Iceland, Japan, Mexico, Norway, Panama, Peru, Seychelles, South Africa, South Korea, Sweden, UK, USA, USSR) would not agree to a sufficiently low TAC and landings consequently continued to fall. The effort on the whale fishing industry was aggravated by the terms of the 1946 Convention which, like those of other high seas fisheries conventions, did not allow the IWC to limit entry to the fishery and, therefore, failed to prevent over-capitalisation. In 1965, with the Antarctic whale fishery close to economic failure and the IWC on the point of collapse, the members finally agreed to catch limits scientifically based on the MSY concept. Management has improved since then, particularly since 1972 when the BWU system was abandoned in favour of quotas for individual species (including zero quotas where necessary), and since 1974 when the New Management Procedure classified stocks according to their conservation needs.

The opinion has been expressed that, whilst the IWC has not been very successful, it has at least slowed the decline of the blue and fin whale stocks, that is, that some conservation is better than none. However, the 1946 Convention has loopholes, and lacks teeth. The 1946 Convention has the very common provision that any member nation may be exempted from a majority decision of the Commission if it lodges an objection within ninety days; and there have even been temporary withdrawals from the Commission (Norway, 1959–60 and Netherlands, 1959–62). The IWC itself has little power to enforce the regulations which it adopts, the system of enforcement being the use of national inspectors and the prosecution of infringements by the home government. (Enforcement has improved since 1972: ships now carry two national inspectors and one bilaterally agreed international observer. Observers are appointed by IWC and report direct to it.) It is, therefore, arguable whether the conservation gained has been any greater than could have been obtained by international negotiation and agreement between the relatively small number of active whaling nations. This is, in any case, the system used for dividing the annual quotas between nations, a function which is again specifically excluded from the convention.

Relatively good progress was made at the 31st session of the IWC in July 1979. For example, a moratorium on pelagic whaling (except for minkes and except aboriginal whaling) was accepted; this will reduce sperm whaling. The Seychelles proposal for a whale reserve in part of the Indian Ocean was also accepted. However, a new and growing problem is that of whaling by non-member countries: Japanese whale imports from such states doubled during 1977. Member states can similarly avoid IWC quotas by the use of 'flags of convenience'. The control of whale product imports by member states is one of the many subjects which must be included in a revision of the 1946 Convention if the IWC is to be enabled to manage the world stocks of whales properly.

Regional Commissions. The regional Commissions range in their functions from discussion groups and advisory bodies to management organisations. Good examples of the latter are the International Commission for Northwest Atlantic Fisheries (ICNAF), established in 1950 by a convention of 1949, and its counterpart the North East Atlantic Fisheries Commission (NEAFC), established in 1963 by a convention of 1959.[30] NEAFC replaced the Permanent Commission of the 1946 Convention for the Regulation of the Meshes of Fishing Nets and the Size Limits of Fish (the 'Overfishing Convention') which was established in 1953. The original members of NEAFC were Belgium, Denmark, France, FRG, Iceland, Ireland, Netherlands, Norway, Poland, Portugal, Spain, Sweden, UK and USSR. They were later joined by Finland, GDR, Bulgaria and Cuba; in 1977 the members of the EEC left NEAFC.

The International Council for the Exploration of the Sea (ICES), originally formed in 1902, acts as a forum for those engaged in fisheries research in the North Atlantic. Within ICES there is a Working Group concerned with each stock, the members of the Working Groups being the acknowledged experts on these stocks from each member state. NEAFC has always taken its scientific advice from ICES and has therefore had available to it the best scientific information of the day. However, NEAFC has not generally been successful in conserving the fish stocks of the north-east Atlantic, and the fact that it has now become necessary to ban fishing for herring, the species most in need of conservation, in virtually the whole of the NEAFC region is a monument to the lack of success. The reasons for this failure are mostly the same as those given for the conservation failures of the previously mentioned Commissions.

The original Permanent Commission did not have any power over herring. The 1959 NEAF Convention included herring but did not provide for the regulation of fishing effort by NEAFC, confining its management measures to minimum sizes for landed fish and net meshes. It became clear that these measures were insufficient, but it was not until 1974 that NEAFC obtained the power to limit effort by the adoption of TACs and national quotas because of the failure by Belgium and Iceland to ratify the recommendation made some years previously. However, the first TAC for North Sea herring was well in excess of that recommended by ICES, a characteristic common to many NEAFC TACs. A further inadequacy of the 1959 Convention was that it gave NEAFC power only to recommend necessary measures and allowed individual states to object to recommendations made by the majority. Even after the introduction of TACs had been approved in principle, agreement on herring TACs could not be reached for 1975/6 because of objections by those nations with fishmeal industries based on herring. Regardless of the constitution of a Commission, it cannot succeed in conserving the fish stocks for which it is responsible without its member states having the will to accept immediate sacrifices for long-term common benefits; this has not been the case with NEAFC members. In fact during the long discussion period leading up to the acceptance of national quotas, fishing effort was maintained at a high level by many member states so that they could eventually benefit from national quotas based on 'historical performance'. When quotas were introduced some states failed to enforce them on their fishermen and once this became common knowledge others also disregarded them for fear of being disadvantaged.[31] NEAFC originally had no powers of enforcement and the Joint Enforcement Scheme with powers of mutual inspection introduced in 1972 is, like that of the IWC, limited to prosecution by the flag state. The greatest stimulus for exceeding quotas is over-capitalisation which, owing to the (until recently) high seas nature of the region, NEAFC has been powerless to control.

Conclusions. The development of a system of fisheries management by international Commissions is logical, given the international nature of many fish stocks, but it does not appear to have worked very well so far. The reasons for this are threefold. First, many of the Commissions have inadequate constitutions which lack provisions for the control of fishing effort (particularly control of entry to the fishery), lack any worthwhile enforcement scheme, and have loopholes written into them allowing individual members to dissent. Secondly, for national and international political reasons member nations have found it difficult to agree to proposed regulations and even more difficult to agree to reductions in catch based on scientific advice. Thirdly, even with the establishment of an international Commission, the high seas nature of the fishery has remained, allowing unlimited entry to the fishery by non-member states. In some cases, even apparent conservation success has been due to good fortune: for example, the occurrence of two good year classes in the early 1970s has brought the Barents Sea cod stock back to a potentially healthy state from the much reduced state to which it had fallen due to recruitment overfishing in the late 1960s.

An unmanaged fishery will experience a natural economic control, that is, unregulated fishing will reduce stocks to a density below which fishing is uneconomic and fishing will cease. Stocks will then recover and eventually fishing will start again. Thus exploitation would go on as a series of peaks and troughs (although in species which are liable to recruitment overfishing there would be only one peak). A good example of this is the sub-Antarctic Kerguelen fur seal, *Arctocephalus tropicalis*, which has been 'exterminated' three times over.[32] This pattern of exploitation will result in over-capitalisation of catching and processing plant, irregularity of supply and periodic unemployment. For the management of a fishery to be declared successful it must eliminate these economic and social ills. This has often not been the case with management by international Commissions. Management itself must also be economic. In 1971 the cost of fisheries research and regulation in the USA was $110 million compared with a total catch value of $600 million;[33] in the UK, annual government expenditure on all sea fisheries R & D runs at $4\frac{1}{2}$ per cent of the value of the British catch,[34] although for certain individual species this ratio is much higher.

The degree of success of the international Commissions seems to have been inversely related to the number of member nations and the ultimate conclusion is that management by individual coastal states would be the best method (although there have been some notable failures of conservation of fish stocks under single nation jurisdiction, for example, the Californian sardine). However, management within the relatively narrow ribbon of the territorial sea would be futile because of the extent and mobility of fish stocks. There has, therefore, been a movement towards the management of fisheries by coastal states within much extended fisheries limits. The Single Negotiating Texts of the Third United Nations Conference on the Law of the Sea (UNCLOS III) provided that coastal states should, in an exclusive economic zone (EEZ) extending to 200 miles from the baselines of the territorial sea, exercise sovereign rights for the purpose of exploring and exploiting their living resources, subject to various conditions. This had no legal status but, in the absence of any firm international agreement, it led to a spate of unilateral declarations of 200 mile fisheries limits in 1976 and 1977, totalling seventy out of a possible 130 by November 1977. This action, which at last establishes control of fish stocks, will have an enormous impact on the future of world fisheries management and provides hope for its eventual success.

FISHERIES MANAGEMENT WITHIN 200 MILE LIMITS

The importance of 200 mile limits can be seen from the fact that the EEZs cover only 35 per cent of the world's sea area but take in 90 per cent of the living resources being exploited commercially at present, that is, the majority of the world's fish stocks will in future be under single nation jurisdiction.

Fish supplies
The social, economic and political significance of 200 mile limits is illustrated by Table 2.3 which shows the 1972 catches of fish, not

Table 2.3   *Estimated World fish catches (thousands of tonnes) by non-local fleets, 1972*

| | Total | | Nationality of vessel | | Location | |
	World Catch *(for comparison)*	Non-local	Developed	Developing	Off Developed	Off Developing
North-west Atlantic	4,329	2,292	2,288	4	2,194	98
North-east Atlantic	10,690	3,667	3,667	0	3,619	48
West-central Atlantic	1,481	143	128	15	37	106
East-central Atlantic	3,356	1,930	1,870	60	0	1,930
Mediterranean/Black Sea	1,137	40	40	0	0	40
South-west Atlantic	805	24	14	10	0	24
South-east Atlantic	3,002	1,771	1,662	109	271	1,500
West Indian Ocean	1,739	201	158	43	0	201
East Indian Ocean	814	88	23	65	9	79
North-west Pacific	14,531	2,936	2,600	336	2,550	386
North-east Pacific	2,775	2,254	2,254	0	2,254	0
West-central Pacific	4,772	479	129	350	0	479
East-central Pacific	979	287	284	3	13	274
South-west Pacific	275	199	123	76	199	0
South-east Pacific	5,562	48	48	0	0	48
Total all oceans	56,247	16,359	15,288	1,071	11,146	5,213

Source: J. A. Gulland, 'World fisheries and fish stocks', *Marine Policy*, vol. 1, no. 3 (1977), pp. 179–89.

including whales, taken by non-local fleets in each oceanic area, with total catches in those areas for comparison. (These figures include catches taken outside 200 miles, but those are almost exclusively catches of tuna which make up only 1 per cent of the world catch.) Of general importance is the fact that non-local fisheries amounted to over a quarter of the total world catch. It can be seen that the non-local catch was taken principally from the North Pacific, North Atlantic and East Atlantic (mainly the West African upwelling areas, that is, the Saharan coast and off Angola and Namibia). Of particular importance is the fact that whilst nearly all of the non-local catch was taken by vessels from the developed countries, about a third of it was taken off the coasts of developing countries. The introduction of 200 mile EEZs therefore presented the developed nations with the problem of maintaining traditional fish supplies, and effectively delivered into the ownership of certain underdeveloped countries fish stocks which they did not have the capability of harvesting.

These problems have been overcome by a whole series of bilateral agreements, at the time of writing still in the process of development, which provide continuity of traditional supplies to the big fishing nations and at the same time grant some kind of compensation to the nations from whose waters the fish are taken. The great range of benefits conferred to either side by such agreements almost defies classification but some typical examples have emerged. The most straightforward is agreement to reciprocal fishing rights in cases where both parties have within their jurisdiction valuable fish to offer. Norway and the Faroes, for example, are granted quotas of mackerel within EEC waters in exchange for quotas of demersal fish to be taken from their own waters by EEC vessels. Then there are the joint ventures where an established fishing nation is granted the right to fish in the waters of an underdeveloped nation if it involves local industry in the exercise or aids the development of a local fishing fleet. For example, Argentina has agreed to the taking of 100,000 tonnes of fish per annum (75 per cent hake) from her waters by West German vessels, on the condition that it is landed at Argentine ports for processing and packing. At the same time the agreement allows fisheries research in Argentine waters by German scientists, but includes provision of a $70m German loan for Argentina to conduct her own research using German supplies and services. West German research boats will be permitted to take direct to West Germany 90 per cent of the fish they catch.[35] Package agreements yet to be made between the EEC and West African countries are likely to include the provision of technical and financial assistance in training local fishermen and developing a local fishing industry.

Less involved are the transhipping and trading agreements. Soviet vessels began fishing for mackerel off south-west England in 1968, and catches increased rapidly to a peak of 300,000 tonnes in 1975. In 1977 Soviet fishing activities ceased abruptly as they were excluded from the waters of the EEC 200 mile EEZs. However, supplies have been maintained by the direct transshipment of mackerel from British fishing vessels to Soviet factory ships. In the 1977/8 five-month season about half of the 188,000 tonne British mackerel catch was exported to the USSR and other Eastern bloc countries in this way and earned nearly £15m. There have been cases of bilateral negotiations for the removal of impediments to external trade in exchange for privileged access to fishing zones, for example, so-called 'fish for beef' deals. New Zealand had hoped to arrange for bigger imports of its farm produce by Japan as part of a *quid pro quo* for granting access to Japanese fishing vessels in the New Zealand EEZ. In the event, an agreement could not be reached and access until 1982 will be a straightforward sale of fishing rights. Each Japanese vessel will be licensed and will pay New Zealand $NZ82 per tonne of cuttlefish caught, and $NZ17 per tonne of demersal fish.[36] The payment of licence fees has become perhaps the simplest and most common bilateral agreement where there is the lack of fishing reciprocity. Another example is Italy which pays over half a million US dollars per annum to fish in Yugoslav waters with 100 small trawlers.

Fisheries Management
The establishment of 200 mile limits has caused remarkably little international conflict. The new limits have been accepted as customary

law, and following that acceptance, negotiations have taken place to establish a new regime of fisheries management with 200 mile EEZs. Whilst negotiations continue, the existing arrangements have in most cases been allowed to stand. That is not to say that there has not been disagreement. A good example of failure to agree concerns Jan Mayen, a small and remote Norwegian island which lies north-east of Iceland between the Atlantic and the Barents Sea. Norway proposes to establish a 200 mile EEZ around the island. Iceland, which has traditionally fished in this area, disputes the legality of this action. Iceland claims that Jan Mayen forms part of the Icelandic continental shelf and that the capelin and herring stocks within the proposed zone are cognate with Icelandic stocks. Even if Iceland were to agree to the Norwegian proposal further negotiations would be required to establish a median line where the new zone would overlap with the Icelandic 200 mile EEZ which was established in 1975. The irony of this particular situation is that whilst the two parties continue to disagree, more than 100 Soviet vessels are industrial fishing in the area. The dispute was resolved in 1980.

Two hundred mile EEZs have, of course, drastically altered the position of the international Fisheries Commissions. The species Commissions with restricted membership like the halibut, salmon and tuna Commissions in the Pacific continued to operate effectively. However, the relevance of most of the regional Commissions was reduced as individual nations asserted their authority to determine catches within their EEZs. A feature of this determination has been a general reduction in TACs, particularly for those foreign vessels allowed to continue fishing in national waters. Indeed, these reductions will put a temporary stop to the growth of the world fish catch. Late in 1978 a much reduced NEAFC agreed to continue in existence but, without the membership of EEC countries, its future role will be little more than that of an advisory body except in respect of the few stocks outside 200 mile limits.[37] Member states agreed, however, to work towards the adoption of a new convention suited to the changed circumstances. ICNAF was disbanded at the end of 1978 and replaced by the Northwest Atlantic Fisheries Organisation (NAFO). Establishment of NAFO was forced by Canada who made it clear to countries intending to fish in the Canadian EEZ, particularly those of the Eastern bloc, that access would not be granted unless they joined a new international agreement on fisheries outside 200 mile limits in the north-west Atlantic.

In many cases the schemes of TACs established by individual states for management purposes within their waters have been indistinguishable from the bilateral agreements on exploitation and supply. In some cases attempts to reach agreement have resulted in the same kind of problem experienced prior to the establishment of EEZs, the inability to keep TACs to a level demanded by the needs of conservation. Some further problems for the management and division of stocks have been experienced where the geography is such that states have very short lengths of coast or where a number of states front on to one fairly restricted body of water like the Baltic. These sorts of problem indicate that even with a 200 mile EEZ regime, where stocks are within national ownership and management can be nationally enforced, there is a place for bodies similar to the old international Commissions. In such a two-tier system 'shared' stocks might be exploited and managed in a more logical way than if simply divided between coastal states.

A good example of such a system might eventually emerge in the EEC itself when its Common Fisheries Policy (CFP) is finally revised. In many respects the EEC Commission has taken the place of NEAFC, since it covers much of the same area, has similar functions and takes its advice on fisheries matters from ICES.

The origin of the CFP, its development and the many proposals and revised proposals that have been put forward in the negotiation of a new CFP, is a long and complicated story which cannot be recited in detail here.[38] Three basic principles of the Community, upon which any CFP must be based, are that there should be no discrimination or unfair competition between member states, that there should be freedom of establishment in each other's territories and that there should be a common policy in the sphere of agriculture, including fish and fish products. To this end the original 1970 CFP comprised two EEC regulations. One provided for a common price and trading system and common rules on market competition for all fish and fish products. The other, more contentious, regulation provided not only for a common structural policy for the industry but also for common rules on fishing and, in particular, equal access for the vessels of all member states in waters under the jurisdiction of individual member states. One aim of this regulation was to encourage the rational use of the biological resources, that is, conservation; it is clear that if this is to be achieved whilst allowing non-discriminatory access to all stocks, then a very strong regime of enforcement is required to ensure adherence to management measures.

Certain limited derogations from the equal access provisions of the CFP were allowed both in 1970 and upon the accession of the three new members in 1972, to allow for adjustment to the new regime in areas where inshore fishing is of particular local importance. These derogations are due to end in 1982, unless they, and therefore the CFP, are renegotiated following a review which is required before that date. The declaration of 200 mile fisheries limits by all coastal member states has had such a momentous effect on their fisheries as to ensure a very thorough and comprehensive renegotiation. The renegotiation needs to take into account the same factors as must be considered by the EEC Commission in the annual division of the TAC of each fish stock between member states, namely:

(1) The proportion of total fish stocks contributed to the community by the EEZ of each member state.

(2) The losses of distant water fishing grounds sustained by each member state as a result of the extension of third countries' fishing limits to 200 miles.

(3) The historic rights of member states to fish in each other's waters.

(4) The historic catch performance of these states.

(5) The particular social and economic importance of inshore fisheries to certain coastal communities.

(6) The size and location of fish stocks which are to be fished by vessels of third countries and the member states which will benefit from reciprocal agreements with those countries.

(7) The effect on common stocks of the different fishing methods used by member states, for example, industrial fishing versus demersal trawling.

(8) The management measures needed for conservation and the relative effects of such management upon the fishing activities of individual member states.

If these factors are not taken into account in renegotiation of the CFP certain member states will be understandably aggrieved. The UK, for example, unless it is awarded a wide exclusive fisheries zone, will be in the position of being both the biggest loser of distant water catches as a result of third countries' extensions to 200 mile limits[39] and the biggest contributor of fish stocks (c.60 per cent) to the Community 'pond'. In addition, the UK would bear the major practical and financial burden of enforcement of conservation measures. This is quite contrary to the spirit of the Community, that is, a fair balance of benefits and disadvantages between member states.

Sea fisheries have become of great political importance within the EEC but they are of little economic significance compared with farming. There has been an attempt to keep these two subjects apart, at least formally. However, most EEC Agriculture Ministers are also Fisheries Ministers and they can hardly be expected to forget this economic position when negotiating fisheries matters. It is uncertain whether the agreement on EEC farm prices for 1979/80 happened by accident or design. If it was by design the UK has already paid the price for French agreement to British fishing demands. In view of the reduction in contribution to the EEC budget being sought by the UK at the time of writing, it is likely that Britain will still have to concede further political points before the CFP is settled.

It is clear that the original CFP, which envisaged a truly communal industry with common access, management, licensing, enforcement, market and structure, is unsuited to the new situation of 200 mile limits. Renegotiation based on this concept will be unsatisfactory. However, a two-tier system providing exclusive national coastal belts for fishing and jurisdiction over fisheries, all within a 200 mile EEC controlled zone, is more likely to achieve success.

Regional bodies established elsewhere will not be fettered by the dogma of equal access, but the question of access will still be important and all the points listed above will need to be considered in determining reciprocity and the division of shared resources. In the previously cited case of the Baltic, for example, it is unreasonable to expect the vessels of coastal states to be strictly restricted to their own EEZ. However, in the absence of agreement on the distribution of TACs between the members of the Baltic Fisheries Commission, this has virtually been the situation in the first two years of 200 mile EEZs.

Two hundred mile EEZs, in establishing control of stocks, have provided the authority for effective fisheries management and fair division of stocks. In the final analysis, however, efficient operation of the new regime will, as before, depend upon the diplomacy and co-operation of neighbouring states.

NOTES AND REFERENCES

It will be obvious from the list of references that certain authors dominate the general field of the biology and management of the world's fisheries. Foremost among them is Dr J. A. Gulland, who is remarkable in having pursued an outstanding career in fisheries science and management, in the UK and with FAO, and at the same time published widely in books and journals. His *The Management of Marine Fisheries* (Bristol: Scientechnica, 1974) is an excellent introduction to the subject. It is a readable book with explanatory material for students unfamiliar with the subject, but it still has room for detailed example topics, many of them taken from Dr Gulland's own experience. The other major author is Dr D. H. Cushing, whose *Fisheries Resources of the Sea and their Management* (London: Science and Engineering Policy Series, Oxford University Press, 1975) is another good introduction to marine fisheries including history, development, basic biology and management. However, the work contains highly condensed material and the interested reader will need to look to other works for explanatory detail. *Marine Ecology and Fisheries* (Cambridge: Cambridge University Press, 1975) by the same author, like Gulland's *The Management of Marine Fisheries*, includes all the information needed to make it a companion to the book above. It does, however, cover a wider range of ecological topics and contains a lot of information on the factors other than fishing which affect fish populations.

Students unused to scientific books might prefer F. T. Christy and A. Scott, *The Common Wealth in Ocean Fisheries. Some Problems of Growth and Economic Allocation* (Baltimore: John Hopkins Press, 1965) as a grounding in international fisheries. The subject is examined from a geographical and economic point of view, and is consequently more wordy than some of the other general works. J. R. Coull, *The Fisheries of Europe, An Economic Geography* (London: Bell, 1972) examines fisheries from the same point of view as Christy and Scott. Despite being more recent, it is more out of date because the fisheries of Europe in particular have been so affected by recent political events.

To understand the subject in depth it is necessary to examine some examples in greater detail than is possible in the general works quoted above. Useful examples are to be found in F. R. Harden Jones (ed), *Sea Fisheries Research* (London: Elek Science, 1974). This is a collection of twenty-one papers on a wide range of topics by scientists from the Ministry of

Agriculture, Fisheries and Food Fisheries Laboratory in England and Wales. The topics include examples of the problems in fisheries biology and management raised in this chapter, but other topics like marine pollution and shellfish culture are also included.

As has been intimated in this chapter, knowledge of the dynamics of a fish population is an essential prerequisite of management measures. J. A. Gulland (ed), *Fish Population Dynamics* (London: Wiley, 1977) provides a wealth of detail on all the aspects of fish population dynamics referred to in the chapter. Using both theoretical models and well-known example stocks, the authors describe how the dynamics of fish populations can be analysed in terms of the factors affecting their rates of growth, mortality and reproduction, with emphasis on the effects of fishing. The book also contains an interesting history of the subject by W. E. Ricker. Papers on fish population dynamics are included in J. H. Steele (ed), *Fisheries Mathematics* (London: Academic Press, 1977), but not exclusively as might be assumed from the title. *Fish Population Dynamics* would be a better buy for students of international fisheries whose interest in the nature of the resource has been stimulated.

Finally, the student who wishes to progress further will need reference sources of facts on international fisheries. J. A. Gulland, *The Fish Resources of the Ocean* (London: Fishing News (Books), 1972) is an excellent treatise on the known or estimated potential of all fish stocks in all the oceans of the world, based on a wide selection of research work. This is due to be updated shortly but is still very useful for comparative purposes. It can be used with advantage if read with the *Atlas of the Living Resources of the Sea* (Rome: FAO, 1972). A. W. Koers, *International Regulation of Marine Fisheries* (London: Fishing News) (Books), 1973) contains a comprehensive guide to the Fisheries Commissions and a full discussion of alternative methods of fisheries regulation, with many useful references. Unfortunately, because of the rapidly changing international situation, it is already a little out of date with respect to the powers and functions of the Commissions.

1   World distribution of phytoplankton and zooplankton is illustrated in the *Atlas of the Living Resources of the Sea* (Rome: FAO, 1972).
2   1968 landings cartographically represented in FAO, op. cit.
3   A. P. Isarankura and G. Kuhlmorgen-Hille, 'Demersal fish resources investigations in the Gulf of Thailand', *Proceedings of the Indo-Pacific Fisheries Council.*, vol. 12, no. 2 (1967), pp. 162–71.
4   J. A. Gulland, *The Fish Resources of the Ocean* (London: Fishing News (Books), 1972); S. J. Lockwood, 'Mackerel. A problem in fish stock assessment', *Laboratory Leaflet*, no. 44 (Ministry of Agriculture, Fisheries and Food, Fisheries Laboratory, Lowestoft, 1978).
5   Gulland, op. cit.
6   ibid.
7   P. Appleyard of FAO quoted in *Eurofish Report*, vol. 41 (22 November 1978). See also J. R. Coull, *The Fisheries of Europe – an Economic Geography* (London: Bell, 1972).
8   G. D. Stroud, 'Squid', *Torry Advisory Note*, no. 77 (Edinburgh: HMSO, 1978).
9   R. V. Tait, *Elements of Marine Ecology* (London: Butterworths, 1968).
10 J. A. Gulland, 'Antarctic marine living resources', in *Adaptations Within Antarctic Ecosystems* (Washington, DC: Smithsonian Institution, 1977).
11 That is, the original signatories (Argentina, Chile, Norway, UK, Australia, France, New Zealand, US, USSR, Japan, South Africa, Belgium) to the 1959 Antarctic Treaty.
12 B. Mitchell, 'Resources in Antartica, potential for conflict', *Marine Policy*, vol. 1, no. 2 (1977), pp. 91–101.
13 See: P. H. Milne, *Fish and Shellfish Farming in Coastal Waters* (London: Fishing News (Books), 1972); E. S. Iversen, *Farming the Edge of the Sea*, rev. edn (London: Fishing News (Books), 1977).
14 N. M. Kerr and S. J. Kingwell, *Progress in Farming Marine Fish 1977* (Edinburgh: White Fish Authority, 1977).

15 Theoretical treatments have indicated that density-dependent growth may be expected, but direct evidence of this is somewhat limited. The effect has been shown to be more important in young fish. This subject is discussed by J. A. Gulland, 'Ecological aspects of fishery research', in J. B. Cragg (ed.), *Advances in Ecological Research*, Vol. 7 (London: Academic Press, 1971).

16 Defined in D. H, Cushing, 'A history of some of the international fisheries commissions', *Proceedings of the Royal Society of Edinburgh (B)*, no. 73 (1972), pp. 361–90.

17 ibid.

18 The problems in using MSY, and some alternative concepts, are discussed in J. A. Gulland and L. K. Boerema, 'Scientific advice on catch levels', *Fishery Bulletin*, vol. 71, no. 2 (1973), pp. 325–35.

19 The many possible reasons are thoroughly discussed in J. A. Gulland, 'Goals and objectives of fishery management', *FAO Fisheries Technical Paper*, no. 166 (1977).

20 For further reading on the subject see: J. A. Gulland (ed.), *Fish Population Dynamics* (London: Wiley, 1977); J. H. Steele (ed.), *Fisheries Mathematics* (London: Academic Press, 1977).

21 The best known use of this treatment is for the North Sea plaice stock. See R. C. A. Bannister in Gulland (ed.). op. cit.

22 Some of the problems involved and methods of overcoming them are described in F. R. Harden-Jones (ed.), *Sea Fisheries Research* (London: Elek Science, 1974).

23 Such interaction is discussed by J. A. Gulland, op. cit. n. 15 above. See also D. H. Cushing, *Marine Ecology of Fisheries* (Cambridge: Cambridge University Press, 1975).

24 B. K. Bowen, 'Management of the western rock lobster', *Australian Fisheries*, vol. 31 (1972), pp. 24–5.

25 Over-capitalisation is discussed more fully by J. A. Crutchfield, 'Over-capitalization of the fishing effort', in L. M. Alexander (ed.), *The Future of the Sea's Resources* (Kingston, RI: University of Rhode Island, 1968), pp. 23–9.

26 P. Pownall, 'Future management of ailing South Australian rock lobster fishery', *Australian Fisheries*, vol. 37, no. 8 (1978), pp. 12–15.

27 Details of the international Commissions, their constitutions, membership and jurisdiction are to be found in 'Report on Regulatory Fishery Bodies', FAO Fisheries Circular no. 138 (1972).

28 For a brief review of the history and functions of the IPHC see *The Pacific Halibut: Biology* (Seattle: IPHC, 1978).

29 For a brief review of the history and functions of the IWC see R. Gambell, 'Whale conservation. Role of the International Whaling Commission', *Marine Policy*, vol. 1, no. 4 (1977), pp. 301–10.

30 For a brief review of the history and functions of ICNAF and NEAFC see D. H. Cushing, 'The Atlantic fisheries commissions', *Marine Policy*, vol. 1, no. 3 (1977), pp. 230–8.

31 North Sea landings of sole in 1976 were 12 per cent above the TAC set by NEAFC, and this was already more than 50 per cent higher than the TAC recommended by ICES. In addition there were non-reported landings of sole. H. A. Cole, 'The conservation of fish stocks: can the lessons be learnt in time?', *Marine Pollution Bulletin*, vol. 9 (1978), pp. 57–8.

32 R. S. R. Fitter, 'Hunting the whale (and others) to death', *Marine Pollution Bulletin*, vol. 9 (1978), pp. 173–5.

33 J. C. McHugh, *Domestic Wrangles and International Tangles* (Washington: Woodrow Wilson International Centre for Scholars, 1971).

34 Anon., *Fisheries Research and Development Board Third Report, 1976–1977* Ministry of Agriculture, Fisheries and Food/Department of Agriculture and Fisheries for Scotland (London: HMSO, 1978).

35 Anon., *Eurofish Report*, nos. 21 and 26 (1978).

36 Anon., *Eurofish Report*, no. 36 (1978).
37 The EEC Commission insists that it is the appropriate body to represent the interests of its member states on international Commissions. The USSR and other Eastern bloc countries refuse to recognise the EEC. These two views are irreconcilable and have resulted in the withdrawal of EEC member states from NEAFC. However, a tacit acceptance of the EEC by the USSR appears to be emerging in other Commissions, for example, the new NAFO and in 1980 also in NEAFC.
38 For such details see P. W. Birnie in *Fifth Report from the Expenditure Committee, Session 1977–78, The Fishing Industry*, Vol. I, Appendix I (London: HMSO, 1978).
39 UK catch off non-EEC North Atlantic states in 1972 was 378,000 tonnes (36 per cent of total UK catch in North Atlantic waters). R. Churchill, 'The EEC fisheries policy – towards a revision', *Marine Policy*, vol. 1, no. 1 (1977), pp. 26–36.

Chapter 3

The Deep Seabed

VICTOR PRESCOTT

In the legal sense the deep seabed refers to the seabed and ocean floor and their subsoils which lie beyond the limits of national jurisdiction.[1] Two principal issues have dominated international negotiations about this area: the first deals with the definition of the outer limits of national jurisdiction on the continental margin, while the second concerns the system by which the extensive mineral resources of the deep seabed are explored and exploited. Before the different attitudes of states to these questions are considered and the proposed answers examined it is necessary to describe the nature and possible occurrence of the mineral resources under the sea.

THE MINERAL RESOURCES OF THE DEEP SEABED

Four categories of minerals can be identified.[2] The first group included liquid and gaseous substances such as petroleum, gas, condensate, helium, nitrogen, carbon dioxide, water, steam, hot water and sulphur and salts extracted in liquid form in solution. The deep seabed is not a favourable environment for hydrocarbon reserves and it is unlikely that exploration for such deposits will be actively pursued in the near future. The few deposits of hydrocarbons identified in the deep seabed are generally associated with the foundered margins of the continental blocks. This means that the deposits were formed in comparatively shallow circumstances, and that the outer portion of the continental margin in which they were originally located has sunk into deeper water through faulting processes. Unlike many deposits on the continental shelf, continental slope and continental rise the sediments on the deep seabed do not contain sufficient organic material to generate oil or gas fields. This deficiency may result from a fast rate of oxidation on the seabed where deposition from the small supply of organisms is very slow.[3]

The second category includes minerals which occur under the seabed at depths greater than 3 metres. While there will unquestionably be such deposits there is no evidence to suggest that they will be sought and exploited until some time in the distant future when low-grade terrestrial deposits are nearing exhaustion. The third group comprehends ore-bearing silts and brines. Massive deposits of such material have been found in four deep basins formed by tectonic movements in the floor of the Red Sea. Unfortunately the present cost of extracting the iron, zinc and copper from these deposits prohibits their commercial use. If it is ever decided to exploit these resources it will be necessary for the Sudan and Saudi Arabia to agree on their common marine boundary which intersects this metalliferous zone.

The fourth category includes useful minerals occurring on the surface of the seabed or at depths less than 3 metres. Calcareous and siliceous oozes, which contain more than 30 per cent by weight of organic remains derived mainly from skeletal debris of planktonic animals and plants, exist in huge quantities. Calcareous ooze could be used in roles presently played by limestone, while the siliceous oozes could be used as a lightweight aggregate for concrete, as a filter in the construction of bricks to withstand heat or sound, and as a mild abrasive.

However, this category also includes phosphorite and manganese nodules, the latter of which constitutes the main prize in the exploration and exploitation of the deep seabed in the near future. While both classes of nodules are found on the continental margin and the abyssal plain the phosphorite nodules occur more frequently on the margin while the main fields of manganese nodules are located in the deep seabed.[4] Phosphorite nodules are most commonly deposited where the upwelling of cold waters rich in phosphates occurs around the continental margins. The offshore regions of southern California are the likely sites which have been most thoroughly explored, but phosphorite fields can be expected along the west coast of other continents.

Manganese nodules have a wide distribution on the deep seabed. While their existence has been known since the *Challenger* expedition of 1873–6, it is only in the early 1960s that a serious research programme was started to explore the economic potential of this resource.[5] Manganese nodules are generally irregularly spherical in shape and vary in size from a cannon ball to a grape. They appear to be found most frequently where there are appreciable water currents; they induce rolling movements which remove sediment and prevent the nodules from being buried, allow an even coating of mineral particles, constantly renew the supply of these particles, and maintain an oxidising rather than reducing environment. The nodules are formed by the accretion of charged manganese and iron particles around nucleii which may be organic, such as a shark's tooth, or inorganic, such as particles of decomposed volcanics. The onion skin structure of the nodules contains valuable metals such as nickel, copper and cobalt dispersed as oxides in the iron-manganese hydrate matrix and is a particularly notable feature of the birnessite-enriched nodules (a comparatively rare form of manganese oxide) found in the abyssal areas of the North Pacific Ocean.

PRINCIPAL KNOWN DEPOSITS OF MANGANESE NODULES

Equatorial Scale

0   5000 km

The exploratory surveys conducted by mining companies and research institutes have demonstrated that economically interesting concentrations of nodules are comparatively rare occurrences. This is not surprising in view of the number of critical factors which must coincide if the site is to be a commercial prospect. Ideally the site should contain a high density of nodules with high assay values over a large area lying on a seabed free from major obstructions and irregularities in less than 3,000 fathoms in an area of the sea which has a high proportion of calm weather and an absence of major storms.

Consideration of only the large-scale patterns of climate and submarine morphology indicate the manner in which the prospective zones for nodule-mining are reduced in area and scattered in location. The long polar winters and the regular tracks of tropical cyclones provide climatic restrictions on the areas of sea where ships can operate for long periods to the precise navigational standards which the mining techniques demand. The extensive Mid-Ocean Ridge, which is the longest and broadest mountain system in the world and occupies about 42 per cent of the deep seabed, and the less extensive ridges and fracture zones are too rugged to permit nodule collection; the trenches which account for 1 per cent of the deep seabed are too deep for nodule mining and in any case the deposition of sediment is probably at a rate sufficient to bury any nodules which might form.[6] This means that the search tends to be concentrated on the abyssal plains and hills, which occupy oceanic basins between 1,600 fathoms and 3,300 fathoms. The level plains have a gradient usually less than 1:1,000 and are interrupted by the hills standing up to 360 metres high. Siapno has noted that even in these areas there are important differences in the concentration of nodules.

Most deposits of interest occur in the abyssal hill provinces. Hills vary from 36 to more than 360 metres high. In general the topography is one of constant undulation. Slopes on these hills commonly are 10° and at times reach 60°. Associated with these hills are several types of obstruction to any type of mining equipment in contact with the bottom. These include escarpments of sheer rock walls ranging from a few metres to several hundred metres high, outcrops of pillow basalt and areas of rocks and boulders up to several feet in diameter.

Preliminary analysis has shown 20 to 25 per cent of a mine site may be inaccessible because of obstructions. Further analysis has shown that high nodule populations are likely to occur in the vicinity of these obstructions. It must be stressed that large smooth portions of the sea floor rarely contain any manganese nodules.[7]

Now that the prize for which international competition is occurring has been described it is possible to proceed to an examination of the two main issues: the first concerns the limits of the area under international control and the second involves the nature of that control.

THE SEABED BOUNDARY SEPARATING NATIONAL AND INTERNATIONAL
JURISDICTION

The boundary separating areas of national and international authority
will either be marked by the outer edge of a state's exclusive economic
zone or by the outer edge of a state's continental margin. The limits of
these two zones are defined in the proposals of the UNCLOS ICNT in
the following terms:

> The exclusive economic zone shall not extend beyond 200 nautical
> miles from the baselines from which the breadth of the territorial sea is
> measured.[8] The continental shelf of a coastal State comprises the sea-
> bed and subsoil of the submarine areas that extend beyond its
> territorial sea throughout the natural prolongation of its land
> territory to the outer edge of the continental margin, or to a distance
> of 200 nautical miles from the baselines from which the breadth of the
> territorial sea is measured where the outer edge of the continental
> margin does not extend up to that distance.[9]

It follows therefore that the limits of national jurisdiction will only
coincide with the edge of the continental margin where that structure is
more than 200 nautical miles wide. The problems of defining the outer
limits of the exclusive economic zone and the continental margin are
quite different. The delimitation of the exclusive economic zone is a
mechanical task once the baseline from which the territorial sea is
measured has been established. The delimitation of the continental
margin is a practical problem in the related fields of geophysics, geology
and geomorphology; it is far from being a simple, uncontentious matter.
Before the difficulties associated with each of these cases are considered
two preliminary points should be made.

First, the bases on which claims are made to the continental shelf and
exclusive economic zone are not identical. This means that different
states may rely on different bases in making their claims. This will
mainly be a problem concerning adjacent states which share a common
coastline and states which are opposite each other and separated by seas
less than 400 nautical miles wide. In such situations it cannot be assumed
that the boundaries separating their exclusive economic zones and
continental shelves will always coincide. Only if the boundary drawn on
the seabed is a line of equidistance are the two boundaries certain to
coincide. If the seabed boundary is not a line of equidistance then the
exclusive economic zone claimed by the country which possesses the
narrower part of the seabed may overlap the seabed possessed by the
opposite country. That situation has arisen in respect of the Timor Sea
between Indonesia and Australia. The seabed boundary agreed between
the two countries in 1972 lies closer to the Indonesian coast and that
country has decided to claim an exclusive economic zone, in respect of

the waters above the Australian seabed as far south as the line of equidistance. Indonesia may decide to make similar claims across the seabed boundary agreed with Malaysia north of Sarawak in 1969 because this boundary favoured Malaysia.

Whether the boundary between the exclusive economic zones of adjacent or opposite states is equidistant or not it will be open to one of the states to claim that the natural prolongation of its land territory extends beyond that boundary. In respect of the definition of the deep seabed this anomaly in the proposals of UNCLOS will only be significant where adjacent states make conflicting claims against each other. In such a situation the international authority would be faced with conflicting claims by two states along the same segment of boundary. Providing both states were claiming the same outer limit this would not be a serious problem for the international authority; however, if they claimed different outer limits the international authority would be faced with an uncertain position.

Table 3.1 *Seas where most or all of the seabed is subject to national claims*

Seas where the entire seabed is claimed	
Andaman Sea	East Siberian Sea
Arafura Sea	Java Sea
Aral Sea	Kara Sea
Baltic Sea	Laptev Sea
Barents Sea	Mediterranean Sea
Beaufort Sea	Persian Gulf
Black Sea	Red Sea
Caribbean Sea	Sea of Japan
Caspian Sea	Sea of Okhotsk
Celebes Sea	South China Sea
East China Sea	Sulu Sea
	Timor Sea
Seas where most of the seabed is subject to national claims	
Bering Sea	
Philippine Sea	
Tasman Sea	

The second point to be made concerns the identification of those seas and oceans where there will be areas of the deep seabed available for international control. Table 3.1 lists those seas where the seabed will be entirely claimed by peripheral states and those where only a small area of seabed will be left for international control. These seas are located between and around the edge of the world's continents, and their elimination as zones of international control leaves most of the Arctic Ocean, Atlantic Ocean, Indian Ocean and Pacific Ocean as the main areas where questions associated with the deep seabed will arise. It should be noted that the multitude of island states in the South Pacific Ocean almost divide it into two major parts, and they enclose some narrow corridors and enclaves of deep seabed between their national claims; the other oceans are not compartmented to the same extent.

It was noted earlier that once the baseline of any country has been established, the delimitation of its exclusive economic zone is a simple matter. The exercise only involves the construction of intersecting arcs of circles with a radius of 200 nautical miles from successive centres along the baseline, and for this reason it follows that if disagreements arise over the definition of the outer edge of the exclusive economic zone they will be directly caused by disputes over the baseline used.

The letter and spirit of the rules which governed the construction of baselines in the 1958 Convention on the Territorial Sea were adopted with three additions into the Informal Composite Negotiating Text published by UNCLOS. A recent survey of baselines proclaimed by seventy countries revealed the following conclusions.[10] First, there are no major rules which have not been breached in both letter and spirit; the only minor rule which does not appear to have been breached concerns the use of harbour works and roadsteads as points on the baseline. Secondly, the majority of baselines which contravene existing and proposed rules have been drawn by countries which could be considered to be members of the Third World. While the use of improper baselines might cause sharp disagreements over the limits of territorial seas and contiguous zones it is unlikely to be a serious matter in respect of the outer limit of exclusive economic zones. The reason for this is found in the irregularity of coastlines and the increasing widths of territorial seas, contiguous zones and exclusive economic zones. It is predictable that the use of straight baselines will have the greatest effect in increasing the area of internal waters and the least effect on increasing the extent of the exclusive economic zone at the expense of the high seas.

For example, measurements were made of the different maritime zones which Australia would obtain if they were measured from the low-water mark of the coast and islands between King Sound and Napier Broome Bay on the northern sector of Western Australia and from a straight baseline joining the outer islands.[11] Using the straight baseline the area of internal waters was increased by 7,666 square nautical miles; the territorial sea incorporated 876 square nautical miles which had previously formed part of the contiguous zone; the contiguous zone enclosed 228 square nautical miles which would otherwise fall in the exclusive economic zone; and no detectable erosion of the deep seabed was caused by the exclusive economic zone. It would be necessary for the baseline to be in flagrant breach of the rules to push the outer limit of the exclusive economic zone seawards. The baseline proclaimed by Ecuador in June 1971 represents one of the worst infringements of the proposed and existing rules.[12] That baseline secures an additional 992 square nautical miles of seabed for the mainland and the baseline drawn around the Galapagos Islands secures an additional 608 square nautical miles. The greatest erosion of the high seas and therefore of the deep seabed by the improper use of straight baselines would occur if archipelagic baselines were drawn around countries composed of small, scattered islands which did not satisfy the four conditions proposed in the Informal Composite Negotiating Text.[13] Such baselines would reduce and in some cases eliminate enclaves of deep seabed which would otherwise exist within and between such archipelagic countries.

Off those coasts where the continental margin is wider than 200 nautical miles the boundary between national and international control will be marked by 'the outer edge of the continental margin'. Ever since the continental shelf was defined in the terms quoted earlier (see p. 58) there has been an awareness amongst delegates to UNCLOS that it would be necessary to refine a more exact, unambiguous definition. The search for a precise limit centred on four alternatives: they are the 500 metre (273·4 fathom) isobath, the 200 nautical mile line and boundaries drawn according to the Hedberg and Irish formulae. Each of these must be examined in turn before the differing attitudes of states to them are considered.

Except in the case of very wide and shallow margins the 500 metre isobath would be the most restrictive, and it would compel many countries to forgo valuable areas of continental slope where hydrocarbon deposits might exist. Further, in the vicinity of submarine canyons the isobath would follow a very convoluted course which would produce an unsatisfactory boundary when transcribed on charts. In addition to this problem there would be enclaves of national seabed where waters shallower than 500 metres were separated from the margin by deeper channels. In short such a boundary would produce an irregular pattern of control which would complicate the administrative problems for both state governments and international authorities.

A line fixed 200 nautical miles from the baseline from which the territorial sea is measured would produce a shelf boundary which was coincident with the outer limit of the exclusive economic zone. There would be no difficulties about locating such a boundary and it would have a much smoother outline than the 500 metre isobath. However, such a limit would exclude several countries from access to the outer edge of wide margins, which could be productive in fuel supplies. The use of a fixed limit would also raise the possibility that attempts could be made to enlarge the area under national control by the construction of baselines remote from the coast.

The Hedberg concept was devised by Hollis D. Hedberg.[14] He advocated that a boundary which would enable each state to claim its reasonable entitlement of the continental margin would be found in a zone stretching at least 100 kilometres (54 nautical miles) from the junction of the continental slope and the continental rise. Such a boundary would avoid the need for countries to abandon potentially valuable areas and would allow the construction of boundaries with long straight segments which would be easy to administer by national and international bodies. The Hedberg concept was subsequently included in the Irish proposal and lost its separate identity. The Irish delegation at UNCLOS proposed two alternative lines. The first corresponded to the Hedberg concept except that the zone was increased from 54 nautical miles to 60 nautical miles. The original part of the Irish proposal concerned a line which was drawn on the continental rise through points where the depth of the sediment was at least 1 per cent of the distance from the point to the foot of the continental slope. It is clear that both the Hedberg and Irish concepts require the junction of the continental slope and continental rise to be identified. The difficulty of this task will depend on the structure of the margin and its geomorphological history. Some margins have no rises; instead they are replaced by deep trenches, as in the case of the Philippine Trench off the east coast of the archipelago. Other margins, in the vicinity of major deltas, such as that produced by the Mississippi River, have rises which have almost buried the continental slope. The only way in which debate about each case could be avoided is for a law of the sea treaty to specify a critical gradient which is regarded as the maximum encountered on the continental rise and the minimum encountered on the continental slope. In order to prevent problems associated with that critical gradient being repeated on a terraced formation it would be necessary to nominate the deepest such change of gradient on the edge of the margin. It would be easier to have a general, protracted debate over the selection of that critical value than to treat each case on an *ad hoc* basis.

The Irish proposal has the added disadvantage that after this junction has been identified it is then necessary to measure the thickness of sediments across the rise in order to select the critical thickness which is at least 1 per cent of the distance to the junction. This will be a harder line to find than one 54 nautical miles seaward of the junction and it will be a much harder line to verify. This is an important point because it is recognised that there will have to be some international authority to certify that boundaries drawn according to either of these concepts have been properly constructed. Hedberg has produced a devastating criticism of the Irish proposal which should be required reading for all delegates concerned with this matter at the Law of the Sea Conference.[15] He lists eight practical difficulties which will face surveyors and administrators trying to map the thickness of sediments on the continental rises.

At the seventh session of UNCLOS in Geneva in 1978 the Soviet delegation proposed that a fifth boundary should be considered. It was suggested that if the continental margin extended more than 200 nautical miles from the coast its outer limit would be determined by the use of scientifically sound geological and geomorphological data, provided that the outer limit does not extend more than 100 nautical miles beyond the 200 nautical mile exclusive economic zone. This simple solution would still deny some states access to the outer parts of very wide margins and would carry the risk of evolving into 300 nautical mile exclusive economic zones.

The influence of this Russian proposal can be seen in the caveat included in the revised Informal Composite Negotiating Text which was produced by the eighth session of UNCLOS in April 1979. After stating that margins wider than 200 nautical miles could be defined either by the Hedberg or Irish proposals, article 76 stipulates that the boundary shall not exceed 350 nautical miles from the baseline or shall not exceed 100 nautical miles from the 2,500 metre isobath. Given the scope for genuine disagreement about the precise location of the junction of the slope and the rise, and the precise thickness of sediments on the rise, it is safe to predict that selected lines will be very close to the maximum limits permitted. It will be very tempting for countries to determine whether a boundary 350 nautical miles distant from the baseline or 100 nautical miles seaward of the 2,500 metre isobath is furthest from the coast, and then to search for justification for adopting the more distant line.

It is now necessary to consider the different appeals of each proposed definition to states with different geographic, economic and ideological characteristics.

Two basic geographic conditions may influence the attitude of states to the definition of the outer edge of the continental margin. The first relates to access to the shelf and the second to the width of the margin. The thirty-one states which have no access to the margin because they are landlocked and those unnumbered states which have very little access because they are shelflocked have no obvious reason to give strong support to definitions which allow wide claims. Similarly, those countries with margins narrower than 200 nautical miles might consider that there is no need to permit wider claims. In contrast to these groups the countries with margins wider than 200 nautical miles can be expected to favour the Irish proposal. There are forty-five countries with wide margins and they are listed in Table 3.2. However, this group may be less coherent than the landlocked and shelflocked community because the nature of the margin outside the 200 nautical mile boundary is important. The states with wide margins have been divided into three groups depending on whether their distant shelf includes parts of the continental shelf, continental slope and continental rise, or only parts of the slope and rise, or only areas of the rise. It is likely to be considerable time before there is any chance of commercial exploitation of hydro-carbon deposits which might exist on the rise. The economic circumst-ances of the state may also have a bearing on attitudes to the definition of the outer edge of the margin. Countries such as Australia, which have no significant fields of onshore petroleum, might be expected to have a firmer attachment to the Irish formula than states such as Canada and the Soviet Union which have large onshore reserves. Similarly, countries such as Canada and the United States, with access to domestic capital and advanced undersea mining technology, may hold more strongly to the widest definition of the margin than states such as Ecuador and Mozambique which might face difficulties in acquiring funds and skills.

Table 3.2 *States which could claim continental margins wider than 200 nautical miles*

States where the distant margin consists of parts of the continental shelf, slope and rise

Australia	Norway
Canada	Soviet Union
Madagascar	United States of America
Mauritius	

States where the distant margin consists of parts of the continental slope and rise

Argentina	Mozambique
Brazil	New Caledonia
Ecuador	New Zealand
Fiji	South Africa
France	South West Africa/Namibia
Iceland	Transkei
Ireland	United Kingdom

States where the distant margin consists of continental rise

Angola	Ghana	Seychelles
Bahamas	Guinea Bissau	Sierra Leone
Barbados	India	Somalia
Cape Verde Islands	Indonesia	Spain
Denmark (Greenland)	Kenya	Sri Lanka
Equatorial Guinea	Mauritania	Surinam
French Guyana	Oman	Tanzania
Gabon	Pakistan	Uruguay

It is entirely possible that none of these factors will prove decisive in determining the attitudes of states to the concept of the outer margin. Instead it is possible that states will support a definition of the margin which gives them no obvious advantage, in return for support on some other section of the law of the sea which is of vital concern. It is generally considered that the final decision on the precise definition of the continental margin will be related to two other questions.[16] The first concerns the arrangements for states with margins wider than 200 nautical miles to share the revenue they derive from that distant sector with other countries, and especially with landlocked developing countries. The second relates to access for landlocked and geographically disadvantaged states to the living resources of the exclusive economic zone of the region or sub-region. Finally, the unpredictability of state attitudes is increased by the chance that ideological blocs, such as that led by the Soviet Union, might adopt common attitudes to the question of the margin which belie their obvious geographic and economic differences. On balance it seems unlikely that any state with a potentially useful section of margin more than 200 nautical miles from the coast will yield the right to control that area or that such states would deny reasonable concessions, in other aspects of the law of the sea, to states with narrower margins in order to secure that right.

THE NATURE OF INTERNATIONAL CONTROL OVER THE DEEP SEABED

No debate at the third UNCLOS has been more protracted and fiercely engaged than that concerned with the system under which the deep seabed will be explored and exploited. The importance of the debate can be roughly measured by the fact that in the Informal Composite Negotiating Text there are thirty-four pages dealing with the deep seabed, which is only one page less than the space occupied by the text dealing with the territorial seas and contiguous zone, straits used for international navigation, archipelagic states, the exclusive economic zone and the continental shelf. Four of the seven negotiating groups at the seventh session in March to May 1978 treated aspects of the regime for the deep seabed. It is also an interesting commentary that while compromise over questions related to the use of baselines or claims to the continental shelf have resulted in the use of increasingly general phrases, which each state can interpret in its own manner, compromise over questions of the deep seabed's administration have produced increasingly detailed articles, which leave less and less chance of ambiguity. The clarification of the calculation of the production ceiling for nickel contained in the very technical article 150 *bis* is a good example of this situation.[17]

The contest over the regulations which will govern the economic use of the deep seabed is between two broad philosophies, which are supported by different groups of states for different reasons. The first philosophy considers the minerals of the deep seabed as a resource which technology has made available and which should be developed quickly with a minimum of necessary international supervision. The second philosophy regards these resources as belonging to a special global category the development of which must be hedged about with safeguards so that the most needy countries benefit most and so that there is the least possible interference to the orderly marketing of existing supplies of minerals from land and to the environment. While the basic division occurs between developed countries favouring the first philosophy and developing countries favouring the second, the separation is not perfect and the two basic groups divide in different ways over particular rules to control deep seabed mining.

Countries which support the early development of nodule mines on the deep seabed act in response to three motives which might operate separately or in concert. First, there are those countries containing companies which have the technical and financial capacity to harvest and process manganese nodules. The expansion of the operation of such companies on to the deep seabed will generate economic activity in engineering and shipbuilding fields, will provide increased employment opportunities, will make higher contributions to the state's income, and might result in technical advances in undersea activities with economic or strategic significance. While the total contribution in these financial areas might be relatively small in the total structure of capital and labour, no government in the depressed economic circumstances of the late 1970s and early 1980s can afford to neglect such an opportunity. Secondly, there are countries which need to import nickel, cobalt and copper. Such countries might welcome production of these minerals from the deep seabed for two reasons. In cases where that production is achieved by domestic companies the cost of raw material imports will be reduced and the state's balance of payments will benefit. In other cases, importers may anticipate lower commodity prices, and that might occur in respect of cobalt. However, all importers will probably welcome the increased number of exporters with which contracts can be negotiated. Thirdly, there may be countries whose leaders have viewed with dismay the increased economic and political power wielded by states which export mineral raw materials and are prepared to develop co-operative policies. These leaders will welcome any development which undermines the corporate power of such groups of states.

Some indication of the interest of countries in the early development of deep sea mining can be formed by an examination of the international companies which are operating in this field. At the beginning of 1979 there were eight international and national consortia, only one of which, called Eurocean and formed by twenty-four European companies drawn from France, Belgium, the Netherlands, Britain, Italy, Sweden, Norway, Spain and Switzerland, was non-commercial and apparently devoted to scientific research and survey. Amongst the other seven there were four which were outstanding: they were Kennecott Exploration Corporation, involving American, British, Canadian and Japanese companies; Ocean Mining Associates, comprising American and Belgian companies; Ocean Management Incorporated which included American, Canadian, West German and Japanese companies; and Ocean Minerals Company made up of American and Dutch companies. Each of these groups had carried out extensive exploration in the Clarion-Clipperton Fracture Zone in the eastern Pacific Ocean, had tested mining systems and had tested pilot processing plants. Further, each of the groups had plans to continue its activities. Two other groups had concentrated on exploration in the eastern and central Pacific Ocean; they were Association Française Pour l'Etude et la Recherche des Nodules, composed entirely of French government agencies and private companies, and Deep Ocean Minerals Association, involving thirty-five Japanese companies. The remaining company, entitled Continuous Line Bucket Syndicate, made up of twenty companies from the United States, West Germany, France, Canada, Japan and Australia, is concentrating on the continuous line bucket mining system using one or two ships.

The major involvement of American mining companies and the determination of some government agencies to reduce American dependence on imported strategic materials are the major reasons which explain the determined efforts of some congressmen to promote a Bill permitting American companies to engage in mining the deep seabed before the final treaty produced by the Law of the Sea Conference. All attempts in the four Congresses ending in 1978 failed, although a measure came close to being passed in 1978. The proposed Bill was passed by the House by 312 votes to 80 votes, but its consideration in the Senate was effectively blocked by Senator James Abourezk, who has since retired. Two new bills were introduced in 1979. Representative John M. Murphy of New York introduced HR2759 in the House of Representatives, and Senator Spark M. Matsunaga introduced S493 in the Senate. Both Bills would require companies to provide plans and information about environmental safeguards before receiving permits, would tax mining revenue at 0·75 per cent, would transfer funds derived from this tax to any revenue-sharing fund set up through international agreement, and would require that nodules be transported by ships owned and operated by American companies. In addition, and most importantly, both Bills require the American diplomats at the Law of the Sea Conference to ensure that American companies would lose neither access nor investments in any transfer to international mining regulations. This so-called 'grandfather clause' is unpopular with the American administration, because it recognises that it might have to recompense companies which suffered losses because of the final international treaty. The administration would prefer to limit the diplomats to ensuring that no new substantial economic burdens were imposed on existing mining operations. The Murphy Bill sought to establish 1 January 1980 as the starting date for the issue of permits; the

Matsunaga Bill set the date exactly one year later. Senator Matsunaga's Bill was passed by the Senate on 14 December 1979. The Bill requires that processing plants be set up within United States territory, and the Senator noted that Hawaii was a leading contender for such a plant. As might be expected the developed and developing countries take diametrically opposed views to the proposed legislation. The developing countries regard such unilateral action as a contravention of various General Assembly resolutions on the deep seabed. The developed countries, led by the United States, regard the legislation as a proper interim measure, which ensures that no group of countries will believe that by delaying final agreement at UNCLOS, developed countries will be coerced into accepting an unsatisfactory treaty as the price for gaining some access to the deep seabed.

The motives of countries which demand very strict international controls over mining the deep seabed are also diverse. First, there are those countries which presently lack the companies, either private or state, with the necessary technical skills and capital to engage in nodule-mining and processing. Some of these countries might reasonably fear that unless mining is carefully regulated, all the richest mine sites will have been claimed and perhaps exhausted by the time their lack of technology and capital is remedied. Secondly, there may be governments of poor countries which do not aspire at any time in the future to enter the arena of deep seabed mining, but which nevertheless hope to benefit from international funds generated from mining royalties and dues. Plainly, unless the activity is strictly controlled by an international body which has a strong representation of poor and developing countries, it will be difficult to extract payments from actual and prospective miners and to ensure that the available revenue is distributed in favour of the poor and geographically disadvantaged states.

Thirdly, land-based producers of cobalt, copper, manganese and nickel from mines on land have a vested interest in seeking controls over deep seabed mining in order to avoid any reduction in export prices or markets for these commodities. Such countries will try to ensure that seabed mining does not proceed without reliable international safeguards against economic interference to established patterns. Fourthly, there may be some governments which perceive that the chief beneficiaries of deep seabed mining will be developed countries because of their technical and financial advantages and because of their import needs. For ideological reasons such governments may have a determination to oppose any arrangements to the advantage of developed, capitalist countries, and will therefore throw their weight behind demands for inflexible controls of seabed mining.

The discussions over the regulations to govern mining of the deep seabed have centred on three main topics: the identity of parties allowed to mine; the conditions under which mining may occur; and the administration which will supervise mining activities and enforce regulations. The first issue has been resolved by adoption of a parallel system which permits national operators, whether states or companies, and the international authority supervising deep seabed mining, to engage in harvesting manganese nodules. The second and third issues have proved less tractable. The most important conditions being attached to mining by states or companies relate to the identification of sites, the transfer of technology, payments to the international authority and restrictions on levels of production.

While much exploration has been undertaken to discover the distribution of manganese nodules, the detailed work necessary to locate potential mining sites is expensive, requiring the use of advanced equipment for a long period. Under the conditions on which contracts will be awarded a prospective miner will have to identify either one site which can be divided into two equally profitable mines, or two sites of equal economic potential. The international authority will then issue a contract for one of the sites and reserve the other site for its own use, perhaps in association with some developing country. It has been calculated that the sites necessary to supply smelters with 3 million dry metric tons of ore each year for at least twenty years would extend for 20,000 to 40,000 square kilometres;[18] this would mean that a prospective company either has to find two comparable sites of this size or a single site between 40,000 and 80,000 square kilometres in extent. The need to prove this additional site represents a significant charge on the applicant for mining rights and an important subsidy for the international authority.

In order that the international authority can initiate mining projects it will require technology to be provided by the mining companies. The transferred technology applies only to the harvesting of nodules and not their processing, and compensation must be based on fair and reasonable commercial terms and conditions. A more controversial proposal requires the miner to use only technology which can be transferred and to assume obligations to transfer technology to any developing country which mines the second site reserved by the international authority.

The question of charges levied by the international authority has proved a difficult one to solve because of uncertainties about the profitability of seabed mining in the future. The flow of funds to the international authority will be used in two ways. Some will be distributed to member nations, with particular consideration being given to developing and landlocked and geographically disadvantaged states, and some will be used to finance mining operations by the international authority either on its own or in association with some other organisation. This means that the countries which will benefit in these two areas want a large and continuous cash flow to the international authority. The countries which will be engaged in mining want the charges to be set at a level which will not deter investment. Three separate charges will be applied. The first concerns the application fee and there is general agreement that it should be no higher than necessary to process the application; in 1978 the figure being discussed varied from $US 100,000 to $US 500,000, with the representatives of members of the European Economic Community favouring the lower figure and the United States of America and developing countries favouring the higher figure. The second charge involves an annual fixed fee which the developing countries argue is necessary in order to ensure diligence by the mining companies, and to provide the international authority with funds before the commencement of mining. The developed countries argue that the scale of investment involved in deep seabed mining will ensure the diligence of companies.

The third and major charge involves either a royalty payment or a nominal royalty payment and a profit-sharing agreement. Reliance on royalties only was advocated by the Soviet Union, Australia and Canada. The former regards such a system as more compatible with its economic ideology and organisation, while the other two states regard it as being easier to administer and uniform in application. Members of the European Economic Community, Japan and the United States of America prefer a nominal royalty and profit-sharing because this avoids the need for large preliminary payments before the mining operation is established and because the international authority would have to bear a share of the risk associated with all mining ventures. The developing countries do not seem to have a particular preference providing there is a large and continuous cash flow to the international authority, but plainly if the latter system is adopted there will be arguments about the method of calculating the profit.

It has been a prime concern of some developing countries to ensure that seabed mining does not adversely affect their mineral exports from production on land. There has been an almost endless debate on the volume of minerals which will be generated by seabed mining of manganese nodules, and because there are so many variables of unknown quantity in the equation both major factions have claimed that their case is proved.[19] Some producing, developing countries are convinced that seabed mining will cause a depression in the prices received for cobalt, copper, manganese and nickel. Importing developed countries are equally convinced that the expanding market for metals will ensure that seabed production is not a vital factor in causing downward price fluctuations. The developed countries are certainly correct in respect of copper because of the very small proportion of the world's copper supply which would be derived from nodules.

The position regarding manganese is uncertain. Until comparatively recently only one company had plans to extract manganese from nodules; other companies intended to use processes which would not yield pure manganese, However, some estimates now show that there are likely to be serious shortages of manganese by 1987. At present about 80 per cent of the manganese supply to the non-communist world comes from six mines in Australia, Brazil, Gabon, India and South Africa. Already Australia and Brazil have restricted exports to conserve domestic supplies, and the Indian mines are not mechanised and produce metal with a high phosphorus content not suitable for steel-making. By 1987 the remaining major producers will be Gabon, the Soviet Union and South Africa. Unless alternative supplies are discovered, and no new major fields have been discovered outside communist countries since 1960, the price of manganese seems sure to rise, and there would be some risk of interruption of supplies being used as a political lever by some or all of those three countries.

Countries which produce cobalt, such as Zaïre, Canada, Zambia, the Soviet Union, Morocco and Cuba, are probably correct in asserting that the price of cobalt will be depressed by seabed mining because it is an expensive mineral serving a small market. Zaïre produces most of the world's cobalt, and in 1974 exports of that mineral accounted for 4·2 per cent of export revenue. However, it should be noted that cobalt can be substituted for nickel in many industrial uses and therefore nickel prices should provide a floor through which cobalt prices would not fall. Most attention has been focused on nickel and regulations have been devised to restrict seabed nickel production to levels related to the cumulative growth segment of world nickel demand. The formulae by which such calculations are made are extremely complicated and include the relationships between future production, demand and price, as well as the productivity and profitability of nodule mines. Some developed importing states argue strongly against limitations on mineral production being used to benefit developed exporting states, which in respect of nickel would be Canada, Australia and the Soviet Union.

While it is generally agreed that the international authority supervising deep seabed mining will consist of an Assembly, a Council and a Secretariat, there is disagreement about the role which should be played by the Council as well as its membership and system of voting. In the opinion of developing countries the Council consists of representatives of special interest groups and geographical regions who act as an executive committee for the Assembly. Developed countries believe that the Council serves as a counterbalance to the Assembly in order to protect the interests of special groups. While each member state sits on the Assembly there will be a limited membership of the Council. In the Informal Composite Negotiating Text it was proposed that the Council should consist of thirty-six members of whom four would represent countries which have made the greatest contribution to developing the technology for mining and processing nodules; four would represent countries importing minerals derived from the seabed; four would represent countries which are major exporters of the same minerals; six would represent developing countries; and eighteen would represent regional interests defined as Africa, Asia, Eastern Europe, Latin America and Western Europe and other countries. At various discussions on this question since 1977 various groups of states have advanced reasons why the representation of the category to which they mainly belong should be increased.

The developed countries generally wanted a weighted system of voting which would enable the investing countries to protect their interests from depreciation through sudden changes in the rules. The developing countries, presumably frustrated by the use of the veto in the Security Council, oppose any system which gives a blocking vote to special interest groups. This does seem to be an issue on which neither major group is disposed to make concessions.

CONCLUSIONS

The identification of the boundary between areas of national and international jurisdiction is an easier problem to solve than settlement of the system under which nodule-mining will be conducted. Unless countries flout the rules for drawing baselines it will be harder to agree on the outer limits of margins wider than 200 nautical miles than on the outer limits of exclusive economic zones. However, discussion has narrowed to two or three promising formulae, and one of them is likely to be selected, providing there can be simultaneous agreement on the sharing of revenue derived from the margins beyond 200 nautical miles, and on the access of landlocked and geographically disadvantaged countries to the living resources of exclusive economic zones in their region.

Although for administrative reasons it seems sensible to eliminate the enclaves of high seas and deep seabed between national claims there will be strong opposition to such a development from landlocked and geographically disadvantaged states; they seem to set great store by the small patches of blue on maps signifying high seas. What is quite clear is that a committee will have to be established to monitor state practice in setting the edge of claims to the continental margin and exclusive economic zones.

The most difficult problem to solve concerning the administration of the deep seabed concerns the structure, functions and voting system of the proposed Council. A compromise has been found to the question of who should be allowed to mine the deep seabed, and agreement is close on the terms under which mining should take place. But the ability to prevent the Council from changing those rules or interpreting them in a discriminatory fashion is crucial to countries responsible for the massive investment in seabed mining. There is no evidence at present that the developing countries will agree to any form of veto or blocking vote. If no agreement is reached on the regime to control deep seabed mining two developments are possible. First, the lack of agreement may dissuade companies and governments from risking capital in mining ventures. Such a development would gratify those countries which hope to delay the onset of mining until they have acquired the technology and capital to compete on equal terms and those which hope to avoid any competition for their land-based mineral exports. The same development would disappoint those countries ready to commence mining operations and those poor countries hoping to benefit by the distribution of royalties from seabed mining. Secondly, the lack of agreement may cause some governments to decide that they encourage unilateral mining of the seabed without international interference. This development would distress many developing countries, especially those which are heavily dependent on the export of nickel and cobalt.

The economic history of the world suggests that the existence of this resource on the deep seabed is sufficient guarantee that it will be used when economic conditions or strategic needs are compelling. The compulsion from one or both motives is likely to occur within the next five years.

NOTES AND REFERENCES

There is no recent comprehensive study of this subject; most writers tend to focus on one or two of the topic's main aspects, which may be identified as mineralogy and mining, national outer limits of the continental margin, the economics and economic effects of deep sea mining, and the politics and law involved in United Nations conferences. The best single volume is S. J. Pearson's *Ocean Floor Mining* (New Jersey: Noyes Data Corporation, 1975); it is a matter of considerable regret that I was unable to see a copy of this book until after this chapter had been completed.

In addition to Pearson's work the best references on mining include the monograph by Metallgesellschaft AG, Frankfurt am Main, entitled *Manganese Nodules – Metals from the Sea* (Klein-Krotzenburg: Metallgesellschaft AG, 1975), and the study by the American National Academy of Sciences dealing with *Mining in the Outer Continental Shelf and in the Deep Ocean* (Washington, DC: National Academy of Sciences, 1975). R. A. Frank's *Deep Sea Mining and the Environment: a report of the Working Group on environmental regulation of deep sea mining* (St Paul, Minn.: West Publishing Company, 1976) provides a useful introduction to this subject which is sure to increase in importance.

Hedberg has produced the best studies of questions connected with the definition of the outer edge of the continental margin subject to national claims. His two papers entitled 'Ocean boundaries and petroleum' and 'Ocean floor boundaries' which appeared in *Science* (vol. 191, no. 4231, 12 March 1976, pp. 1009–18; and vol. 204, no. 4389, 13 April 1979, pp. 135–44) are essential reading on this topic.

Information on the economic debate between developed and developing countries is contained in a variety of sources. Some of the useful ones include the collection of source documents by the editors of *Ocean Science News* entitled *United Nations Source Documents on Seabed Mining* (New York: Nautilus, 1975); an analysis from the point of view of the Third World by D. M. Leipziger and J. L. Mudge called *Seabed Mineral Resources and the Economic Interest of Developing Countries* (Cambridge, Mass.: Ballinger, 1976); J. I. Charney's useful survey of problems and options entitled 'The equitable sharing of revenues from seabed mining' in *Policy Issues in Ocean Law* (New York: The American Society of International Law, Studies in Transitional Legal Policy No. 8, 1975, pp. 53–120); and N. W. Cornell's provocative economic analysis of one aspect of nodule-mining contained in 'Manganese nodule mining and economic rent', *Natural Resources Journal*, vol. 14 (1974), pp. 518–31.

The basic source for information on legal issues relating to deep seabed mining remains the *Informal Composite Negotiating Text* issued by the United Nations (New York: United Nations, 15 July 1977) and its supplement *Reports of the Committees and Negotiating Groups on negotiations at the Seventh Session contained in a single document for the purposes of record and the convenience of delegations* (Geneva: United Nations, 19 May 1978). No doubt subsequent sessions will also result in the issue of further reports and texts. Such documents represent the prevailing consensus; some outline of the debate which produced them can be gauged by the changes in successive texts. However, there are several surveys of these developments; the best include S. Oda's *The Law of the Sea in Our Time: The United Nations Seabed Committee 1968–73* (Leyden: Sijthoff, 1977); Volumes II, III and VI of *New Directions in the Law of the Sea*, edited by R. Churchill, M. Nordquist and S. H. Lay (New York: Oceana, 1973–7); R. P. Anand's *Legal Regime of the Seabed and the Developing Countries* (Leyden: Sijthoff, 1976); and the *Law of the Sea Conference Status Report Summer 1978* issued by the House of Representatives Committee on International Relations (Washington, DC: US Government Printing Officer, 1978).

1 United Nations, *Revised Single Negotiating Text* (New York: United Nations, 6 May 1976), p. 11. In later versions, including the Informal Composite Negotiating Text (New York: United Nations, 15 July 1977), the corresponding article simply notes that 'This Part of the present Convention shall apply to the "Area".'

2 United Nations, *Informal Composite Negotiating Text*, p. 73.

3 Exxon, *Deepwater Capabilities* (New York: Exxon Corporation, 1976), p. 12.

4 F. T. Christy, 'Marigenous minerals: wealth, regimes and factors of decision', in J. Sztucki (ed.), *Symposium on the International Regime of the Sea-bed* (Rome: Accademia Nazionale Dei Lincei, 1970), pp. 113–53.

5 W. D. Siapno, 'Exploration technology and ocean mining parameters', *Mining Congress Journal*, vol. 62, no. 5 (May 1976), pp. 16–22.

6 A. J. Guilcher, 'The configuration of the ocean floor and its subsoil; geopolitical implications', in Sztucki (ed.), op. cit., pp. 3–27.

7 See Siapano, op. cit., p. 20.

8 United Nations, *Informal Composite Negotiating Text*, p. 42.

9 ibid., p. 52.

10 J. R. V. Prescott, 'Drawing Australia's marine boundaries', in G. W. P. George (ed.), *Australia's Offshore Resources* (Canberra: Australian Academy of Science, 1978), pp. 22–46.

11 Prescott, ibid., p. 34.

12 J. R. V. Prescott, *The Political Geography of the Oceans* (Plymouth: David & Charles, 1975), pp. 95–7.

13 United Nations, *Informal Composite Negotiating Text*, pp. 37–8.

14 H. D. Hedberg, 'Ocean boundaries and petroleum resources', *Science*, vol. 191 (1976), pp. 1009–18. Apart from the 500 metre isobath, the other boundaries are shown on a map prepared by the UNCLOS Secretariat at the request of the Second Committee, *Map illustrating various formulae for the definition of the continental shelf, Mercator projection* (Geneva, 1978).

15 H. D. Hedberg, 'Ocean floor boundaries', *Science*, vol. 204 (1979), pp. 135–44.

16 See United States of America, House of Representatives, Committee on International Relations, *Law of the Sea Conference Status Report Summer 1978* (Washington, DC: US Government Printing Officer, 1978) p. 37.

17 United Nations, Third Conference on the Law of the Sea, *Reports of the Committees and Negotiating Groups on negotiations at the Seventh Session* (Geneva: United Nations, 19 May 1978), pp. 6–7.

18 Metallgesellschaft AG, Frankfurt am Main, *Review of Activities: Manganese Nodules – Metals from the Sea* (Klein-Krotzenburg: Metallgesellschaft AG, 1975), p. 18.

19 D. M. Leipziger and J. L. Mudge, *Seabed Mineral Resources and the Economic Interest of Developing Countries* (Cambridge, Mass.: Ballinger, 1976), 5–8.

Chapter 4

Offshore Resources: Oil and Gas

PETER ODELL

AN INTRODUCTION TO OFFSHORE OIL AND GAS DEVELOPMENTS

The extension of the search for oil and gas into marine areas and the production of large quantities of these energy sources from under some of the world's seas is a recent phenomenon. Shallow water exploration and exploitation from enclosed water areas such as Lake Maracaibo in Venezuela and the Gulf of Paria in Trinidad and from the territorial waters of the states of Texas, Louisiana and California in the United States, go back over a much longer period (to the 1940s) but in terms of technology and economics, as well as of politics, they represented nothing more than limited extrapolations of the requirements and challenges of the oil industry in its onshore guise.

Since the late 1950s the technology of offshore oil and gas exploration and production has developed rapidly and has enabled the industry to sever its links with the land surface and so move out beyond the water depth limitations of jack-up rigs. Such 'jack-up' facilities had to have, as their name implies, contact with the seabed so that considerations of stability severely limited the water depths in which they could work. However, in some shallow sea areas even such jack-up operations sometimes extended beyond traditional territorial waters and so raised problems of sovereignty; as, indeed, in the case of offshore Texas and Louisiana where the question of state's or federal jurisdiction of the marine areas beyond the 3 mile limit was important in both political and economic terms. As maritime issues, however, they remained unimportant in these conditions, simply because the areas which were both geologically interesting and politically attractive to oil companies – as well as being in shallow enough water to make oil exploration possible – were small in geographical extent. The recent removal of the severe water depth limitation on marine oil exploration by the development of alternative technologies such as the semi-submersible platform and, even more recently, the self-positioning drill ship, has taken the industry well beyond those marine areas within which questions of sovereignty and control had already been established in connection with other non-oil and gas considerations. At this point in its history the development of the offshore oil and gas industry has, thus, generated new types of marine policy issues. These are of political and economic as well as of legal importance and arise in respect not only of relationships between governments and oil companies, but also of relationships between governments and governments. Obviously, if offshore oil and gas promises to become a large new source of wealth for a country then the question of its government's relationships with the exploiting companies automatically becomes a matter of national and regional economic and political importance. The same is true in respect of the consideration necessary of the effects of oil and gas developments on other uses of the marine environment as well as on the environment itself. At the same time any individual country which becomes concerned with offshore oil and gas developments needs to take appropriate action against possible competing claims by adjacent and other countries in order to secure its interests in the offshore areas which, in its view, fall under national control and responsibility.

In overall terms, therefore, the developing technological potential for offshore oil and gas exploitation has, for many nations, opened up the possibility of a new resource frontier in areas hitherto defined as outside their national territories and, hence, outside their control. Moreover, this is a potential in respect of a commodity which, even in the period before the massive increases in the price of oil in 1973–4, was already widely recognised as being of great significance in terms of its influence on the economic well-being of nations. This, of course, made the prospects for offshore oil and gas developments even more important than would otherwise have been the case. The impact of such considerations was, for example, seen in the speed with which the nations surrounding the North Sea agreed, more or less, on its division between them for purposes of determining national control over its gas and oil resources, the great potential for which had been indicated by the discovery of the giant onshore gas field under the northern Dutch province of Groningen in 1959. Indeed, with hindsight it is possible to argue that these north-west European countries were so anxious to ensure their ownership and control over possible oil and gas resources lying under the North Sea, in a situation in which they felt that the absence of an agreement between them might well allow powers external to the region to declare an interest in it, that too little attention was given to particular individual circumstances in the decision process and to the enormous economic consequences arising from the decisions. Thus, West Germany alone reserved its position in respect of the median line arrangement for determining its seaward limits with neighbouring Denmark and the Netherlands and, indeed, later negotiated an extension to its offshore waters at the expense of its neighbours, following advice given to the parties concerned by the International Court of Justice.[1] On the contrary, neither the United Kingdom nor Denmark chose to reserve their positions in respect of the proposed median line basis for a division of the North Sea between themselves and Norway in spite of the fact that the deep water trench off the west and south-west coasts of Norway created the possibility of a limitation on the Norwegian claim to the sea areas extending up to the median lines with Britain and Denmark. The latters' under-appreciation of the potential significance of the oil and gas resources, under those parts of the North Sea which could have been disputed, has led to immense benefits for Norway – given that the richest oil fields of the whole North Sea province to date have been found in the immediate vicinity of the median lines concerned. Indeed, Norway as the beneficiary in this respect is, as a result, the first country in the world with known offshore resources whose value seems likely to exceed that of the total natural resources of the country itself. And, on the other hand, of course, Britain and Denmark are considerably less well off than they might have been. Now, however, less than twenty years since the division of the North Sea for purposes of oil and gas exploration and development, there is a general appreciation of the potential economic value which offshore hydro-carbons represent and a much better understanding of the fact that continuing technological developments will enhance the likelihood of this potential value being converted into real economic advantages for the nations concerned. As a consequence the possibility of disputes between states over competing claims to offshore waters with possible underlying oil and gas rich strata is now much increased and constitutes a maritime dimension to future economic policy-making by many of the world's nations which seems certain to be spelled out with heightening tensions over the next two decades.[2]

CONTINUING TECHNICO-ECONOMIC RESTRAINTS ON OFFSHORE
DEVELOPMENTS

In spite of rapid advances in recent years there remain severe technical and economic limitations on the degree to which maritime areas can be exploited for oil and gas. These limitations are related basically to depth of water considerations for no oil or gas has yet been produced from fields lying under the seabed where the water depth exceeds 350 metres. Even production in this depth of water is exceptional and most oil and gas has, so far, been from fields lying under the continental shelves – that is, by means of offshore facilities built in water depths of up to 200 metres. The continental slopes beyond the shelves are still being opened up only very slowly and tentatively and even then only in good politico-economic conditions and in locations having favourable meteorological circumstances.

These conditions do, indeed, have a powerful general impact on oil and gas exploration and exploitation decisions relating to maritime areas, especially, of course, on the continental shelves, the generalised

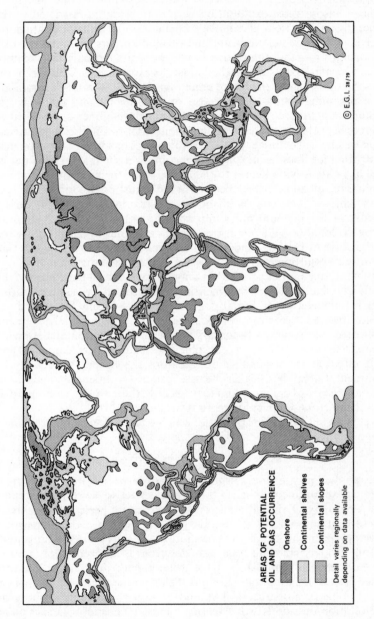

AREAS OF POTENTIAL
OIL AND GAS OCCURRENCE

Onshore

Continental shelves

Continental slopes

Detail varies regionally
depending on data available

© E.G.I. 28/79

Figure 4.1 The World's Continental Shelves and Slopes

worldwide distribution of which is shown in Figure 4.1. For meteorological reasons most exploitation was, until recently, restricted to the generally calm waters of relatively sheltered, low-altitude continental shelves. North Sea exploration and production has provided the first important breakthrough in this limitation – though only at a level of costs which has far exceeded the industry's expectations. This means, as we shall show below, that there remain important economic constraints even on middle-latitude expansion of offshore oil and gas reserves' exploitation in spite of the technological developments which have overcome problems of frequent and intense storm conditions. However, where such local extreme weather conditions coincide with the incidence of drifting ice floes, as in some marine areas in the middle latitudes as well as in areas lying nearer to the North Pole, the attempts to date to explore for oil and gas have been hesitant, whilst no production has yet been achieved. Less stormy offshore polar regions where winter ice is a regular *in situ* phenomenon (and which can thus be allowed for) are being explored to a limited degree (as, for example, in the Beaufort Sea to the north of Canada) and finds have been made. The first production from such environments has, however, yet to be achieved.

In brief, one may conclude that only quite restricted parts even of the relatively shallow-water continental shelves of the world's maritime dimension have, so far, been opened up technologically for oil and gas exploration and, yet more so, for production. It seems likely to be the last decade of the twentieth century before all the continental margins of the marine environment are accessible for oil and gas developments and well into the twenty-first century before the deeper waters of the continental slopes become an effective resource frontier even in terms of technological possibilities. And then, as now, there will be economic and political factors which continue to restrain the efforts of the industry to develop all of the offshore potential which is technologically accessible.[3]

OFFSHORE ACTIVITIES IN TRADITIONAL OIL AND GAS PRODUCING AREAS

This applies very strongly in the contemporary situation. The limited areas of the continental shelves that are under active development reflect the geography of the oil industry in terms of its preferred regions of investment interest. First, in this respect, there are those maritime developments which constitute offshore extensions of pre-existing areas of oil production. This one can describe as a process of natural development as companies have followed through their onshore successes in locating oil and gas fields in near-coastal geological formations. In parenthesis, it should be noted that most onshore oil exploitation outside North America has been coastal or near-coastal, given that success in such locations ensures low cost transportation of the oil to export terminals and to tidewater-located refineries so that the extension offshore has generally been a local development. One has seen this 'natural process' at work in Venezuela, Mexico, Texas/Louisiana, Indonesia and in the Persian Gulf in respect of all the surrounding nations' waters. In these circumstances the pre-existing availability from the onshore operations of geological and other relevant knowledge pertaining to the offshore possibilities, the existence on the spot of all the elements which go to make up the infrastructure of an oil exploration and development situation and the ability of a company simply to incorporate any offshore production into the marketing and/or refining system already developed for its onshore output from these important oil-consuming and/or exporting countries, mean that the new maritime dimension of the oil industry does not present any really serious political and/or economic considerations. Thus, because the process has been so 'natural' within the context of the pre-existing geography of the oil industry's activities, little special or separate attention has really been devoted to these examples of new offshore activities.

In total, to date, this sort of offshore oil and gas development has formed the bulk of the industry's commitment to the maritime dimension though, as we shall see below, its share in the total has been falling as a consequence of the rapid development of offshore oil and gas exploration and development elsewhere in the world. This relative decline has had more than a little to do with recent changes in the international oil industry; most notably with the nationalisation of the international oil companies' interests in almost all of the world's major petroleum-exporting countries. This has, to a high degree, isolated the latter from the offshore oil and gas expertise, more than 90 per cent of which is concentrated in the hands of the important international companies. Within the context of nationalised oil industries in the main oil-exporting countries, the state companies have not, of course, had either the incentive or the opportunity to pursue the offshore search for oil and gas in the regions concerned, with the result that many of the regions concerned have become relatively quiescent in this field of development.

This, however, does not apply to offshore Texas or Louisiana in the United States where the volume of offshore activity in these important oil-producing states has continued to increase: as it would have done in the other main area of interest in oil in the United States – namely, California – had it not been for the serious blow out of a producing well some years ago in a major offshore field, with consequential serious oil pollution along the coastline of the southern part of the state.[4] Neither has there been a decline off the coasts of Mexico. Quite the contrary, indeed, for there the long-established state entity (PEMEX), which took over from the nationalised private oil companies as long ago as 1938, has developed the technological know-how and the necessary funds to continue to expand its offshore exploration effort – with very encouraging results. Elsewhere in the world of the traditional oil-producing countries, however, the recent changes from private to state enterprise have certainly slowed up the creation of new offshore developments, even in areas which were already known to be potentially prolific as a result of adjacent onshore oil and gas developments. However, projects for new and expanded offshore exploration and/or exploitation in such areas are now once again getting under way – as, for example, in many parts of the Persian Gulf and in the Orinoco delta and the Gulf of Venezuela in Venezuelan offshore waters. Given the continued ability of the OPEC countries to find markets for their oil, then their offshore potentials will be developed: though certainly at a slower rate than if the international oil companies had remained responsible for oil exploration and production decisions in these countries.

NEW AREAS FOR EXPLORATION

Meanwhile, partly as a consequence of the nationalisation of the industry in most OPEC countries and partly in response to their need and wish to diversify their production interests geographically, the companies have turned their attention to some of the most highly prospective offshore regions for oil exploration in other parts of the world. In the context of many such prospective areas in many parts of the world (see Figure 4.1) their choice has been orientated to those which lie in proximity to major centres of energy demand and within which, moreover, the companies evaluate the politico-economic conditions as favourable for the heavy investments required in major offshore oil and gas operations. These considerations have, to date, had the effect of largely limiting the oil companies' interests in maritime exploration and exploitation to the energy intensive and politically safer member countries of the International Energy Agency (IEA) – the somewhat separate part of the Organisation for Economic Co-operation and Development (OECD) which has had the responsibility since 1974 for trying to ensure the medium- to long-term, as well as the short-term, availability of energy supplies to the rich, industrialised nations of the world.[5]

In this context, new offshore areas of the United States and Canada have been viewed with increased interest though, in both cases, environmental lobbies as well as disputes between the federal and the state/provincial entities over responsibilities and, even more important, over the allocation of the royalties and taxes expected from the production of oil, have limited the degree and the speed at which developments have got under way. Thus delays in initiating the search for oil and gas and/or in developing production from successful exploration have been experienced off the east coast of the United States and off Labrador and Newfoundland. Similarly, offshore areas of both

Australia and New Zealand have attracted a great deal of interest from the oil companies but, again, there have been political and/or environmental problems which have served to slow down the rate of exploration and development – most significantly in respect of the large opportunities for the exploitation of natural gas from the north-west continental shelf of Australia. The companies expected to develop this production in order to serve the Japanese market for liquefied natural gas but the development was held up for the best part of a decade as a consequence of Australia's unwillingness to commit large quantities of its gas resources to Japan. Production is not now expected to start before the mid 1980s.

It is thus Western Europe which has provided the outstanding attractions for offshore exploration by the international oil companies over the past decade and most especially, of course, since the oil supply crisis of 1973–4. The opportunities taken have included some developments in the Mediterranean, in the Adriatic and in the Aegean Sea and in a limited number of the many potential regions for oil and gas occurrences around the long and much indented coastline of Western Europe with its broad areas of continental shelf – as shown in Figure 4.2. The great centre of attraction and of activity has, however, been the North Sea in which the international oil industry has recently concentrated no less than 50 per cent of its total worldwide offshore effort. Thus, the effort which has gone into this region has, by far and away, been the world's most intensive one as far as the maritime dimension in the search for and the production of oil and gas is concerned. It should be noted, however, that the intensity of drilling to date does not match, by a wide margin, that which has taken place over a much longer period of time and in the much less hostile environmental conditions of the United States' part of the Gulf of Mexico. This latter development was, as previously indicated, essentially a continuation in the offshore areas of the long-lived onshore activities in Texas and Louisiana. By contrast, the developments in the North Sea represent a new frontier in the evolution of the industry in a region where onshore exploitation for oil and gas had hitherto been very limited with the single and relatively recent exception of the massive gas field of Groningen, in the northern part of the Netherlands, the discovery of which initiated the excitement about the North Sea's prospects, given the continuity of geological conditions from Groningen into the North Sea. The challenges and the problems that have had to be faced in respect of oil and gas developments in the North Sea are thus important not only in their own right, but also because of their relevance to the expansion of the oil and gas industry into the extensive maritime regions of potential in many other parts of the world. The relevance is apparent not only in respect of the technological aspects of the industry's development,[6] but also in respect of political and economic considerations which have proved to

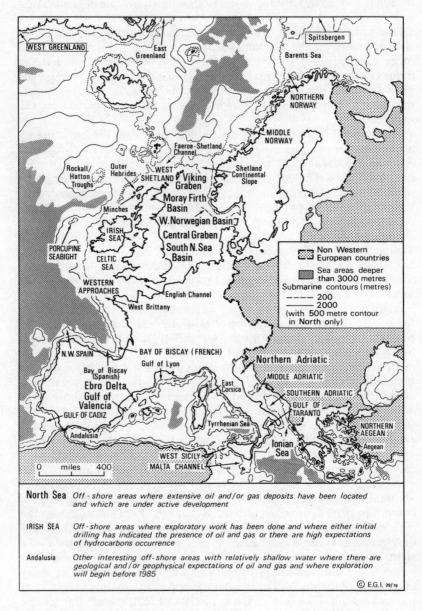

WEST GREENLAND

East Greenland

Spitsbergen

Barents Sea

NORTHERN NORWAY

MIDDLE NORWAY

Faeroe-Shetland Channel

Shetland Continental Slope

Rockall/ Hatton Troughs

Outer Hebrides

WEST SHETLAND

Viking Graben

Moray Firth Basin

W. Norwegian Basin

Central Graben

South N. Sea Basin

Minches

IRISH SEA

PORCUPINE SEABIGHT

CELTIC SEA

WESTERN APPROACHES

English Channel

West Brittany

N.W. Spain

BAY OF BISCAY (FRENCH)

Gulf of Lyon

Bay of Biscay (Spanish)

Ebro Delta

Gulf of Valencia

GULF OF CADIZ

Andalusia

East Corsica

Tyrrhenian Sea

Northern Adriatic

MIDDLE ADRIATIC

SOUTHERN ADRIATIC

GULF OF TARANTO

NORTHERN AEGEAN

Aegean

Ionian Sea

WEST SICILY

MALTA CHANNEL

| | Non Western European countries |
| | Sea areas deeper than 3000 metres |

Submarine contours (metres)
- - - - 200
——— 2000
(with 500 metre contour in North only)

0   miles   400

North Sea   *Off-shore areas where extensive oil and/or gas deposits have been located and which are under active development*

IRISH SEA   *Off-shore areas where exploratory work has been done and where either initial drilling has indicated the presence of oil and gas or there are high expectations of hydrocarbons occurrence*

Andalusia   *Other interesting off-shore areas with relatively shallow water where there are geological and/or geophysical expectations of oil and gas and where exploration will begin before 1985*

© E.G.I. 29/79

Figure 4.2   Western Europe: Areas of Offshore Hydrocarbons Potential

be important in determining the pattern and speed of expansion of the activities in the North Sea.

THE NORTH SEA: A CASE STUDY IN OFFSHORE OIL AND GAS EXPLOITATION

Background
Figures 4.3 to 4.7 illustrate several aspects of North Sea oil and gas exploration and exploitation and the results to date of the efforts that have been made. The hydrocarbons province is delimited by the occurrence of basement (that is, non-productive) rocks at or near the surface around the periphery of the North Sea. As in the rest of the world, the underlying geology which determines the potential – or the lack of potential – for oil and gas is no respecter of contemporary coastlines – let alone of national frontiers – so that the province includes parts of eastern England and of the mainland of Europe in the Netherlands and western Germany, as well as most of the North Sea area itself. Moreover, as shown in Figure 4.3, there are large parts of the marine areas themselves in which the potential for oil and gas is not high, because the basement rocks are relatively near the surface so limiting the depth of potential hydrocarbon-bearing strata. Away to the north the North Sea province is not terminated geologically in that similar geological conditions extend northwards beyond the 62nd parallel. However, effective areas for the search for oil and gas become non-existent (given present technology), as the continental shelf itself disappears where the deep water trench off the south-west coast of Norway links with the North Atlantic, so providing a sea depth limit to the North Sea province. (Further north off the coast of Norway, as seen in Figure 4.2, continental shelf marine conditions are re-established and these provide large additional regions of offshore oil and gas potential for that country.) Worthy of note, however, is the fact that Norway and the UK have recently agreed to an extension north of 62° of the median line between their waters. This newly defined extension to the marine areas over which Britain and Norway have established their rights to oil and gas exploitation reflects the impact of developing technology whereby exploration in waters deeper than those of the continental shelf can now be undertaken. Indeed, one block (214/30) in this area, with a water depth of over 300 metres, has already been allocated for exploration in the British sixth round of offshore licensing awards.

Within the North Sea proper, the decisions on the extent of national sectors were, as indicated above, generally a result of agreements between the countries concerned – the United Kingdom, Norway, Denmark, West Germany, the Netherlands and Belgium. The basis of the agreements was that of median line boundaries. Only in the case of West Germany were there disputes with the neighbouring countries over

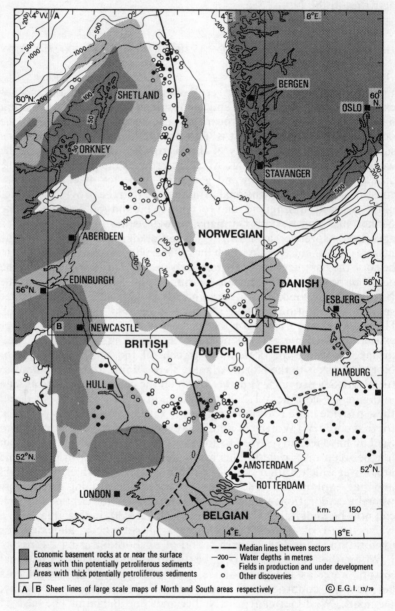

Figure 4.3   The North Sea Oil and Gas Province: Geology, Sectors and
Discoveries

the seaward boundaries to the sectors and these went for judgement to the International Court of Justice. Its judgement favoured the arguments of West Germany and the resulting negotiations between the parties led to a narrow extension to the north-west of West Germany's sector. This brought it up to the median line with the UK in an area of the North Sea originally claimed by Denmark and the Netherlands (see Figure 4.3). The fact that both these countries had permitted drilling in parts of the disputed areas before the dispute was resolved accounts for the irregular shape of this part of the German sector. The agreement between the three states concerned, following the court's decision, permitted the two other countries to maintain their interests in the areas which had already been drilled. So far, however, this extension of the West German sector has not proved to be very prolific in resources (though some discoveries have been made, as shown in Figure 4.5). This is far from being the case for the other main area of possible dispute over the geographical division of the North Sea. This, as mentioned earlier, is in respect of Britain's early acceptance of the median line arrangement with Norway in spite of the existence of a non-continental shelf maritime area just off the south-west coast of Norway. The existence of this deep water geographical feature might well have been used to challenge the extent of Norway's seaward interest. As one can see clearly from the information on Figures 4.4 and 4.6 this, 1963 mistake – if such it was – by the UK has cost the country dearly, given the discovery of many of the largest North Sea oil fields to date immediately to the east of the agreed UK–Norwegian median line.

Developments to Date

Over 200 separate discoveries of oil or gas (or oil and gas) fields had been made in the North Sea by mid 1979 – after fifteen years of increasingly intensive exploration activities. Their locations, declared sizes and other attributes are shown in Figures 4.4 and 4.5 whilst Figures 4.6 and 4.7 show the transport facilities which have been built or which are under construction or planned to link the fields under development with their connecting coastal terminals and/or refineries.

These maps show something of the complexities of the production and transportation developments that have already occurred. Fields have been discovered in all sectors (except the small Belgian sector in the extreme south) so that the area of production or of potential production stretches for more than 1,000 kilometres from north to south. The fields are highly variable not only in terms of their size (they range from under 50 million barrels of oil and oil equivalent to 3,500 million barrels) and their hydrocarbon type (for example, oil or gas; or oil and natural gas; and with or without significant quantities of natural gas liquids and other gases such as ethane), but also in terms of their distance from shore, the depth of water in which they occur, their depth in the

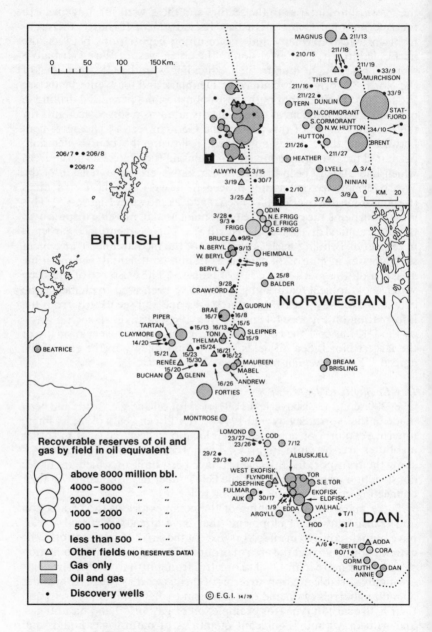

Figure 4.4   The North Sea north: discoveries and developments to mid 1979

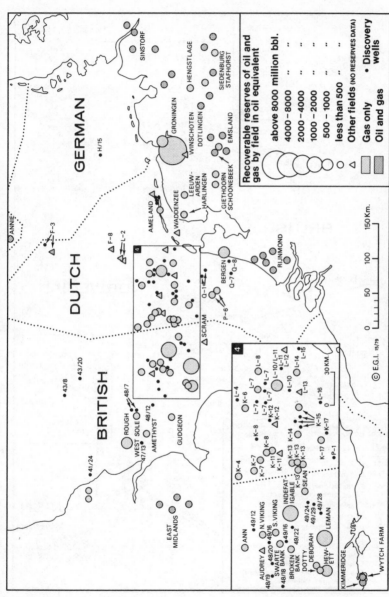

Figure 4.5   The North Sea south: discoveries and developments to mid 1979

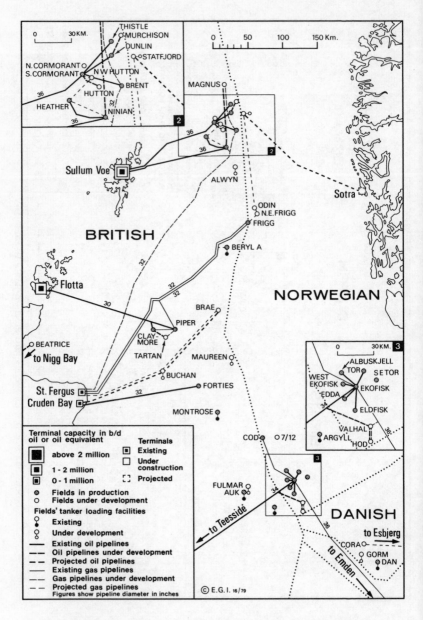

Figure 4.6   The North Sea north: oil and gas transport facilities, 1979

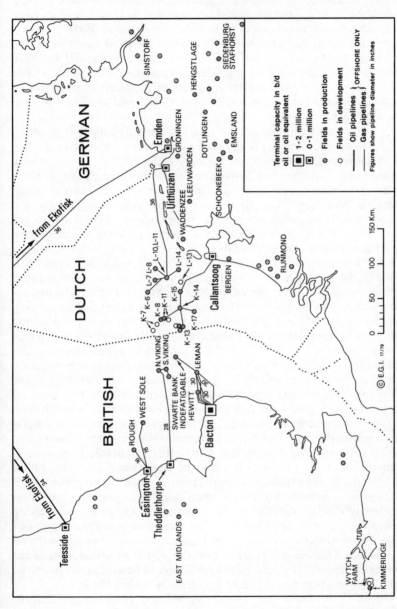

Figure 4.7   The North Sea south: oil and gas transport facilities, 1979

underlying strata, the nature and qualities of their reservoirs, in their geographical relationships one with another and in terms of their ownership (state or private company) by one or more of the many oil companies involved. All these factors affect the production of the oil and/or gas both in technical and in commercial terms and so make predictions on the evolution of production patterns difficult. Moreover, the uncertainties are still further enhanced by political considerations – as we shall show below – in respect of both national and international considerations.

Problems over the size of the reserves are particularly difficult to resolve in the uncertainties of the marine environment given that the size of an individual field involves not only technical but also economic considerations. Both sets of considerations embrace subjective elements so that no single reserve figure provides an unequivocal answer to the question, how large is a particular oil field? And moving from the calculations for one field to the total of reserves from all fields discovered and from there to the total potential for the province multiplies the problems considerably and leads to wide variations in the estimates. Table 4.1 shows how these estimates have varied over time – even when made by the same company – though as uncertainty has been reduced and as successes have exceeded companies' expectations, the estimates have generally moved to higher levels. Currently, as the table also shows, one can count on total North Sea oil and gas reserves discovered to date over 50×10^9 barrels (= 7,000 million tons) of oil equivalent – about half as oil as such (the 28×10^9 bbl. at 1(a) in the table) and half as natural gas and natural gas liquids. Production from the fields already in production or under development will rise by the mid 1980s to over 350 million tons of oil and oil equivalent per year under the stimulus of the high demand for both oil and gas in the nearby industrialised nations of north-west Europe. On the basis of the oil and gas reserves of the discoveries already made and on the assumption that agreements will be reached that enable the oil companies to develop the many other smaller finds profitably, then this level of production could be maintained into the 1990s. Moreover, as the exploration opportunities have by no means been exhausted – indeed, both new areas and new parts within areas previously drilled remain to be explored – there are continuing possibilities for new finds, again on the assumption that the conditions laid down by the countries concerned remain attractive enough to the oil companies. This means, at least, that the period of production at the level indicated above could be extended and, at best, that the potential annual production could rise to significantly higher levels.

On all these counts the North Sea oil and gas province may be considered to be a major one by world standards. As such its reserves represent assets of enormous significance and their exploitation opens up questions of both an economic and a political character. These

Table 4.1   *North Sea oil reserves and resources: estimates and forecasts compared*

	bbl. × 10⁹
1 *Reserves declared economically recoverable*	
(a) By simple addition of reserves declared from 55 fields	about 28

(b) After adjustment to a *summed* 90 per cent
         probability assuming each of the 55 fields is
         declared at a 90 per cent probability
	±35

2   *Reserves declared recoverable plus additional
     discovered reserves not yet defined as
     commercial*	

(a) Following average upward revision of
         recoverable reserves from declared fields
         (including ±35 in lb) above
	40–45

(b) From another 18 fields discovered but with reserves not yet declared	3–6
(c) From 45 other discoveries not yet declared as fields	4–8
3 *Reserves from new discoveries 1979 to end of exploration period*	12–20
Total	59–79

4   *As forecast by 1975 Rotterdam simulation
     model[a] on the full development of the
     province with an assumption that all oil
     found and technically recoverable will
     eventually be produced*	

(a) at 90 per cent probability	78
(b) at 50 per cent probability	109
5 *As forecasts by various oil companies*	
(a) by Shell in 1972 (for 1980 reserves)	17·5
(b) by BP in 1973	38
(c) by BP in 1974	44
(d) by Shell in 1975	35
(e) by Conoco in 1975	45–67
(f) by Shell in 1976	35
(g) by BP in 1976	±50
(h) by Shell in 1978	45–52
(i) by BP in 1979	70
6 *Current expectations of governments with North Sea interests*	62–75

Notes: *a*   P. R. Odell and K. E. Rosing, *The North Sea Oil Province: An Attempt to Simulate its Exploration and Development, 1969–2029* (London: Kogan Page, 1975).
   b   Forecasts given by the companies in papers presented at various North Sea oil and energy conferences between 1972 and 1979.

questions arise first over the relationships that the governments have to have with the international oil companies concerned; and secondly, over the relationships between the different countries involved – either as producers and/or as potential users of the oil and gas resources.

Government–Oil Company Relationships
First, of course, a government has to establish conditions for the exploration of its offshore areas which have a potential for oil and gas occurrences. The conditions have to be attractive enough for oil companies to be willing to seek to participate in the effort in a situation in which most of them have several or, indeed, many alternatives open to them for exploration efforts in various parts of the world. Initially, therefore, the conditions must not be so tough as to inhibit companies from joining in the search: but neither, of course, must the conditions be so 'easy' that companies can secure acreage, not with the intention of exploring and developing it, but with the idea of preventing rival firms from having access to its potential. The choice of government policy is thus critical to having the potential explored properly – as it is to the later ability of the state to secure a return from any developments which eventually proceed. The relative strength of the positions of governments and of companies, moreover, change over time as a consequence, first, of the perceived geological and the economic attractions of a given region and, secondly, of the evolving international oil supply and demand situation. Both of these very dynamic aspects in the relationships between state and oil company are, of course, open to contrasting interpretations so creating an inherent propensity for conflict between governments and oil companies in respect of offshore oil and gas developments.[7]

Such a propensity for divergence between government and company interests is also apparent over questions relating to the development and production of individual offshore fields.[8] Once a company has discovered a field which it considers it can profitably develop then it will normally wish to do this as quickly as possible in order to recover the investment it has already made in its search for oil in the province and in order to provide a cash flow for its continuing work both in the province itself and in other parts of the world. In this respect it will not be interested in the development decision of other companies which have found fields in the maritime province concerned, given that the oil it intends to produce is marketable worldwide and not just locally so that it does not have to fear the possibility of oversupply being created by its single decision to develop a new field. For the government concerned, however, other considerations prevail, as national policy towards oil development in the province may be aiming specifically at, say, sufficient production in total to meet estimated levels of indigenous demand. In these policy circumstances a field development decision has to be evaluated by the government in the light of its likely contribution to national production needs. Sometimes a delay in development could be required, so creating possible tension with the company concerned.

Also in the context of an individual field's development plan a company may wish to keep the degree of the development of the field to a level below that which is technically possible in order to ensure an adequate rate of return on the investment involved. This means that less than the field's technically recoverable reserves will be produced and this could also create a possible conflict with the best interests of the government for which maximum possible recovery will usually be viewed as the most appropriate and the most advantageous policy to follow.

Exploration and development decisions in respect of offshore oil and gas are obviously important ones, creating company–government tensions. The exploitation of onshore resources has not given rise to such tensions which are a consequence of the particular technological and economic circumstances of oil developments in the maritime dimension. However, it is only in the case of the North Sea to date that the issues involved have been effectively exposed and, already, they have led to claims by governments that the companies are avoiding their obligations and to counter-claims by the companies that the governments are inhibiting the development of the offshore resources by dint of their regulatory and fiscal policies.[9] In essence it is, perhaps, the very 'internationalism' of the oil companies, which are alone able to undertake offshore oil and gas exploitation on a large scale, that leads to the problem. This is because national governments are naturally suspicious of the companies' ability so to organise their affairs that they seem able to avoid nationally orientated rules and regulations. This problem was perceived by many governments to be serious enough when oil and gas developments were onshore. Now they have moved offshore, where national authority is so much less firmly established in respect of control and regulation mechanisms and of the ability of governments to collect taxes both from companies and individuals, the enhanced concern by governments about the activities of the companies and their employees can be readily understood.

National Political Considerations
Superimposed on the problems between governments and oil companies in respect of the development of the North Sea are questions of a political and economic character affecting relations both within and between nation states. These emerge, in part, from the fact that petroleum geology is no respecter of pre-existing patterns of economic development and of political organisation. Thus, the successful exploitation of a country's oil and gas resource base will only rarely, by coincidence, serve simply to confirm the influences of the previously

significant factors which determined the patterns of national development and of organisation. This is seen very clearly in the case of Britain's North Sea oil reserves, most of which – to date – have been found off the coast of north-east Scotland and east of Orkney and Shetland. As a direct consequence of oil industry activities the economies of these previously stable or relatively depressed parts of the United Kingdom, dependent on traditional industries, agriculture and tourism, have become overheated. This has happened, moreover, during a period since 1973 when the country's economy generally has had a rather 'thin' time as a consequence of international economic problems. In this period the regions with the ability to serve the offshore oil activities have enjoyed higher relative levels of economic activities than those regions without such opportunities. There have also been unexpected shifts in population. Thus, for the first time in many decades, the population of northern Scotland has been increasing along with that of Orkney and, especially, Shetland, where one of the world's largest crude oil handling terminals is being constructed, which offers job opportunities in a range of activities new to the region.

In political terms these regional economic consequences for the northernmost parts of the UK have been generalised to involve Scotland. Narrowly, there has been the political slogan of 'Scottish Oil' and this has been accompanied by claims that the disbursement of the revenues from the oil produced should reflect the 'geography' of oil production. Much more broadly, the prospects for continuing wealth from the offshore resources sustained the momentum of the Scottish separatist movement. Without the influence – or rather the potential influence – of North Sea oil, it seems unlikely that the concept of the devolution of political power from Westminster to Scotland would have made the rapid progress it achieved between 1973 and 1978.[10]

The impact of offshore oil on Scotland in both economic and political terms can thus be judged to be favourable. In the context of such important gains the impact of the physical and social environmental problems which arise from offshore oil and from related onshore developments may be judged to be relatively minor except, of course, locally where the problems affect people directly and continuously. On the other side of the North Sea in Norway, however, the situation seems likely to be different, for that country's offshore oil and gas potential creates the possibility of a huge disturbance both in national economic and in even more general societal terms. Norway's small population and its limited GNP and range of onshore economic opportunities and resources are overshadowed by the country's maritime oil and gas prospects. The extent of the hydrocarbon provinces under the offshore areas (including the much larger potential areas to the north of latitude 62°) is so great that the development could become the dominant component in the Norwegian system. This involves not only consequential macro-economic effects at the national level but also carries the prospects of severe environmental impact in the localities most closely concerned with the oil industry. It is in this possibility (which, one should note, the Norwegians are trying to control by severely limiting the degree and speed of offshore oil and gas exploration and exploitation) that there lies the prospect for the first time – the development of a country in the modern period whose economy and society will be principally influenced by the maritime rather than the land dimension of the realm.

Some International Political Aspects
The development of the North Sea's resources of oil and gas also has important international implications. First, there are the continuing important issues between the countries which own the resources as a result of the division of the North Sea into national sectors (see Figure 4.3). The boundaries of the sectors have, of course, been agreed but there remain problems associated with the location of the exploitation efforts. These include complicated issues, with technical, legal and economic components, such as those involved in the unitisation of the development of a field which lies astride a median line between two countries. (Norway and the UK have already had three such joint discoveries.) Agreement is necessary on the calculations of the field's reserves and on their division between the countries (and the companies) concerned and their exploitation involves jointly approved development plans by the various parties concerned. There is also a set of problems arising from the need for international agreement on the pipelines required to take the oil and gas ashore – as, for example, in respect of the gasline from the Norwegian Ekofisk complex of fields. This traverses both Danish and West German waters *en route* to Emden and carries gas for the Netherlands, Belgium and France, as well as for West Germany itself (see Figures 4.6 and 4.7). The development of such physical facilities related to the rapid expansion of the oil and gas industry in the North Sea and on its seabed do, of course, involve much international negotiation and, to date, these have been of an *ad hoc* nature between the two or more countries involved in particular enterprises. Many of the developments involved are, moreover, of a kind which necessitate specific negotiations – as in the case, for example, of decisions on the unitisation of a field which lies partly in one country's sector and partly in that of a second country. Similarly with the routes of pipelines and the conditions under which they may be laid: in this respect it seems unlikely that any country would be prepared to allow decisions to be taken by an international body, though the prospect of a set of generally agreed principles between some or all of the six nations concerned cannot be excluded. The evolution of an agreed legal regime, in respect of some common problems to which North Sea oil and gas developments give

rise for all the countries concerned, does, however, seem to be increasingly necessary – and thus likely. Such common problems include the safety and security of the installations, their defence from external powers and from terrorists, their status in taxation terms and in terms of local administration, the navigational problems which they create and their status and treatment once they are time-expired in terms of the purposes for which they were built.[11] The evolution of general international agreements in north-west Europe in respect of such oil and gas related problems of the maritime dimension could well set the pattern for legal developments in other multinational maritime environments for oil and gas related activities.

International issues of a different kind between the nations involved in the North Sea developments arise as a result of the contrasting regimes established by the five countries concerned for the exploitation of the oil and gas resources. No single country with a North Sea sector can afford to be too far out of line with the others in respect of the conditions it establishes for exploration and production. Otherwise it will lose the interest of the companies which will look instead to the possibilities they have in the other sectors where conditions are less onerous. Norway suffered a decline in the companies' interests when its regulatory and fiscal regime on offshore oil development and exploitation was tightened up. Those companies which also had interests across the median line in British waters preferred to concentrate their attention in the latter area. Even in terms of discoveries of fields actually made, the oil companies involved may not want or need to develop those found in a particular national sector. For example, the companies in the consortium responsible for successful exploration in Danish waters have been unenthusiastic about committing their resources to these fields' development, given the much better opportunities which they have had to date for investment in fields in the British sector and the absence of any means whereby Denmark could force the companies to develop the resources.

In the light of both the technical and the politico-economic problems which are arising between the nations with the joint responsibility for developing the oil and gas resources of the North Sea province, it is perhaps surprising that no attempt has yet been made to establish any kind of joint framework for tackling them given, on the one hand, the close relationships of the countries with each other and, on the other, the limited technical and human resources available to each of the countries concerned in contrast with the wealth of expertise available to the multinational corporations with which each country has to negotiate. Perhaps the failure of any collective governmental organisation to emerge, as a means of effectively countering the undoubted strength of the large oil companies arising out of their superior knowledge and access to technology, is a measure of the degree to which the potential for creating wealth from the exploitation of the North Sea's reserves creates an enhanced nationalistic approach in the policies of the countries concerned.

Nationalist Responses to North Sea Oil and Gas
The impact of nationalism is, moreover, even clearer in the attitudes and the policies of those countries which have achieved considerable oil and/or gas production towards their near neighbours and/or their partners in the EEC. The Netherlands, where hydrocarbons production from the North Sea province was initiated on a large scale (from the onshore Groningen gas field), did at least start off in the 1960s with an open export policy. Between 1963 and 1971 it concluded arrangements for the large-scale sale of its gas to Belgium, West Germany, France, Luxembourg, Switzerland and even Italy. In the early 1970s, however, Dutch policy changed radically and government restraints were then placed on the export of gas from the country's first offshore field to be developed. As the company concerned wanted to sell its gas in West Germany where it had found a willing buyer at a price higher than that which could be obtained for the gas on the Dutch market, this raised the question of Dutch discrimination against a customer in the neighbouring country and so introduced the likelihood that this made the Netherlands in default of the non-discriminatory regulations of the Treaty of Rome. This raised the possibility of a case coming before the European court in respect of a sector of the economy to which the EEC had given very little attention at that time. It thus seems that the prospect of a legal judgement in respect of a matter on which all member countries of the Community were, in effect, reserving their positions was not particularly welcome to any of the parties concerned – except, of course, the willing seller of the Dutch gas concerned (an American oil company) and the willing buyer in West Germany. In the event, a political compromise was sought and found (in which the gas concerned was shared 50/50 between domestic and West German use) and no European court case emerged. The Netherlands was obviously satisfied that its neighbours and fellow members of the EEC were hardly likely to press for policies which reflected the non-discriminatory clauses of the Treaty of Rome in the light of their own possible exposure to counter-claims in respect of their own energy policies, and thus in 1974 there was a Dutch government decision that no further gas export contracts would be permitted. All remaining natural gas was to be kept at home to meet long-term national needs. The validity of Dutch policy in this respect in terms of its EEC membership has never been called into question.

It is, therefore, perhaps not very surprising that the United Kingdom, a later and a less enthusiastic member of the EEC than the Netherlands, and Norway, which failed to join the EEC partly because of fears about what the Community would do to its oil policy, have been even more nationalistic towards the development of their resources. All UK offshore oil and gas has to be landed in the UK and this policy has been rigidly observed. An application to the government in 1971 for permission for gas from the southern part of the UK sector to be piped directly to West Germany was refused and now, even with the prospects of too much gas being available for the domestic market – in spite of the fact that the market is growing very quickly – there has been no serious consideration given to the possibility of exporting it to countries such as France and Belgium, where the gas would find a ready sale and serve to substitute imports of oil from elsewhere in the world.[12] And as far as oil is concerned, current UK government policy is to control the level of production rather than to allow more than a quite limited amount (of a maximum of about 25 million tons per year) to be exported. Norway, too, in spite of its own very limited demand for energy (given its small population and a ready availability of low-cost hydro-electricity) has not been prepared to allow the development of its oil and gas resources beyond a severely controlled limit. This was imposed partly to ensure the availability of the resources on a long-term basis for national use. Given the absence of a large demand for oil and gas in Norway this, of course, means that the incentive to look for oil and gas is much reduced.

POLICY RESPONSES TO THE NORTH SEA CHALLENGE

Such various national policies in the geographical context of one of the world's most energy intensive regions and one which is dependent, moreover, to a high degree on imports of oil from the member nations of OPEC with both price and security of supply considerations, indicate the divisive impact which the oil and gas resources of the North Sea province have had on the region. This, moreover, has to be seen in relation to the possibilities of co-operation over energy policy which the offshore resources of the North Sea have created in a situation in which the revolution in the world of oil power since 1973 had served to emphasise the need for a European approach to the important energy sector of the continent's economy. The absence of effective co-operation to date does not, however, lie by any means solely with the Western European oil and gas producing countries. Until very recently the non-producing countries such as France, Belgium, Sweden and West Germany showed remarkably little interest in the development of the North Sea and the potential of its oil and gas reserves as a means whereby the structure of their energy sectors could be changed – in particular, their dependence on imported oil.[13] This, in part, seems to have been the result of continuing ignorance about the offshore oil and gas possibilities on the part of the governments of the countries concerned. The potential from the new maritime dimension in Western Europe's resource base did not enter their calculations. Thus, enter-prises from these countries (except in the case of France) only sought involvement in the offshore opportunities at a relatively late stage – as with Deminex of West Germany and Petroswede of Sweden. In part, it was also because the countries concerned had already decided to concentrate their attention on two other ways of meeting their energy needs, first, by planning to try to expand nuclear power very rapidly and, secondly, by attempting to achieve some kind of 'special relationship' with the countries from which they traditionally imported their oil. The political, economic and other risks associated with both these aspects of post-1973 energy policy making in Western Europe were high, as subsequent events continue to show, and it is all the more surprising that co-operation with neighbouring countries with North Sea oil and gas potential was, for so long, not considered to be a viable policy alternative – an attitude which, it must be stressed, emerged out of the general lack of appreciation of the significance of the maritime dimension in respect of future oil and gas developments and availabilities.

Moreover, following the compromise over the Netherlands' initial refusal to allow its offshore gas to be sold to customers outside the country – a compromise which meant that the European court was excluded from concerning itself with the production and use of these offshore resources – the EEC also failed to take positive steps early enough to ensure that the extensive maritime dimension to its territorial extent was properly evaluated for the oil and gas potential. The evolution of the Community's fishing policy could obviously be related to the totality of the sea areas surrounding the member countries. This was an aspect of the maritime dimension with which there was general familiarity. On the other hand, there was far too little knowledge and understanding of the nature of the hydrocarbons potential lying underneath the extensive continental shelf of the Community members and, basically, it was thus ignored. Instead EEC energy policy planning was based on the impossible (the rapid development of expensive nuclear power) and the unlikely (the speedy recovery of the European coal industry from its twenty year period of decline since 1955). Even now, in 1979, the EEC is still only tentatively accepting the idea of a large contribution from offshore oil and gas to future energy needs. Its lack of knowledge of the issues is, moreover, now compounded by the fear that its involvement will only serve to stimulate rather than reduce the intensely nationalistic attitudes to which offshore oil and gas around Western Europe has now become subjected.[14]

This lack of appreciation of the significance of West European offshore oil and gas does not apply to the attitudes of the two major world powers – the USA and the USSR – towards the exploitation of the North Sea, though the motivations behind the policies of the two countries towards these maritime hydrocarbon resources are by no means identical. In the case of the United States its interest in the North

Sea reflects the dominance of American companies in offshore oil and
gas technology. As a direct consequence of this, most of the concessions
in British, Norwegian, Danish, West German and Dutch waters were
originally allocated to US oil companies. This remains the case, in spite
of later attempts in the allocation of concessions to give preference to
national entities, except in the cases of Norway and Britain both of
which decided that such American domination of their maritime
hydrocarbon resources was an unacceptable situation and thus decided
that their newly formed national state oil companies should automatically secure at least a 51 per cent holding in all new concessions. Conflict
between American commercial interests, which, of course, continue to
dominate the international oil industry, and the interests of the countries
with offshore areas of oil and gas potential is certain to be a continuing
one in the near to medium-term future exploration and exploitation of
marine areas. Indeed, it seems likely to be even more intense than has
been the case in respect of onshore oil developments, given the much
more complex and expensive technology which is required for successful
offshore activities. This can, for example, be seen in the case of Brazil
where, in spite of the state monopoly over oil stretching back some thirty
years, the government has been obliged to invite foreign oil companies
to participate in offshore exploration given the financial and technical
barriers to Petróbras, the state oil company, undertaking sufficient
offshore work. However, one may expect nationalist responses to
American leadership and control in the exploitation of offshore oil and
gas resources and these will serve to slow down the pace at which the
resources are discovered and produced from underneath the world's
seas and oceans – particularly in respect of activities beyond the
relatively shallow waters of the continental shelves, where only a
handful of the major international oil companies are currently technically capable of undertaking oil exploration activities.[15]

For the Soviet Union interest in what has been happening in the
North Sea in respect of oil and gas and, indeed, on the other parts of the
continental shelf of Western Europe (see Figure 4.2), is related to its
great strategic concern for this part of the Western industrial world's
system. In economic terms the development of the offshore resources
represents such a major change in the politico-economic prospects of
Western Europe overall, and for a few countries in particular, that it is
an important component in the Soviet Union's appraisal of the region's
strength. This can be seen from Figure 4.8 and Table 4.2 showing the
potential of the North Sea (and of other offshore oil and gas in other
areas) for reducing the exposure of Western Europe to dependence on
imports of oil from politically unstable parts of the world. More
specifically for the USSR in economic terms there must be concern for
the impact that large indigenous resources of oil and gas could have
upon the opportunities available to the Soviet Union for continuing its

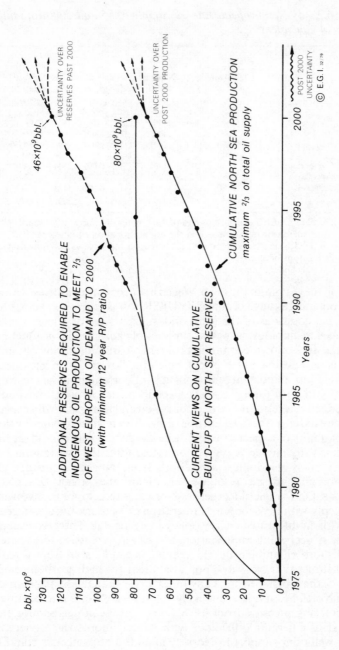

Figure 4.8 The potential North Sea Contribution to Western Europe's Oil Supply

Table 4.2   *West European Energy Supply 1985 and 2000 (in million tons coal equivalent)*

	1985				2000			
	Early 1970s[a] Estimates		Alternative Estimates		Early 1970s[a] Estimates		Alternative Estimates	
	m.t.c.e.	%	m.t.c.e.	%	m.t.c.e.	%	m.t.c.e.	%
Total	2,870		1,950		5,000		c.2,700	
Oil	1,845	64	1,150	60	3,200	64	1,100	41
(of which imported)	(1,650)	(89)	(750)	(66)	(3,000)	(93)	(200–400)	(18–36)
Natural gas	385	14	400	21	500	10	900	33
(of which imported)	(85)	(22)	(60)	(15)	(300)	(60)	(150–300)	(16–33)
Coal	310	11	280	14	300	6	450	17
(of which imported)	(90)	(29)	(50)	(17)	(100)	(33)	(100)	(22)
Primary electricity[b]	330	12	120	6	1,000	20	250	9
(of which imported[c])	(140)	(42)	(20)	(17)	(250)	(25)	(50)	(20)
Total imported	1,965	68	880	45	3,650	73	500–850	18–31

Notes: a OECD, EEC and various national estimates of future energy supply patterns made prior to the change in the international oil situation in 1973.

b Hydro and nuclear power calculated on the heat value equivalent of the output of electricity.

c Dependent in part on imports of uranium for nuclear power.

sales of these commodities to Western European countries. In recent years oil and gas have become the USSR's most effective exports to the industrial countries of the West and in exchange for which it receives advanced technology, as well as supplies of capital and consumer goods essential for its own economic progress. A diminution in oil and gas exports or a decline in the prices which the Soviet Union gets for these could be an important component in worsening its medium-term opportunities for foreign trade; especially as the Soviet Union does not have effective alternative outlets for the oil and gas it currently expects to continue to sell in Western Europe. Finally, in respect of Norway there is the possibility of a special relationship which may arise should the Soviet Union try to pursue a policy for integrating the two countries' oil policies. This possibility arises both from Norway's attitude to its offshore oil and gas resources and from the Soviet Union's own interests. On the one side, there is Norway's reluctance to involve itself too deeply with the economic integration of Western Europe in general, and with an integrated energy policy in particular. This has been noted above. A deepening appreciation of Norway's massive total potential for offshore oil and gas developments (as can be seen from Figure 4.2 which shows that Norway's potential areas for hydrocarbon resources north of the North Sea are many times larger than the Norwegian sector of the North Sea itself), seem likely, however, to cause it to be subjected to increasing pressure from its Western European neighbours. In this context of emerging difficulties with its neighbours the Soviet Union could well offer support to Norway in a kind of protective role. Given that Norway and the Soviet Union share a common frontier in the far north and that agreement has yet to be reached on the way in which this frontier is to be extended out into the Arctic Ocean in order to delineate the highly prospective offshore areas for oil and gas between the two countries, then it is quite clear that a firm basis for a common interest in the subject of marine hydrocarbons resources does exist. It could, indeed, quickly evolve into the most important issue between Norway and the Soviet Union whose ships, in the meantime, are giving close attention to the oil and gas developments already under way in the North Sea itself.[16]

The North sea constitutes a very small part of the world's maritime areas with oil and gas resources. Nevertheless, its position in the context of both European and more broadly international political and economic issues – together with the speed at which the development has taken place – makes it a case study of great importance in respect of the attention which must increasingly be given to the maritime areas of the world from which a large part of the future supply of oil and gas can be expected to come.

NOTES AND REFERENCES

As this is only a general, introductory article on the exploitation of offshore oil and gas resources detailed referencing seemed to be inappropriate. Much of the description and analysis remains scattered in relatively inaccessible technical and industry journals but there are now a number of books which deal with the issues that are involved in this relatively recent development of the use of the maritime environment for oil and gas exploitation. On offshore oil and gas developments in general the book by D. E. Kash *et al.*, *Energy under the Oceans: A Technology Assessment of Outer Continental Shelf Oil and Gas Operations* (Norman, Okla.: University of Oklahoma Press, 1973) provides an assessment by an interdisciplinary team of social and natural scientists, engineers and a lawyer on the opportunities and problems involved in offshore oil and gas development. However, because the region of study was the United States there is no consideration of the international political and legal problems involved in the designation of maritime areas for oil and gas activities. D. M. Leipziger and J. L. Mudge's book *Seabed Mineral Resources and the Economic Interests of Developing Countries* (Cambridge, Mass.: Ballinger, 1976) mainly deals with offshore oil and gas. It is particularly concerned with the division of the seabed for oil and gas exploitation in order to achieve production efficiency in the operations and equity in the division of the returns from the value of the production. In terms of the latter it treats the problem as to how geographically disadvantaged states could secure access to the revenues from subsea hydrocarbon resources. It thus takes the international aspect of the use of maritime resources beyond the question of the geographical division of the seabed between nation states. By contrast the study by F. W. Mansvelt Beck and K. M. Wiig, *The Economics of Offshore Oil and Gas Supplies* (Lexington, Mass.: Lexington Books, 1977) is essentially a technico-economic appraisal which attempts to quantify the ultimate availability of oil and gas from the US offshore areas and the costs involved in exploiting them. The methodologies described in the book could be applied to other offshore areas and it thus provides guidance for approaching the economic aspects of the exploitation of maritime hydrocarbon resources.

On the North Sea, in particular, two monographs by P. R. Odell and K. E. Rosing, *The North Sea Oil Province: An Attempt to Simulate its Exploration and Development, 1969–2029* (London: Kogan Page, 1975) and *The Optimal Development of North Sea Oilfields* (London: Kogan Page, 1977), deal with the technico-economic aspects of North

Sea oil and gas exploration and exploitation. They indicate the large number of variables involved and demonstrate the complexity of their inter-relationships. K. Chapman's *North Sea Oil and Gas* (Newton Abbot: David & Charles, 1976) surveys the process of development of North Sea exploration and exploitation highlighting the main issues involved including onshore effects, the use of oil and gas produced and the importance of the resource at the Western European level. C. Robinson and J. Morgan, *North Sea Oil in the Future: Economic Analysis and Government Policy* (London: Macmillan, 1978) contains a great deal of information on the economic aspects of North Sea oil in this book and a great deal more speculation on its future, based on the limited range of ideas both on reserves and on policy that the authors are prepared to consider. It is, however, a book which is most interesting from a negative point of view: as an example, that is, of the way in which economic analysis can be so unconcerned with the specific environment of a major development. The maritime dimension to the North Sea oil and gas production process is ignored. By contrast, the somewhat older book by D. I. MacKay and G. A. Mackay, *The Political Economy of North Sea Oil* (London: M. Robertson, 1975) on the economics of North Sea oil recognises the specific problems arising from the maritime nature of the development. It is thus, in part, concerned with the question of the ownership and use of offshore resources and, in particular, with the influence of developments on Scotland and on the basis of the authors' claim that most of the oil discovered in the British sector lies to the north of an English/Scottish median line.

1 The North Sea Continental Shelf case, 1969, International Court of Justice, Den Haag.
2 A prime example of the great potential for international disputes lies in China's claims over its adjacent waters as these impinge on Korean, Japanese and even Philippine interests. See S. S. Harrison, *China, Oil and Asia: Conflict Ahead?* (New York: Columbia University Press, 1977) for a discussion of the issues involved.
3 The large multinational oil companies have been unable and/or unwilling to operate in many countries of the Third World for up to several decades. This situation applies equally, of course, to offshore areas. See P. R. Odell, *Oil and World Power*, 5th edn (Harmondsworth: Penguin Books, 1979), Ch. 7.
4 See D. E. Kash *et al.*, *Energy under the Oceans* (Norman, Okla.: University of Oklahoma Press, 1973) for a background to US offshore oil and gas exploitation.
5 Note, however, that France, an OECD member, declined to join the IEA as it considered it to be an anti-OPEC organisation. France considered that its membership of the IEA might thus prejudice its attempts to maintain its special relationships with the Arab countries.
6 This is reflected, for example, in the way in which hundreds of US companies associated with the oil industry in Texas and Louisiana have set up subsidiaries in the UK, Norway and the Netherlands to do business in the North Sea.
7 See P. R. Odell and K. E. Rosing, *The Optimal Development of North Sea Oilfields* (London: Kogan Page, 1977) for a detailed discussion of this inherent conflict of interest between governments and companies in respect of offshore developments.
8 ibid.
9 As, for example, in the dispute in the summer of 1979 between the chairman of the British National Oil Corporation, Lord Kearton, and the international oil companies over the responsibility for the decline in oil exploration in the UK sector of the North Sea. See the *Guardian*, 27 July 1979, p. 1.
10 See D. I. MacKay and G. A. Mackay, *The Political Economy of North Sea Oil* (London: M. Robertson, 1975) for a discussion of the Scottish component in the evaluation of UK oil exploitation.
11 See J. J. Holst, 'The strategic and security requirements of North Sea oil' and P. W. Birnie, 'The legal background to North Sea oil and gas developments', in M. Saeter and I. Smart (eds), *The Political Implications of North Sea Oil and Gas* (Oslo: Universitetsforlaget, 1975) for consideration of these issues.

12 The possibility of UK gas exports to France and Belgium is at last under discussion. It is reported that British and Norwegian energy ministers are to meet late in 1979 to discuss the options open for gas-gathering and transmission lines for moving north North Sea gas to markets in the mainland of Europe. See *Noroil*, August 1979.

13 See Saeter and Smart (eds), op. cit. for a discussion of these questions in the light of the situation up to 1974.

14 Fear of EEC control over its offshore oil and gas helped to swing Norwegian votes against membership of the Community. More recently, concern has also been expressed in the UK over the possibility of EEC interference in decisions on the exploration and exploitation of offshore oil and gas.

15 P. R. Odell and L. Vallenilla, *The Pressures of Oil* (London: Harper & Row, 1978) discuss the role and the problems of the multinational oil corporations in contributing to the development of oil resources in Third World countries. See especially Chapter 15.

16 See Holst, op. cit. for an evaluation of Norwegian/USSR interests in offshore oil and gas developments in areas of shared interests.

Chapter 5

The Marine Environment

R. P. BARSTON AND P. W. BIRNIE

INTRODUCTION

Within the past two decades many significant threats to the marine environment have developed as a result of the intensified use of the sea for an increasing number of purposes. The Geneva conventions paid little attention to the control and prevention of marine pollution. However, the spread of industrialisation and the corresponding rapid increase in transportation of goods, especially oil, by sea and use of the sea for the disposal of waste has forced states to pay much greater attention to the regulation of these and other sources of pollution. A number of major maritime disasters has recently made states acutely aware of the urgency of the need for more effective control. However, the problem of negotiating an effective and comprehensive regime has been complicated by the diverse nature of the sources of pollution.

Scale of the Problem
The major source of contemporary marine pollution, accounting for up to 80 per cent of all pollution, is land-based activities such as industrial discharges, factory effluents, agricultural wastes and sewage. Moreover such activities as the testing of nuclear weapons inevitably produce fall-out which adds to the levels of radioactive pollution, and many other pollutants discharged into the atmosphere eventually contribute to marine pollution. Disposal of waste also takes place by direct dumping at sea; this use of the sea has proved particularly controversial since it has come to include dumping of nuclear wastes, nerve gases and highly toxic substances.

It is, however, regulation of oil pollution from vessels, caused either by deliberate discharges or maritime casualties, such as the *Torrey Canyon* and the *Amoco Cadiz*, that has received the greatest attention from the international community, partly because oil spills are visible, widespread and pose a potential threat to public amenities and fisheries, and partly because of the international nature of shipping. Ships not only navigate the high seas but regularly also cross areas within other states' jurisdictions, whereas land-based sources remain permanently within one state's jurisdiction.

The number of ships plying the oceans today has increased to over 70,000 and the total tonnage now exceeds 400 million gross registered tons, compared with 36,000 and 125 million respectively in 1959.[1] In many sealanes the density of shipping movements has greatly increased; in the English Channel, for example, some 300 vessels transit north or south every day and another 250 make cross-channel passages; by 1970 the Straits of Gibraltar averaged 215 passages, the Cape of Good Hope 160, the Straits of Japan 100, the Straits of Malacca 85 and the Persian Gulf Straits 80. Moreover there have been significant changes in the types of vessels; in 1959 the largest cargo vessel in operation was *Universe Apollo* of 104,520 dwt whereas now vessels of over 500,000 dwt are in operation. By 1975 623 of the oil tankers were super tankers of over 100,000 dwt, making up half the world tanker tonnage at that date. Tankers, because of their size, were carrying 50 per cent of the total cargoes, and a much higher proportion of the tanker fleet (79 per cent) was at sea at any given time than of the cargo fleet (20 per cent). Container ships, along with chemical and liquid gas carriers, were not developed until the 1960s. Although liquid gas and chemical carriers comprised a small proportion of world tonnage (for example, 2,415,000 dwt and 748,000 dwt by 1975), nevertheless the potentially hazardous nature of their cargoes is a further source of concern for coastal states. Despite the world tanker recession which developed during the late 1970s, the anxiety of coastal states has not lessened concerning the potential threat to their environments posed by the size and type of the present world fleet.

Following the Geneva Convention on the Continental Shelf, exploration and exploitation of offshore seabed resources soon took place and rapidly expanded throughout the world. By the end of the 1960s, for example, there were about 6,000 installations in the Gulf of Mexico; in the UK sector of the North Sea the first commercial oil find, the Montrose field, was made in September 1969, followed by the Forties field in October 1970. By 1979 there were twelve oil fields and one gas field in production and a further eleven fields under development.[2] These developments have created new pollution hazards: blow outs, tanker spillage, collisions, oily water discharges and dumping of oil-related debris. Offshore installations also generate pipelines which could be fractured, for example, in the process of trawling, and the installations themselves add to the navigational hazards for fishing and other vessels. In enclosed and semi-enclosed seas, any pollution occurring may not be confined within one national sector but could cross the boundaries of other states' sectors. The hazards to marine life and public amenities are increased proportionately when installations are located in estuaries or near coastal waters, although the precise effects of oil and other forms of pollution are the subject of considerable controversy amongst scientists.[3]

THE CONTROL OF POLLUTION: INSTITUTIONS AND CONVENTIONS

The approach to the international control of marine pollution from all sources has long been strongly influenced by the customary doctrine of freedom of navigation on the high seas which was codified in the Geneva Convention on the High Seas. This convention specifically referred to other freedoms (fishing, laying of submarine cables and pipelines and overflight), and acknowledged the existence of others 'recognised by the general principles of international law' (article 2). States have consequently assumed that they are free to use the seas for the disposal of wastes from a variety of sources and for testing weapons. This article confirmed, however, that such freedoms must be exercised by all states with reasonable regard to the interests of other states in their exercise of the freedom of the high seas. The efforts to develop an international framework for the control of marine pollution have therefore been characterised by the need to achieve a reasonable balance between the exercise of freedoms.

However, since the United Nations Conference on the Human Environment held in Stockholm in 1972, the international community has taken an increasing interest in protecting the marine environment by taking account of its ecological interdependence and this concern is evidenced in some of the more recent agreements such as the Oslo Dumping Convention (1972)[4] and other regional conventions.[5]

The techniques for establishing marine pollution regimes have varied. For example, the regime for vessel-source pollution has largely been built up within the Inter-Governmental Maritime Consultative Organisation (IMCO) which has its headquarters in London. Several conventions concerning crew standards have also been developed through the International Labour Organisation (ILO) in Geneva. Also within the United Nations framework the United Nations Environment Programme (UNEP), established in Nairobi by the Stockholm Environment Conference, has accepted a special role for promoting regional agreements. In other cases *ad hoc* diplomatic conferences have been used to negotiate specific conventions such as the London Dumping Convention, [6] and the Paris Convention on Land-based Pollution.[7] Increasingly resolutions and recommendations have also been adopted in an attempt to develop norms and codes of conduct for environmental protection.

The IMCO Conventions
IMCO was established in 1958 as an inter-governmental organisation for the purposes of developing rules and practices concerning the technical aspects of international shipping and encouraging the adoption of the highest practical standards for maritime safety and efficient navigation. The membership of IMCO has risen from twenty-one in 1958 to 107 in 1979 with one associate member. IMCO, as an inter-

governmental organisation, is dependent on the consent of its member states for the adoption and implementation of resolutions and conventions. The entry into force of these is dependent on the fulfilment of certain specified conditions. Examples of these conditions are the achievement of a specific number of ratifications, ratification by certain named states, or ratification by states with a certain amount of tonnage registered under their flag.

There are now at least thirty IMCO Conventions and protocols but it is proposed to discuss only the main conventions directly concerning pollution from ships. The first convention regulating vessel-source pollution, the International Convention for the Prevention of Pollution of the Sea by Oil,[8] was adopted in 1954 before the IMCO Convention entered into force, but its administration and subsequent amendment has been taken over by IMCO. The purpose of the 1954 Convention was to control pollution by prohibiting deliberate discharges of oil or oily mixtures containing 100 parts of oil per million parts of mixture or more in designated zones 50 miles from the coast (extended to 100 miles in 1962). It also introduced an administrative control – oil record books, which can be inspected in port. This was the first tentative move towards giving the port state, as well as the flag state, some role in inspection. The convention, however, can only be enforced by flag states; if inspection reveals a violation the port state's powers are limited to reporting the incident to the flag state. This convention has become the most widely ratified of all IMCO's conventions dealing with vessel-source pollution. By the end of 1978 some sixty states had ratified it. In 1969 the convention was amended in order to tighten the definition of oily mixture to include any oil content; and to take account of a new appreciation of an acceptable level and distribution of oil discharges. The ban on discharges in certain areas was therefore replaced with a permissible discharge per mile formula for tankers proceeding *en route* at least 50 miles from land which enabled them to operate the load on top (LOT) system for cleaning ballast tanks.[9] Because of the conditions laid down for entry into force, which proved difficult to fulfil, the amendments did not become effective until 20 January 1978.

In 1973 IMCO adopted an International Convention for the Prevention of Pollution from Ships (MARPOL)[10] which covers all forms of pollution from ships (except ocean dumping of wastes). It was innovatory in many respects. The convention includes provisions relating to pollution by oil, noxious liquid substances carried in bulk, harmful substances carried in, for example, freight containers, sewage and garbage. This new major comprehensive convention is, however, still aimed at the prevention of pollution by discharges (whether accidental or deliberate) into the sea, and not the prevention of accidents giving rise to pollution. When it comes into force, and if it is widely ratified, the convention will be a major advance. However, even then parties may not accept the whole of the convention since it has several optional annexes of detailed provisions, which along with the two protocols and several resolutions make up by far the largest part of the instrument.

Annex I maintains the oil discharge criteria laid down in the 1954 Convention and its 1969 amendments, with minor amendments. It requires LOT and provision of reception facilities for discharges and carriage of appropriate equipment for monitoring discharges, and its construction requirements include provision of segregated ballast tanks (SBT) for new tankers of and over 70,000 dwt. This annex in addition introduces the concept of Special Areas which are designated to include the Mediterranean Sea, the Black Sea, Baltic Sea, Red Sea and 'Gulfs' Area, most of which have since become the subject of regional conventions. Originally acceptance of both Annex I and II (relating to noxious liquids) was required for ratification but since 1978 acceptance of the former alone is sufficient. Annexes III and IV relating to packaging requirements for harmful substances and discharge of sewage and garbage respectively are also optional.

Under the enforcement provisions of the 1973 Convention the flag state retains primary responsibility, but provision is also made for coastal state jurisdiction: since no limit is referred to, its jurisdiction could, to the extent provided at UNCLOS or elsewhere, extend beyond the territorial sea. The powers of the port state (a state party to the convention into whose port a ship enters) are also considerably extended by this convention to include verification of required construction and equipment certificates; inspection in order to monitor observance of the discharge requirements; and detention of substandard and other ships, such as those without certificates. The convention is unusual in that states party are obliged to apply the requirements of the convention to vessels of states which are not party to it.

A further unusual feature of the convention is the introduction of tacit acceptance procedures to allow for technical amendments to the annexes in order to expedite their entry into force. Unless one-third of the states party, or parties representing at least half of the global merchant gross registered tonnage (grt), object to an amendment it will enter into force by a specified date. However, none of these new procedures has yet become binding upon states since the convention has not entered into force, only five states having ratified the convention to date – Jordan, Kenya, Tunisia, Uruguay and Yemen. Indeed its oil prevention provisions have already had to be amended by protocol to introduce new requirements concerning surveys and certificates.

The *Torrey Canyon* disaster in 1967 led in 1969 to the conclusion of the Intervention Convention[11] enabling coastal states to take action in defined circumstances against foreign vessels on the high seas which have become maritime casualties. It is worth noting however that the absence of a convention did not prevent the UK taking the action it thought necessary to deal with the *Torrey Canyon* incident since, in its view, the right to take such action already existed under customary international law. Article 1 of the convention permits states to take the measures necessary to prevent or reduce 'grave and imminent danger'[12] to their coastlines and related interests from pollution of the sea by oil from maritime casualties. A protocol adopted at the 1973 MARPOL Conference will extend these provisions to substances other than oil when the MARPOL Convention comes into force. The Intervention Convention entered into force in 1975 having achieved the necessary fifteen ratifications; there are now thirty-five states party to it.

Increasingly human error has been perceived to be at the root of many vessel-source pollution problems; valves may be left open, adequate watch may not be kept, signals can be inadequate or misread, navigation is often poor. Although there are a series of ILO Conventions relating to standards of crew and certification of officers these are not widely ratified. The ILO is a tripartite organisation: seafarers share equal representation with shipowners and governments in its decision-making processes and adoption of its conventions. Recent disasters have led IMCO, where the interests of shipping states and shipowners are more closely linked and the economic implications of conventions are taken into account, to adopt in 1978 a Convention on Training, Certification and Watchkeeping for Seafarers.[13]

Ocean Dumping
Dumping at sea of toxic wastes generated on land, especially radioactive wastes and redundant nerve gases, some of which have reappeared or were accidentally recovered by fishermen, led to such international protest that in 1972 both a regional and an international convention to prevent or control it were adopted. The Oslo Convention,[14] adopted by twelve states in the North Atlantic area, preceded the international London Dumping Convention[15] for which it was a model, though there are some differences. Both institute a system of annexes into which pollutants are graded according to their harmfulness. Highly dangerous ones are prohibited from being dumped in any circumstances, others can only be dumped on certain conditions under special permits; the rest can be freely dumped. These are often referred to as the 'black', 'grey' and 'white' lists respectively. IMCO acts as the Secretariat of the London Convention, which has no Commission of its own, but the Oslo Convention instituted a Commission of all states party to it to administer and interpret its provisions. It now shares a Secretariat with the Paris Commission described below. Allocation of pollutants under the annexes has caused some difficulty because of the economic costs that flow from such decisions and which give rise to political difficulties, especially as not all states have alternative sites on land for disposal. The

conservation lobby has campaigned strongly against disposal of radioactive waste on land and in the sea even if done under the recommendations of the International Atomic Energy Agency (IAEA) as is required under the convention.

Enforcement under both conventions is left to flag states and coastal states within their territorial jurisdiction, though the ICNT in article 210 proposes to extend this, for dumping only, to the EEZ and the continental margin, which would impose a major enforcement burden on coastal states and perhaps create problems for landlocked states, such as Switzerland, which also need to dispose of wastes at sea, and find the high seas area available to them for the purpose shrinking.

Dumping is also controlled under the more comprehensive Helsinki Convention for the Baltic Sea[16] and the Barcelona Convention for the Mediterranean[17] promoted by UNEP. The former establishes a Commission, whereas UNEP provides the secretariat for the latter, but both aim to regulate all sources of pollution in their regions. It has proved difficult under the Barcelona Convention, because its parties include both developed and developing states, to promulgate standards for the Mediterranean, since it is the industries of developed states bordering it that have caused its chronic pollution; developing states which do not create such industrial pollution do not want to be restricted by the regulations necessary to control it. Several regions are now also, encouraged by UNEP, considering adopting pollution conventions, for example, the Gulf of Guinea, the Caribbean, the East Asian Seas, the Gulf and the Red Sea.

Land-based Sources
International concern about the impact on the marine environment has grown acute though it is difficult scientifically to establish the biological effects. In 1974 North Sea and North Atlantic states concluded the Paris Convention[18] to prevent and control pollution from these sources, categorising pollutants under annexes, as in the Dumping Conventions, and establishing a Commission (which now shares the Oslo Secretariat) to administer them. Difficulties have been encountered in grading pollutants and interpreting the convention's terms. The EEC, in promulgating drafts of directives and regulations concerning water quality as part of its Action Programme for the Environment,[19] has encountered similar problems. They stem partly from the different capacities of states' coastal waters to degrade pollutants: cold water and fast flowing currents, as in the eastern North Sea, dispose of them more effectively than the more sluggish warm waters of the Mediterranean. The UK therefore prefers to take advantage of this and set environmental quality standards verified by monitoring, whereas other states support uniform emission standards so that the economic burdens are uniform. The solution has been to leave the choice to states concerned.

Other problems are handled by establishing Working Groups on particular pollutants or issues. The Oslo and Paris Commissions have some Joint Working Groups, for example, on hydrocarbons. This group bases its work on national research programmes which follow a framework laid down by ICES. Definitions of terms used in the Paris Convention such as 'pollution', 'harm to the marine ecosystem', 'persistent oils' and 'elimination' has invariably proved contentious because of the economic and political consequences stemming from the categorisations which flow from them, and the debates are still continuing on these questions. The Paris Commission has accepted that the inclusion of pollution from man-made structures in the convention covers offshore installations, which could lead to some overlap with the Oslo Convention's coverage of dumping from them, and the MARPOL Convention's treatment of installations as vessels for the purpose of regulating oil discharges from them. The overlap is at present more theoretical than practical but points to the dangers of allowing *ad hoc* functional Commissions to proliferate without a co-ordinating body.

Offshore Installations
The Continental Shelf Convention was silent on pollution from this source except that it required shelf states to take the measures necessary in the 500 metre safety zones to protect the living resources of the sea from harmful agents. It has been left to individual states through their national legislation to develop offshore pollution prevention regimes. This they have done. Good examples are provided by the UK and Norwegian Continental Shelf regimes, which have adopted different approaches – the UK favouring broad enabling Acts supplemented, as experience was gained, by a series of specific regulations, whereas Norway included detailed requirements in its Acts and decrees. The original differences have, in the course of time, narrowed. The Paris, Oslo and the MARPOL Conventions have since, as mentioned above, imposed some specific international obligations on their states party and the EEC has also considered producing relevant regulations.[20]

Problems have also arisen concerning the harmonisation of safety and pollution regulations on offshore platforms. North Sea states have met several times since 1973 in an informal diplomatic conference on Safety and Pollution Safeguards in the Development of North West European Mineral Resources. The conference established Working Groups on different aspects – safety of the installations, of the personnel and on pollution safeguards – but has been undecided whether to produce a treaty or a code of conduct on these topics. It does not meet again until 1980 but now favours the latter course. In 1976 the states concerned in this conference signed a Convention on Civil Liability for Oil Pollution Damage Resulting from Exploration and Exploitation of Seabed Minerals. States could not agree on the 'worst case' analysis. There was serious disagreement in the conference concerning the financial limit of liability; Ireland favoured a high limit, Norway wanted unlimited liability and the UK insisted on relating it to what was insurable. The treaty did set a limit but left states the option nationally of imposing no limit. The convention has not yet been ratified by any state.

The only other convention relating to offshore oil spills is the regional Bonn Agreement for Cooperation in Dealing with Pollution of the North Sea by Oil.[21] It, however, relates only to co-operation in sighting and monitoring oil slicks and is primarily directed to those emanating from tankers, not blow outs, in the North Sea, but after the Ekofisk disaster the parties agreed that it did cover spillages from offshore platforms. The convention had been dormant until this incident but meetings of the parties have since taken place and its extension to spillages of substances other than oil is under consideration. The EEC's indication of its interest in adhering to the agreement as a community has, however, held up further progress for the moment.

THE EFFECTIVENESS OF INTERNATIONAL REGIMES FOR CONTROL OF MARINE POLLUTION

As we have suggested in the previous sections the development of international machinery for the control and prevention of pollution has in the main taken place in an *ad hoc* manner. Conventions have emerged from a variety of international and regional organisations and many are as a result serviced from headquarters in various parts of the world – London (IMCO, Oslo and Paris Commissions), Geneva (ILO), Nairobi (UNEP). This reflects the lack of a co-ordinated approach both to the development of pollution control measures and to administration. However, the major problem common to nearly all conventions is securing their entry into force within a reasonable period of time for a sufficiently large number of states. For example, although the 1954 Oil Pollution Convention entered into force in 1958, the more important 1969 amendments to it did not enter into force until 1978. This was partly because the latter required to be accepted by a two-thirds majority of states party to the former and thus the influx of new parties to the 1954 Convention paradoxically postponed entry into force of the amendments. Another reason has been that some states have preferred not to sign the 1969 amendments in view of the conclusion of the 1973 Marine Pollution Convention, yet the latter has not entered into force and because of the economic implications of its technical requirements (such as provision of reception facilities on shore, monitoring and separation equipment and SBTs) is not likely to do so for some considerable time. Some maritime states take little or no part in conventions, preferring the economic and administrative advantages arising from minimal international regulation. It is, however, extremely difficult to find methods of improving this situation since IMCO has no mandatory powers as an organisation and cannot compel member states to ratify its conventions.

IMCO has recently resorted to setting target dates for entry into force of the newer conventions and protocols; for example, the 1978 protocol to the 1974 Convention on Safety of Life at Sea which requires the installation of inert gas systems on tankers of 70,000 dwt and above has a target date of June 1981. The delay in entry into force often means that when the convention does become effective the measures which it has provided have become technically outdated; IMCO has as a result been forced to amend conventions which have not entered into force.

The entry into force of the regional conventions has not been subject to such long delays, because of the smaller number of states party and their geographical proximity to the area regulated. The Commissions have encountered difficulties in operating the conventions, however, because the economic costs of harmonised regulations do not always fall equitably on the states party to them. This is sometimes due to the different levels of development of states concerned but is often occasioned by the varying ability of receiving waters to degrade pollutants.

Enforcement of the conventions is frequently poor since IMCO has no powers itself to enforce conventions and enforcement is therefore left primarily to flag states, not all of which stringently observe their obligations under the conventions. Some moves have therefore been made in recent IMCO Conventions towards giving both coastal and port states limited powers of enforcement, but these are very carefully circumscribed. It has been left to UNCLOS to endeavour to introduce major improvements in the present regime of predominantly flag state jurisdiction over vessel-source pollution and to effect improvements in the regimes dealing with other sources of pollution.

In the meantime, following the *Amoco Cadiz* disaster, eight states bordering the North Sea decided that there was limited scope within existing ILO and IMCO Conventions and recommendations for regional arrangements to improve enforcement. Accordingly their administrations (not their governments) adopted a Memorandum of Understanding requiring inspection of all vessels entering their ports to ascertain whether they conform to various standards laid down by IMCO and ILO, in the form of both conventions and recommendations, even though the flag state concerned may not have accepted these standards. Vessels cannot be detained; any deficiencies found can merely be reported to the flag state. For this agreement to be fully effective a higher level of inspectorate would be required than is currently in existence in most of the countries concerned, though all of them are important maritime states.

There are, of course, many other weaknesses in existing conventions for prevention of pollution from all sources. It is not possible, however, within the context of this chapter to examine these further but some of them have been highlighted by a number of recent large-scale disasters such as those described below. These have tended to stimulate the most international action, yet at the same time have emphasised the inadequacies of the above arrangements for controlling and preventing pollution.

The Amoco Cadiz

The grounding of the supertanker M/T *Amoco Cadiz*, a VLCC of 109,700 grt, off the coast of Brittany after her steering gear had broken down, eight miles north of the island of Ushant, on 16 March 1978, resulted in the greatest single discharge of petroleum in maritime history. The tug *Pacific* had been unable to prevent the *Amoco Cadiz* from drifting on to a rock outcropping about a mile offshore. The vessel was carrying a full load of Iranian crude oil and lost the entire cargo of 210,000 tons and bunker fuel amounting to 4,000 tons, which heavily polluted nearly 140 km of the Brittany coast from Portsall to the Ile de Brehat in the course of the next fifteen days, affected other areas, and extended 60 km offshore, damaging recreational beaches, mariculture areas and a substantial amount of fisheries.[22]

The interim inquiry held by Liberia[23] concluded that factors contributing to the stranding of the vessel included the failure of the steering gear and the close proximity of the vessel whilst in passage to the French coast. As a result of this case the French government adopted a strong position at the seventh session of UNCLOS, advocating strict channel separation schemes and requiring reporting in of vessels in transit. They also initiated proposals at IMCO to strengthen the powers of coastal states, and introduced new national legislation. The incident also drew attention to the fact that in salvage operations there is no obligation to resort to Lloyds Open Form of Salvage agreement and that delays in negotiating salvage terms might contribute to such disasters. The disaster also demonstrated the inadequacy of existing conventions and agreements concerning liability and compensation to cover losses of this scale. Claims for damages from the disaster raised in the United States courts could reach more than $1.7 billion; the French government alone is claiming $300 million.

The Betelgeuse

The explosion of a French tanker *Betelgeuse* in Bantry Bay in the Irish Republic on 8 January 1979 illustrated clearly that marine pollution damage can also arise even during the unloading of tankers in harbours or offshore terminals. The tanker in this case had unloaded about two-thirds of its cargo of 120,000 tons of Middle Eastern crude oil when it exploded.[24]

The Enskeri case

In March 1975, the case of the Finnish tanker *Enskeri* caused, against the background of the 1975 session of the Law of the Sea Conference,[25] considerable international controversy. The 114,450 dwt *Enskeri* had left Helsinki in March bound for the Gulf in ballast with a deck cargo of waste, which included several tons of arsenic trioxide. The tanker, owned by the Finnish state oil company, Neste, intended to dump the waste in the South Atlantic without the knowledge or approval of the Finnish government. Difficulties arose when the deck cargo began to leak and became unsafe; at first no state would permit the *Enskeri* to enter its ports to transfer the waste to new containers. Entry was refused into Gibraltar and Las Palmas by the United Kingdom and Spain respectively. Meanwhile the plight of the vessel had attracted great international concern and, moreover, the planned dumping was strongly criticised by environmentally minded states such as Canada. South Africa too was highly critical of the proposed operation.[26] It appeared that the *Enskeri* might become rather like the *Stella Maris* of some four years earlier – a ship without a port – until the Portuguese government allowed the vessel into Lisbon, where the deck cargo was properly containerised in the hold, and the *Enskeri* subsequently returned directly to Finland with the waste cargo. The episode proved not only expensive for the Finnish government but diplomatically embarassing, partly because the *Enskeri* was state owned, and partly too because of the restrictive public position of the Finnish government on ocean dumping. More generally, the case is unusual in a number of respects. It occurred against the background of the third session of the Law of the Sea Conference and served to underline (as *Amoco Cadiz* did for oil pollution) the need for adequate international control of dumping – though such control can only be exercised effectively if conventions are both widely ratified and enforced. The *Enskeri* case drew attention to a related issue: the question of the geographic area covered by a convention. In this case the proposed dumping site in the South Atlantic fell outside the Oslo Convention area and under the London Convention. The former entered into force only the following month; the latter a year later. However Finland, whilst being a party to the regional Oslo Convention, is not party to the international London Dumping Convention. The case too raised the important issue of the reception of vessels which have dangerous cargoes requiring attention; in this case, for example, facilities at Gibraltar for offshore transhipping were inadequate and the vessel fortunately was able to enter Lisbon. It is clear, however, that in this and similar cases involving the shipment of dangerous cargoes technical support and port entry may not always be available or forthcoming.

The Ekofisk and Ixtoc I Blow outs

On 22 April 1977 an oil and gas blow out occurred in well B–14 on the Bravo production platform in the Ekofisk field 175 miles south-west of Norway.[27] The blow out occurred during the installation of the blow out preventer valve. The well is the largest producer in the Norwegian sector of the North Sea and about 22,500 tons of crude oil and 1.7 million Nm³ of gas escaped. The Norwegian commission of inquiry concluded that the accident was due to a combination of circumstances in which human error played a major part. The underlying cause, however, was found to be deficiencies in the organisational and administrative systems for supervising the work. The blow out was stopped and the well eventually brought under control on 30 April 1977 by a specialist team from the United States led by the redoubtable Red Adair. This was the first major blow out in any North Sea sector and it revealed that not even the detailed regime prescribed by Norway could prevent an accident of this kind. Norway's handling of the incident demonstrated the difference between its approach and the UK's: Norway refused to use chemicals to disperse the oil because of the environmental risk. It also demonstrated the absence of readily available specialist personnel and equipment capable of dealing with such an emergency.

Two years later the Ixtoc I[28] well, 80 km north-west of the Mexican Yucatan peninsula, blew out on 3 June 1979 and again the episode emphasised the difficulties of preventing and controlling blow outs. The estimated oil loss has been between 10,000 and 30,000 bbl. per day. By 12 June the oil slick was 180 km long and up to 80 km wide and gave rise to great concern for the rich fisheries on the neighbouring Campeche Banks. Attempts to cap the well, including those of Red Adair, failed and use of dispersants, booms and skimmers was of very limited value in containing the pollution. It is feared that there may be serious damage to the rich shrimp fishing grounds in the coastal area; shrimp boats recently took catches valued at £20 million.

UNCLOS

The weaknesses of the existing regimes are apparent: the slowness of entry into force of conventions, their poor ratification, inadequate enforcement, and the *ad hoc* manner in which conventions and institutions have been developed. UNCLOS provides an opportunity to remedy some of these deficiencies. An important feature of the ICNT produced at the seventh and eighth sessions of UNCLOS is its provision within a single text of regimes for land-based[29] and seabed sources,[30] dumping,[31] pollution from vessels[32] and from the atmosphere,[33] as part of an overall package on the law of the sea. In Part XII of the text dealing with the protection and preservation of the marine environment a significantly large number of the articles are devoted to control and prevention of vessel-source pollution. This part of the text has attracted the widest consensus at UNCLOS; by the eighth session (1979) negotiations had been substantially concluded. This suggests that even if the conference fails to adopt a treaty, or alternatively during the period of entry into force, some provisions of Part XII are likely to be adopted into customary international law, as has been the case with some of the provisions concerning 200 mile fisheries jurisdiction.

Intensified negotiation on the articles concerning vessel-source pollution since 1975 has produced a text which provides for a careful balance between continued jurisdiction for the flag state and increased powers of regulation and enforcement for coastal states, together with limited port state jurisdiction. Powers to prevent vessel-source pollution would also be strengthened by provisions in other parts of the text such as the proposal in article 3 that the breadth of the territorial sea should be extended to 12 nautical miles. Article 19(2) now defines the activities which make passage through the territorial sea non-innocent. These include 'any act of wilful and serious pollution' and 'any other activity not having a direct bearing on passage'. The rights and jurisdiction of coastal states within the 200 nautical miles exclusive economic zone, which is provided for in articles 55 and 57, include in article 56(1)(3) the preservation of the marine environment as governed by the relevant provisions of the convention.

Freedom of navigation on the high seas beyond the EEZ is preserved by article 87. The customary flag state system is retained, though a 'genuine link' is required between the registering state and the registered vessel, but again no criteria are laid down for establishing this link. The specific duties of the flag state to ensure safety at sea are, however, now laid down in detail in articles 74 and 217. In straits used for international navigation, as defined in article 37 of ICNT, whilst ships have a right of transit passage, that is to say, they can proceed freely, they must comply with generally accepted international regulations for safety of life at sea, including collision regulations and the rules and standards for prevention of vessel-source pollution. Article 41 enables states bordering straits to designate sealanes and prescribe traffic separation schemes, after first submitting them to the competent international organisation.

The articles of Part XII of the text which are exclusively concerned with vessel-source pollution first of all require states in article 211, acting internationally through diplomatic conferences or the competent organisation, to establish international rules and standards for prevention, reduction and control of pollution from vessels and to enforce these on their flag ships. Coastal states can also establish national laws in their territorial sea but only to the extent that they do not hamper innocent passage. In their EEZs, however, they can only establish such laws for the prevention of vessel-source pollution which conform to and give effect to generally accepted international rules and standards. After the *Amoco Cadiz* stranding article 211 was amended at the eighth session to require states to adopt routing systems to minimise the threat of accidents. Further amendments require states which establish conditions for prevention of pollution as a prerequisite of port entry to publicise them and inform the competent international organisation. It is envisaged that some states, in an effort to harmonise policy, might establish identical conditions, and in such cases the relevant international organisation must also be informed of the states participating in the co-operative arrangements. A foreign vessel navigating in the territorial sea of a participating state must, at the request of that state, indicate whether it is proceeding to a state which is taking part in the co-operative arrangements, in which case it must inform the port state of its destination of its compliance with that state's port entry requirements. This would give states a better opportunity to monitor the movement of foreign vessels and to verify their condition but it is doubtful whether in practice this will tighten up enforcement since it would require a high degree of administrative co-operation between flag, coastal and port state.

The concept of special areas introduced by the 1973 IMCO Convention has been extended by article 211(6). If the international rules and standards are considered inadequate to meet special circumstances and an area of the EEZ is especially vulnerable to pollution for various reasons, a special mandatory system can be imposed by the coastal state after the competent international organisation has been consulted. The coastal state cannot, however, contrary to the initial demands of some states, such as Canada, regulate standards of design, construction, manning or equipment except for those generally accepted internationally and approved by the organisation concerned. In ice-covered areas, however, within the EEZ, coastal states have the right (article 234) to establish and enforce their own non-discriminatory laws and regulations to prevent or control pollution.

In addition to the above proposals considerable improvements in enforcement are provided for at the flag state, port state and coastal state level, but the relevant articles still place the primary responsibility on the flag state since many states remain reluctant to accept a primary role for port or coastal states. Flag states, however, under article 217(3) will have to ensure that their vessels carry certificates (which can be inspected by port states) and must prohibit the sailing of vessels which do not conform to the certificated standards. They must also inspect their flag ships and investigate and institute proceedings if violations occur, on their own initiative or on the initiative of other states. A port state, under article 218(1), can take action irrespective of where a violation occurs only when a vessel voluntarily enters its port or an offshore terminal if investigation reveals that violations have occurred.

It can also take action for discharge violations occurring in the territorial sea or EEZs of other states, but only if the state concerned requests it to do so. The port state can institute proceedings in such cases only if the flag or coastal state concerned does not do so. Coastal states are also given wider powers by article 220. If there are clear grounds for believing that a vessel in passage in the territorial sea has violated national laws which conform to the international rules the coastal state can physically inspect the vessel, detain it and, if there is sufficient evidence, take proceedings against it. If the violation occurs in the EEZ, however, the discharge must be substantial and also threaten to cause significant pollution of the marine environment before action can be taken. The coastal state can even then only physically inspect the vessel if it has refused to give information, or gives wrong information. Proceedings can be instituted only if there is clear evidence of a violation resulting in major damage, or a threat of it, to the coastline, related interests or resources of the coastal state.

The large number of safeguards, qualifications and the careful balance of jurisdictions in this part of the text reflect a compromise between the major maritime states which, with some exceptions, have sought to sustain the primacy of the flag state system, and other groups of states seeking to extend the powers of coastal states to protect themselves against the present scale of environmental threats. The problems of negotiating a revised regime were summarised by the Chairman of the Third Committee at UNCLOS, Ambassador Yankov:

> to keep a viable balance between ecological considerations and the legitimate demands of expanding navigation, between national legislation and enforcement measures on the one hand and the international rules, standards and regulations on the other, between coastal and flag state jurisdiction, between the interest of developed maritime powers and developing countries.

CONCLUSION

The United Nations Stockholm Conference in 1972 introduced a new international perspective into the protection of the marine environment from pollution. The principles laid down require states to ensure an environment of quality and to take account of the complex ecological interrelationships of the oceans. The international community is still struggling to evolve the appropriate organisational response. The traditional approach to dealing with marine pollution problems had been the *ad hoc* diplomatic conference, such as the UNCLOS I, which laid down only very general principles, which were developed and enforced by national means, and the pace of development was slow, being dictated by a large variety of national interests. The growing awareness of the international community of the scale of the threats to their national waters posed by industrialisation and the fact that the sources of pollution often lie outside national control, the seas being a particularly facile medium for the transferring of pollution from the jurisdictions of other states or from international areas, has led to a spate of international activity to regulate all sources of marine pollution.

Although for this purpose the *ad hoc* diplomatic conference is still used, as in the case of the London Convention and Oslo Convention on Ocean Dumping and the Paris Convention on Land-based Sources of Pollution, international organisations are playing an increasing role at both the regional and global level. UNCLOS III is stimulating this approach; the ICNT makes numerous references to the need to develop laws, regulations and principles not only by diplomatic conferences but also by use of 'competent international organisations'. The ICNT does not name the relevant bodies but present practice suggests that both IMCO and UNEP will play a major role, the former continuing to provide the forum for achieving the balance of interests between shipping and coastal states and between the relative costs of protecting the environment and maintaining international seaborne trade, and the latter stimulating the growth and increasing powers of regional bodies and pointing the need for harmonisation and integration of laws and standards in the field of prevention of marine pollution. The present system of co-ordination of the numerous conventions and institutions remains predominantly loose. There is room for more co-ordination but it is unlikely that any overarching new organisation will be developed for this purpose. The UN ACC's (Administrative Co-ordinating Committee) role is not strong and is confined to UN bodies.

Co-ordination and harmonisation present serious problems. Marine pollution is a complex issue; scientists disagree about its existence and its effects and control has important economic implications. Developing states are particularly anxious that their industrialisation and development should not be impeded by requiring them to adopt controls made necessary mainly by the activities of developed industrialised states. They are aware of the pollution problems but require their developmental interests to be taken into account in any system of regulation as in the case of the negotiation of controls for land-based pollution for the Mediterranean, both developed and developing states being parties to the Barcelona Convention. The economic implications also make it difficult for developed states to reach political agreement on standards; the Paris Commission has thus encountered problems in relation to land-based sources of pollution, as has the EEC. The costs of total protection are too high to bear for most states at a time of economic recession; the negotiation of the margins of safety is likely to continue to present political problems for the resolution of which the community must provide international forums. A notable gap remains: there is no

international convention controlling pollution from offshore installations. States have, for reasons of economics and control over energy
supplies, developed this regime within their national frameworks. Even
in a semi-enclosed sea like the North Sea, the only functioning
agreement, the Bonn Convention, is limited to co-operation in monitoring spills; the Civil Liability Convention remains unratified.

None the less, it is now widely recognised that marine pollution is in
many respects an international problem and that its control requires
international co-operative effort. A major problem now, because of the
ecological inter-relationships of the marine environment, is to find
means of co-ordinating the activities of all the new bodies concerned in
the regulation of pollution from a variety of sources and relating them
also to the work of the Fishery Commissions, since pollution can
adversely affect fisheries. Serious problems are still presented by
enforcement and by participation in existing conventions. As yet the
international community is barely tackling the main problems, most
states being reluctant to create new agencies to exercise a co-ordinating
role.

NOTES AND REFERENCES

Since numerous actual and threatened disasters have focused so much attention on marine
pollution and a strong environmental lobby has grown up, a corresponding increase in the
literature on the topic has occurred. An alarmist introductory work is Colin Moorcroft's
Must the Seas Die? (London: Temple Smith, 1972) which states, but exaggerates, the
problems in a readable form. A more sober analysis is given by Edward D. Goldberg in
The Health of the Oceans (Paris: UNESCO Press, 1976) and in the US factual study
Assessing Ocean Pollutants (Washington, DC: National Academy of Sciences, 1975). A
useful comprehensive collection of research and teaching materials covering the inter-
national law of pollution, including international agreements and cases, evidencing
transnational action taken to date and assessing future trends, is J. Barros and D.
Johnston's *International Law of Pollution* (New York: Free Press and London: Collier
Macmillan, 1974). It includes several reading lists. The study by the David Davies
Memorial Institute of International Studies edited by M. M. Sibthorp, *The North Sea:
Challenge and Opportunity* (London: Europa, 1975) admirably covers all the conflicting
uses of a regional sea as well as outlining the problems of a regional regime and calls for a
new regional Commission. One of the most recent works covering all the legal aspects of
vessel-source pollution is David Abecassis's *Oil Pollution from Ships* (London: Butterworths, 1978) which presents a more balanced, if less readable, picture than Noel
Mostert's *Supership* (Bristol: Western Printing Services, 1975). A wide internationalist
view of the environmental problems and developing law is given in J. L. Hargrove (ed.),
Who Protects the Ocean? (St Paul, Minn.: West, 1975) in which the chapters on various
aspects of marine environmental protection are contributed by a variety of experts in the
particular fields and include one on 'Ocean ecology and the world political system' by R. L.
Friedheim. There are also many journals which frequently have good articles on relevant
theses, examined from the viewpoint of different disciplines, in particular *AMBIO*, a
Journal of the Human Environment Research and Management (Royal Swedish
Academy of Sciences/Universitetsforlaget), and *Marine Policy*, the international journal
for economics, planning and politics of ocean exploitation (IPC Science and Technology
Press). Finally mention must be made of the Proceedings of the Law of the Sea Institute

126 *Maritime Dimension*

(originally attached to Rhode Island University, Kingston, USA, now at the University of Hawaii, Honolulu, USA). Its annual conferences, since 1968, have included a large number of excellent papers on all sources of marine pollution.

1 *The International Conference on Tanker Safety and Pollution Prevention* (IMCO, 1978), p. 12; a detailed analysis of the numbers and types of vessels navigating the oceans is given by C. Bates and P. Yost, 'Where trends the flow of merchant ships', in John K. Gamble, Jun. and Guilio Pontecorvo (eds), *Law of the Sea: The Emerging Regime of the Oceans* (Cambridge, Mass.: Ballinger, 1974), pp. 249–76.
2 Scottish Economic Planning Department Information Sheet (August 1979), Annex B, pp. 8–12.
3 GESAMP (Joint Group of Experts on the Scientific Aspects of Marine Pollution) Reports and Studies 6 (1977), *Impact of Oil on the Marine Environment* (Rome: FAO, 1977). GESAMP's definition of pollution is frequently used by international organisations but has been subject to some criticism and the definition of 'pollution' remains contentious.
4 *Convention for the Prevention of Marine Pollution by Dumping from Ships and Aircraft*, Oslo, 15 February 1972, Cmnd 4984 (1972). The convention entered into force on 7 April 1974.
5 For example the Paris Convention for the Prevention of Marine Pollution from Land-based Sources, 1974; the Helsinki Convention for the Protection of the Marine Environment of the Baltic Sea, 1974; the Barcelona Convention for the Protection of the Mediterranean Sea against Pollution, 1976; all of which are in force; the Kuwait Convention for Cooperation in the Protection of the Marine Environment from Pollution, 1978, which is not yet in force. Action plans are under consideration or negotiation at UNEP's instigation for the Red Sea, the Gulf of Guinea, the Caribbean, the East Asian Seas and the Pacific. For an analysis of these see 'The role of regional agreements in the protection and preservation of the marine environment from pollution', in *Report of the British Branch Committee on the Law of the Sea* (International Law Association, Manila Conference, 1978).
6 *Convention on the Dumping of Wastes at Sea*, London, 13 November 1972, Cmnd 5169 (1972); entered into force 27 September 1975.
7 *Convention for the Prevention of Marine Pollution from Land-based Sources*, Paris 4 June 1974, Cmnd 5803 (1974); entered into force 6 May 1978.
8 *International Convention for the Prevention of Pollution of the Sea by Oil 1954*, London, 12 May 1954, Cmnd 595 (1954); entered into force 26 July 1958.
9 Load on Top is a system of tank washing *en route* whereby one tank receives the washings from the others, the oil separates from the water, rises to the top and can eventually be discharged into special facilities on land at the end of the voyage; only the relatively clean water is discharged *en route*.
10 *International Convention for the Prevention of Pollution from Ships 1973*, at London, 2 November 1973; not yet in force.
11 *International Convention Relating to Intervention on the High Seas in Cases of Oil Pollution Casualties 1969*, at Brussels, 29 November 1969, Cmnd 6056 (1969); entered into force 6 May 1975
12 Article 1, s. 1.
13 *International Convention on Standards of Training, Certification and Watchkeeping for Seafarers*, London, 5 July 1978; not yet in force.
14 *Convention for the Prevention of Marine Pollution by Dumping from Ships and Aircraft*, Oslo, 15 February 1972, Cmnd 4984 (1972); entered into force 7 April 1974.
15 *Convention on the Dumping of Wastes at Sea*, London, 13 November 1972, Cmnd 5469 (1972); entered into force 27 September 1975.
16 *Convention for the Protection of the Marine Environment of the Baltic Sea Area*, Helsinki, 22 March 1972, *ILM*, vol. XXIII, no. 3 (May 1974), pp. 544–610.

17 *Convention for the Protection of the Mediterranean Sea*, Barcelona, 16 February 1976, *ILM*, vol. XI, no. 2 (March 1976), pp. 285–310.

18 *Convention for the Prevention of Marine Pollution from Land-based Sources*, Paris, 4 June 1974, Cmnd 5803 (1974).

19 *EEC Action Programme on the Environment 1973*, OJ no. C112 20, pp. 12–73; for subsequent developments see 'Environment Programme 1977–1981', *Bulletin of the European Communities*, Supplement 6/76.

20 *Draft Council Resolution on Measures for the Prevention, Control and Reduction of Pollution Caused by Accidental Discharges of Hydrocarbons into the Sea*, COM (77) 265 final (7 June 1977).

21 *Agreement for Cooperation in Dealing with Pollution of the North Sea by Oil*, Bonn 9 June 1969; entered into force 9 August 1969.

22 *The Amoco Cadiz Oil Spill: A Preliminary Scientific Report NOAA/EPA Special Report*, US Department of Commerce and US Environmental Protection Agency (August 1978).

23 *Republic of Liberia, Interim Report of the Formal Investigation by the Marine Board of Investigation* (23 February 1979).

24 T. F. Cross, T. Southgate and A. A. Myers, 'The initial pollution of shores in Bantry Bay, Ireland, by oil from the tanker Belelguese', *Marine Pollution Bulletin*, vol. 10, no. 4 (April 1979), pp. 104–7.

25 *The Times*, 27 March 1975.

26 'Deep sea dumping furore', *Marine Pollution Bulletin*, vol. 6, no. 5 (May 1975), p. 68.

27 'Uncontrolled blow-out on Bravo, 22 April 1977', *Report from Commission of Inquiry appointed by the Royal Decree of 26 April 1977, submitted October 10, 1977* (unofficial translation from Norwegian; preliminary edition).

28 'Mexican offshore blow-out rivals Ekofisk', *Marine Pollution Bulletin*, vol. 10, no. 8 (August 1979), pp. 215–16.

29 Article 207.

30 Article 208 and 209.

31 Article 210.

32 Articles 211, 213.

33 Articles 212–35.

Chapter 6

International Shipping

CHRISTOPHER HAYMAN

Shipping is one of the few genuinely international, some might call it supranational, industries that exist in the world today. In no other industry would it be possible to set up a transaction that involved so many different national entities as can be lumped together in one shipping deal. Imagine a modern supertanker, which may be owned by a Greek through a Liberian company. The ship may well have been built in Japan, but powered by Danish engines. It will no doubt be manned by a crew of mixed nationality, including, let us say, some Italian officers and Filipino crewmen. It may have been financed through a New York bank and insured in London. It is time chartered to a multinational oil company for three years to carry Saudi Arabian crude oil from the Gulf to Rotterdam.

This by no means unusual case illustrates one end of the shipping spectrum, where the concept of nationality is blurred at best in a transaction which benefits interests in a range of different countries. Yet there is another side to the story, and an example from the other end of the spectrum illustrates powerfully how nationalism may make itself felt on the industry. Two countries of South America forge between them a bilateral shipping agreement splitting the general cargo trade carried on regular liner services on a 50:50 basis. At least one of the countries in question has a domestic shipbuilding industry, and it encourages its shipowners to expand their fleets by providing soft loans for ships which are ordered locally. The vessels which ply in this particular trade, therefore, fly the flag of the country in question, they are manned by a national crew and wholly owned by a local shipowner. Government credit has been provided, so that the ship in question may only look overseas for its insurance and for certain components in the ship's construction which may not be manufactured (yet) under licence in the country in question. With the bilateral pact between the two countries, 'third flag' ships, those flying the flag of countries other than the two partners, are excluded, providing a totally protected trade.

These two cases show clearly how difficult it is to generalise about sea transport. Shipping is not actually one but several different industries bound together by one common element, the ship itself, and many generalisations about it have suffered because of this flaw. The movement towards more expensive purpose-built ships, designed to perform a very specific task with optimum efficiency, has naturally hastened this trend. Developments in the trade itself have had a similar effect.

The most fundamental division in shipping, between liner and tramp operations, is worth looking at in some detail to illustrate this point. The establishment of a regular 'liner' service between two ports requires a set of disciplines and an operating machinery if it is to work. The user of the service requires to be able to rely upon a set frequency of sailings and efficiency of performance so that the ship operator must build up a system that gives the shipper what he needs. If containerisation appears to be the optimum means for handling cargo then he may be required to invest in highly expensive container ships for the trade. If a computer is necessary to maximise efficiency on a complex trade he may also be required to invest in that. The formation of liner conferences and their continual justification is defended on the grounds that if a shipowner is to provide an efficient regular service he needs a guarantee of reasonable stability in the trade to secure his investment, and a rating structure that provides him with a reasonable return and the resources to undertake replacement of tonnage when this becomes necessary.

By contrast to this admittedly simplified picture of liner shipping operations is the tramp sector. The movement of the major bulk cargoes, oil, coal, iron ore and grain, is more erratic and subject to market conditions than the liner trades. The matching of ships to cargoes is effected in a less regimented way, with charterers securing the tonnage they need to perform a particular function as and when it is required. Thus a major oil company may take a tanker on charter for a period of years or a number of consecutive voyages, or an owner may be awarded a contract of afreightment, under which he is contracted to perform a transportation task within a period of time. Such transportation requirements of bulk commodities as are not catered for by one or other of these techniques are handled through the 'spot' market, where 'unfixed' vessels may be chartered for a single voyage. A major and unexpected purchase of grain by the Soviet Union or an acceleration of crude oil loadings in the Persian Gulf in anticipation of an oil price rise are two simple examples of incidents which create a sudden and unforeseen demand for 'spot' tonnage, lifting freight rates for single voyage charters.

In the tanker trades, something like 60 per cent of the tonnage requirement is owned by the oil companies themselves, but a fair chunk of the world's tanker fleet and the lion's share of the world's dry bulk carrier fleet is in the hands of individual shipowners. These individuals or companies may adopt a conservative approach to the market, only ordering new ships against a first class time charter which guarantees employment at a reasonable rate throughout the loan repayment period, or they may prefer to expand their fleets as a speculation, gambling on the more lucrative returns that may become available in the spot market. Whichever approach a shipowner may take to the bulk market, his success or failure in the business depends as much upon his judgement of the market, and of the likely shifts in demand for particular classes and sizes of ship, as it does on the successful operation of the fleet.

It is an oversimplification to divide sea transport into these two general segments. There are specialist sectors, such as the carriage of chemicals or goods requiring refrigeration, and indeed the passenger ship market, which all have their own special considerations. Nevertheless, the majority of shipping transactions fit into the broad pattern of liner or tramp shipping described.

It is no exaggeration to say that these two functions require skills and disciplines that have almost nothing at all in common. Success in liner shipping requires planning and marketing ability and above all the establishment of an organisation that is capable of handling a myriad of problems as they materialise. In contrast, the bulk shipowner must know the market that he serves, must keep in constant touch with it and anticipate its fluctuations. It is no accident that there are very few cases of shipowners who have been truly successful in both liner and tramp shipping, the most notable exception perhaps being the Hong Kong-based C. Y. Tung Group which boasts a substantial bulk shipping fleet and a fast expanding liner operation, Orient Overseas Container Line.

Despite the major differences that divide them, the two sectors are still frequently regarded as one, often to the disadvantage of the individual making the judgement. Shipping shares on the London and Wall Street stock markets are severely hit by bad news from the international tanker market even though the vast majority of quoted companies' balance sheets will be unaffected by movements in these rates simply because they do not own tankers that participate in this market.

There is however a much more significant area in which a failure to appreciate the basic differences could have serious consequences, namely, in attempts to regulate the industry as a whole and to impose upon both sectors a pattern of regulation that may only be suited to one. This point will be dealt with in greater detail after consideration of some of the ways in which the shipping industry as a whole has been subject to interference from outside interests.

PROTECTIONISM

The twentieth century, and in particular the 1960s and 1970s, has seen a steady erosion of the principle of the 'freedom of the seas', a principle much beloved by the independent shipowners of the traditional maritime nations but far from universally popular. This move towards the limitation of freedom of action of those who own and operate ships has taken a number of different forms. The most controversial of these undoubtedly is the move towards protectionism in shipping. Maritime protectionism is not a twentieth-century concept. In fact Britain as a major opponent of the notion in this century has been rightly tagged as the initiator of it in the seventeenth, when Oliver Cromwell's Navigation Acts reserved portions of English seaborne trade to domestic flag ships, in order to guard against encroachment from the Dutch.

Protectionism in shipping takes many forms and it is by no means exclusively practised in any one economic or political bloc of countries. Cabotage and the principle of reserving a country's coastal trade to its own ships and its own seamen is widespread. The US Jones Act of 1919 is a case in point, requiring US-built and US-manned vessels to perform all coastwise trade, including of course the attractive market transporting Alaskan oil to the lower forty-eight states. France and Japan are two major importers of foreign oil that operate a *de facto* policy of reserving this trade for their own flag ships. Yet it is in fact the maritime nations of South America which have earned that continent the distinction of being known as 'the cradle of protectionism' by their policies of reservations since the Second World War and it is amongst the Group of 77 'developing' nations that the impetus lies for further extensions of this philosophy.

Before examining the form which such arguments have taken it is worth looking at the rationale behind the principle, strongly espoused by the establishment of UNCTAD, that it is a good thing for developing countries to develop their fleets.[1] A variety of arguments are used to support this thesis. One such argument applies to those countries which are major exporters, the suggestion being that a raw materials exporter needs to be able to control a proportion at least of the transport of its exports to insure both availability and price. The logic of this argument is borne out, to some extent, by the long-standing policy of the major oil companies to protect themselves against violent shifts in demand for tanker space by controlling a substantial proportion of their requirement themselves. The weakness in the theory, however, lies in the fact that generally speaking a non-traditional maritime nation will not be able, initially at least, to achieve the levels of efficiency of operation that their experienced competitors from, say, Norway or Greece are likely to be able to provide. Thus the use by an exporter of its own shipping may actually have a detrimental effect on the competitiveness of its export commodity.

A second reason put forward is that an involvement in shipping will broaden the industrial base of a developing country with various spin-off advantages. Shipping is of course primarily a capital-intensive rather than a labour-intensive industry and there is little to offer in terms of providing better-paid jobs and opportunities from such an industry. If a nascent shipping industry is supported by a domestic shipbuilding industry, as is the case in a number of emerging maritime countries including Brazil, South Korea, Taiwan and Argentina, then undoubtedly the beneficial spread is significant, although under current market conditions the desirability of major investment in shipbuilding facilities must be highly questionable.

Shipping is often cited as a major earner of foreign currency, and this certainly is the case, although this may well be counterbalanced by the need to obtain hard currency loans for the initial fleet acquisition programme. As long as the traditional shipbuilding countries continue to provide ships to developing countries on virtual give-away terms then the foreign exchange argument is a much more real one, however. There is little doubt that one of the Soviet Union's principal reasons for vastly increasing the size and scope of its merchant fleet is the goal of earning more hard currency. Unlike the majority of countries in the developing world the Soviet Union is able to acquire its fleet from its own yards or those of its near neighbour, Poland.

The least convincing argument for emerging countries to invest in shipping is that it provides prestige to the country in question. There is something to be said for a country wishing to establish its own line with its own flag fleet if this makes sense in a hard commercial world, but if such a venture requires subsidisation from an already overworked exchequer then it may easily work against the country's foreign trade. A fledgling exporter of semi-manufactured or manufactured goods which reserves a percentage of its exports for its own flag ships risks harming the competitiveness of its goods in world markets as long as its own shipping operations are less efficient and therefore more expensive than shipping services obtainable on the open market. Efficiency in shipping is not something that can be learned overnight.

DEVELOPING COUNTRIES

In shipping, as in any other sphere of economic activity, there are huge differences between the standard of development of the various member countries of the Group of 77. The broadly based fleets of countries like India and Brazil on the one hand have very little in common with the collection of vessels which fly the flags of some of the smaller African states. Nevertheless, within the domain of UNCTAD this group of nations, numbering in practice more like 115 than 77, has acted with broad unanimity in its approach to the question of shipping. Working from the principle that liner conferences have been abusing the shippers of the developing world, the principal rallying point for expression of this sentiment has been since UNCTAD III in Santiago de Chile the search for a Code of Conduct for liner conferences.

First signs of protectionist legislation outside the traditional maritime nations came from South America after the war. One of the first moves made was by Argentina in reserving government cargoes for its own ships, a preliminary that has become a virtual mandatory first step for any would-be protectionist. Brazil made its intentions clear by a unilateral intervention in the conferences serving the country and by the establishment of a government agency with the express intention of reducing the amount of foreign currency required to charter in foreign flag tonnage. Since that move in the sixties, Brazilian shipbuilding has blossomed as both the government and private shipping companies have been encouraged to expand their fleets dramatically, always by ordering tonnage in one or other of the six or more domestic shipyards which have sprung up to meet the needs of the situation.

The dissatisfaction on the part of the governments of the developing world with the conference system, which they had come to regard as monopolies working against their interests by maintaining excessive freight rates or by excluding their own lines from participation in the trade, reached its zenith in the emergence in Santiago in 1972 of the UNCTAD Liner Conference Code, as has already been said. The Code was then radically revised before adoption by the UNCTAD Shipping Committee in 1974. In recognition of the fact that the conference system was in need of a campaign to demonstrate its fairness, if not to correct any unfairness in the system, work had already been put into the formation of a Code by the traditional maritime nations of Western Europe and Japan even before the UNCTAD Code saw the light of day. The difference between these two documents illustrates the basic differences between the two sides on how the liner shipping business should be conducted.[2] It is worth noting in passing that root and branch abolition of conferences has not been a demand of the Group of 77.

The first fundamental difference between the UNCTAD Code and the so-called CENSA (Committee of European and Japanese National Shipowners' Associations) Code is that while the former is conceived as a legally binding document, the latter is based on the principle of self-regulation. There are other differences. The UNCTAD Code is very specific about membership of conferences, providing an automatic right to join for all 'national lines', and a much more stringent set of entry qualifications for cross-traders. The CENSA Code does not involve itself in this issue at all, but its supporters would argue that there are few if any cases of a national line having been excluded from a conference that it wished to join. Another difference is that the UNCTAD Code seeks to impose minimum periods between rate increases, whereas the CENSA Code, perhaps predictably, does not. The main difference between the two, and the issue which has come to be identified with the UNCTAD Code, is cargo-sharing. Implicit in the terms of this instrument is the notion that cargo should be divided on the basis of

40 : 40 : 20 (that is, shares of 40 per cent to each of the two flags between which the trade is operated, leaving a 20 per cent share for cross-traders). This principle, which was first mooted by the Shipping Division of UNCTAD in the 1960s, is not in fact written into the Code in black and white; nevertheless, in its present form (the original Santiago draft spoke of a mandatory 50 : 50 split in cargo-sharing) the cargo-sharing element is the one which has attracted most of the controversy.

In order for the UNCTAD Code to come into force it requires ratification from countries representing a minimum of 25 per cent of the world's liner tonnage. Some support for the Code was provided early on from the developing countries but a measure of concrete support from the traditional maritime countries and the socialist bloc would be necessary to bring it into force. All but the hardest line supporters admit to there being some horrendous problems in application of this principle. To name just one major weakness, the Code takes no account of the activities of 'outsiders', those lines which operate in a trade outside the conference structure. Nevertheless, the idea of introducing a new world order for liner shipping is one which has done more than any other issue to drag politics into the industry. Never before had shipowner associations in the traditional maritime countries felt the need so strongly for governmental support on an issue. Many owners who had equated government interference of any kind with flagrant restriction of their freedom of action were now to be seen in animated conversation with civil servants whose help they sought for protection from a threat that had never manifested itself in such a form before.

The reaction of the developed countries to the Code has been an exercise in gradual acceptance of the reality of a changing order, in which some role for governments in shipping is necessary. Some of the West European countries took an early decision that a Code which promoted the conference system, regulated relations between shippers and conferences and introduced a measure of cargo-sharing that was less extreme than the bilateral 50 : 50 agreements that had gone before it was worth a second look. If some concessions were not made to the Third World, it was argued, all hell would break loose. The Scandinavian countries and the UK, all of them major cross-traders and with a strong historical commitment to freedom of the seas, have taken a far more cautious approach to the problem.

The Code issue has been instrumental in bringing shipping into the political arena in one very particular way. Since the formation of the EEC, the question of whether the general rules of the Treaty of Rome should be applied to shipping had been unresolved. A European Court of Justice judgement in April 1974 made it plain that shipping could not be regarded as an area outside the Community's integration process. The judgement was handed down just prior to the meeting in Geneva in which the UNCTAD Shipping Committee adopted the Code, and the Commission immediately argued that EEC member nations could not unilaterally act on the issue, and that France and West Germany's decision to sign the Code was contrary to the Treaty of Rome. The legality of the pro-Codist position having been called into question, the Commission then argued for a common EEC position on the Code, arguing that the instrument should be accepted or rejected by all nine member countries. The task of finding a compromise position on so controversial an issue as this amongst the nine took several years to achieve, but it is now a matter of fact that a Community consensus, accepting much of the Code but accepting the application of the cargo-sharing principles only on trades that are not between OECD member countries, has now been achieved, representing what many see as a first step towards an EEC common shipping policy. Acceptance of the Code by the EEC countries in a restricted form has given an impetus to the negotiation which was badly needed and the Liner Conference Code issue is now well on its way.

CARGO-SHARING

One of the principal fears of the European shipping nations about the Code was that, given some success, the cargo-sharing formula might be applied very quickly by the developing countries to the bulk trades. Although it was an argument used by some European supporters of the Liner Code that support for this measure would satisfy ambitions in the Third World and prevent an escalation of demands, proposals for a bulk shipping Code were on the agenda of the UNCTAD V Conference in Manila in 1979. What supporters of a cargo-sharing formula for the bulk trades have forgotten is that there is, as already discussed, a very fundamental difference between liner and bulk shipping, and that what is applicable to one may well not be applicable to another. The irregular patterns of bulk shipping movements require the existence of spare capacity to provide for 'spot' needs on a single voyage basis. As shipowner Sir Yue Kong Pao, the chairman of the International Association of Independent Tanker Owners (Intertanko) pointed out in a speech at UNCTAD V, the amount of oil movements catered for by single voyage charters has been increasing in recent years and that in 1978 it reached 25 per cent. As put forward by the UNCTAD Secretariat, whilst regular oil movements would be catered for by the producers' and consumers' tankers, the unforeseen demand would be covered by the independent cross-traders. The risks in the spot market are such that only the boldest of the existing independents would be willing to concentrate wholly on this area. The result, it is argued, would be the destruction of a viable spot market; unforeseen transport needs would then have to be catered for by the long-term charter owners, leading to inefficiencies, higher transport costs, and higher oil prices.

Although the bulk cargo sharing proposal can by no means be said to have taken off at Manila, there exists already a widespread body of unilateral cargo reservation legislation in the producer countries, particularly the oil-exporting countries. A number of Arab oil producers have statutes reserving percentages of their crude oil cargoes for their own ships and many of them have started down the road towards the build up of fleets to fulfil these targets, although there is still a huge gap between their present capability and the size of their ultimate ambition. The Arab flag tanker fleet[3] is now approximately some 5 million dwt, something like 1.5 per cent of the world tanker fleet, or some 3 per cent of the tonnage needed to transport oil produced by the Arab countries. Dr Abdulhady Taher, governor of Petromin, the Saudi Arabian national oil company, and chairman of the Pan-Arab tanker company, the Arab Maritime Petroleum Transport Company (AMPTC), has made it clear that Arab producers see 40 per cent as being a 'reasonable' percentage of transport needs to supply themselves.[4] Assuming a fleet of 180m dwt to carry Arab oil exports he gives 70m dwt as the size of the fleet which needs to be achieved, and fifteen years as the time needed to achieve it. The irony is that despite having embarked upon a tanker-building programme Arab governments have so far acted on a sound commercial basis as far as transportation is concerned and not enforced the use of their own ships, with the result that during the worst period of the tanker crisis, tankers flying the Saudi flag were laid up whilst Saudi Arabia was still exporting around 8 million barrels of crude a day. Sheikh Yamani has made it clear that Aramco could be instructed by decree to transport Saudi Oil in AMPTC tankers but this would only be done on commercial grounds, and therefore only when the Arab tankers were offering competitive rates.[5] Much progress has been made in the Arab world and elsewhere in acquiring the skills to operate ships and to manage them correctly but a vast amount still needs to be learned. It is clearly in this area that the best opportunities exist for joint ventures between the emerging countries and the independent companies of Scandinavia, Greece and the UK, the first supplying the cargoes and the right to carry it and the second supplying the expertise.

GOVERNMENTS AND SHIPPING

Whilst it is first and foremost on issues of cargo reservation that traditionally reticent shipowners have sought help from their governments, these have not been by any means the only ones. The build up of the Soviet merchant marine has provoked one such response and the tough line by the US on conferences and competition in the liner trades has been another area. Just how significant has been the build up of the Soviet merchant fleet in the seventies is impossible to identify accurately, but incursion by USSR lines into lucrative liner trades, nearly always as non-conference outsiders offering substantial savings to shippers, has created a reaction from European and US liner men that has on occasion come close to panic. The Western executives argue that whilst they are prepared to take on all comers if the ground rules are the same for everybody, they consider it unfair practice to have to compete with a political system whose cost-accounting method is entirely different from their own.[6] A true picture of actual costs to a Soviet shipowner is impossible to determine, but, say Western shipowners, heavy subsidies and state aid programmes allow companies like the Soviet Fesco (Far East Shipping Company) to undercut sometimes by as much as 30 per cent the conference tariffs on the trans-Pacific trades, thereby securing valuable foreign currency, and, more sinisterly, it is suggested, gaining footholds in certain trades that can be used to promote political as well as commercial objectives.

There is no doubt that the Soviet merchant marine has been successful in a number of trades in gaining a substantial amount of cargo by these tactics. It is also the case that the rating policy of many Soviet lines offers the best discounts on the most lucrative commodities, and very minor savings on low rates cargoes that have much less carrier appeal. It is also the case that Soviet crews, despite comparatively low wages, have extremely high standards in maintaining their ships. The problem unresolved is twofold. What are the ultimate ambitions of the Soviets and what, if anything, can or should be done by the Western shipping nations to curb their expansion?

As far as the first question is concerned, it has been answered in a number of ways, both by hawks who take the view that Moscow is intent on a commercial maritime dominance that has only just got off the ground, and by milder observers who feel that the current tactics are merely isolated cases of Soviet lines wishing to make nuisances of themselves in certain trades to such an extent that the conferences will bow to pressure and admit them on favourable terms, whereupon they will become arch-conservative establishment carriers.

Stung by criticism and attacks which they fear may prejudice shippers against using Soviet lines irrespective of freight rates, *Morflot*, the Soviet Merchant Marine Ministry, has issued a number of rebuttals to the charges made. It points out that at 1 January 1978 the world fleet of general cargo ships consisted of 128·8m dwt, including roll on/roll off and container ships. Of this some 6·4m dwt or less than 5 per cent of the world fleet was registered under the Soviet flag. A mere 1 per cent of cellular container tonnage was under Soviet flag at that date. The world order-book for general cargo ships then totalled some 14·4m dwt, of which some 378,000 dwt or 2·7 per cent was for Soviet account. Assuming these to be accurate figures, there undoubtedly is a limit to the amount of additional impact that the Soviets can make in the short term on world liner trading, without in any way discounting the degree to which they have cut into cargo patterns on existing trades. Significantly, Western comment on Soviet merchant shipping encroachment has been diverted to comment on the development of the Trans-Siberian Railway which is cutting into the cargoes of the Far East Freight Conference on trades to Europe.

The Soviet 'threat' was considered to be an issue on which agreement would quickly be reached by the EEC countries, providing another plank in a Community shipping policy. Due to French opposition unanimity on anything more than a decision to monitor the activities of East bloc lines has yet to be achieved by the EEC Council of Ministers. Nevertheless, shipowners in Europe and the US alike have been hammering on the doors of government for a concerted reaction.

An almost equivalent amount of dust has been raised by European liner men over what they see as meddling in its liner trades by the US government. At the heart of the problem lies the US's traditional sensitivity on anti-trust issues, and a resulting deep suspicion about the ability of the conference system to allow the kind of rugged open market competition which red-blooded American capitalism is supposed to thrive on. Spearheading the attack on the *status quo* in a Washington that has been deeply divided on shipping issues for most of the 1970s is the Department of Justice, which has never gracefully accepted the amendment to the Sherman Act which provides anti-trust exemption for certain aspects of liner shipping operations. The Department of Justice also has difficulty in accepting the role of the Federal Maritime Agency as the body charged with responsibility for regulating the shipping industry. In a case which is certain to cause ripples for some time to come, seven North Atlantic shipping companies were fined a total of $6m resulting from indictments alleging that they had fixed rates outside the scope of anti-trust exemptions between 1971 and 1974. Some Europeans have interpreted this as a move by the Justice Department to continue its campaign to weaken and ultimately abolish the conference system. Strong reaction from European governments whose nationals had been indicted was one result of this action.

The US attitude to the conference system has yet to be determined but ideas on how to resolve this and other issues, and legislative packages to put these ideas on to the statute-book, have not been in short supply. The latest in a series of regulatory reform proposals suggests a reversal of traditional views that could bring US practice much closer into line with European traditions. The idea would include the legalising of both closed conferences and shippers' councils, both granted full anti-trust exemption for the first time. The Department of Justice would cease to have a role in international shipping matters and the Federal Maritime Commission would exercise complete control of the activities of both the conferences and the shippers' council. The closed conferences would be obliged to permit access of national lines, and a self-policing structure would be established. In addition to ensuring competitive rates for the US shipper, this package would be a revolutionary step in the development of US maritime policy and go a long way towards bringing that country in line with international thinking.

MARKET PRESSURES

As we have seen, political pressures have in a number of ways accelerated the politicising of the shipping industry, but market pressures have themselves exerted a similar push. The tanker market slump resulting from the 1973 oil price increases is without question the most severe crisis to have hit the industry in its history. The problems which were principally felt by the tanker owners had a ripple effect into other areas, so that bulk carrier rates were almost as badly affected as tanker rates, due to the movement of combination oil/bulk/ore carriers out of the tanker market into the dry cargo trades, as well as to the slump in demand. Shipyards have been as badly hit as anybody as contracting for new tonnage is at a virtual standstill, at a time when supply and demand are already so badly out of touch with the existing fleet.

As the crisis developed in 1974 the industry made manful attempts to sort out some of its problems, with the formation of the International Maritime Industries Forum, a unique gathering representing shipowners, shipbuilders, banks and oil companies. The IMIF has had some success in creating a general awareness of what the crisis could mean and what sorts of actions were likely to aggravate it. It has not, and perhaps it was never expected to, come up with a more dramatic catch-all practical solution to the problem. It has recognised, and helped the industry to realise, that a problem of this sort needs governmental action.

CONCLUSION

The dangers of letting rip on government intervention in such a situation lie in the risk of each affected government competing with the next in support grants and aid programmes for its shipyards and easy credit terms for its owners, and thus aggravating the situation still further. On the question of whether common-sense, though politically sensitive, counsels will ultimately prevail over national self-interest, the jury is still out. Discussions on concerted scrap and build policies have taken place, so far without much concrete result, but in the main the world's foremost shipbuilding nations have acted with understandable, if ultimately self-defeating, self-interest. The years since the crisis worked its way through to the shipyards, when the backlog of orders became thinner, have seen a proliferation of schemes offering give away terms to those few owners that retain an inclination to order tonnage. Accusations of cheating on OECD credit ceilings for shipbuilding have occurred within Europe and Japan. The practice of giving away ships virtually free as part of aid packages to developing countries has angered shipowners who see potential competitors being supplied, sometimes by their own government, with a vessel on terms that will enable them to compete highly favourably in a trade.

Support for troubled shipowners has also been widespread, but not perhaps in as generous a form as for shipyards, partly because, as shipowners are inclined to point out, they command far fewer votes in elections than yards, and partly because the owners themselves have always been wary of asking for help in the past and have not always rushed forward to claim it now. The establishment in Norway, surely the country whose owners have been most critically hit by the crisis, of a Guarantee Institute to provide government help to owners with unsupportable obligations to the banks on ships ordered in happier times but now not earning, was clearly set up to prevent a series of forced sales of Norwegian assets overseas. It was however by no means an open-ended commitment to any owner for unlimited support. Ships ordered for delivery beyond a certain date had to be cancelled and performance was to be carefully monitored. Similar if less elaborate schemes have been applied elsewhere in Scandinavia but not enough to prevent a dramatic transfer of tonnage out of the Swedish and Norwegian flags, mostly to ultimate control by Hong Kong owners whose careful chartering policy has enabled them to survive the crisis far better than most other independents.

·It is then both market pressures and national self-interest in maritime development that have occasioned a rather dramatic atmospheric change in the shipping industry. The pattern of the industry, evolved over a period of years, is full of anomalies. Major trading nations, both developed, like Canada, and developing, like Saudi Arabia, still have minute merchant fleets, while the major cross-traders have little domestic trade to support them. There is no reason to suppose that the events of the last fifteen or twenty years will bring into much closer alignment the distribution of merchant shipping and world trade patterns. Liberian, Panamanian and other flags of convenience will continue to provide the legitimate environment for individual entrepreneurs to operate in. Perhaps shipping is the last industry where it remains possible for an individual, by guessing right, to establish a personal fortune in a relatively short time. Much more than that, though, the skills of maritime operation are skills which will remain in overwhelming demand and those countries which possess them are certainly not about to lose their market for them.

NOTES AND REFERENCES

Surprisingly little has been written about the international shipping industry in the English language, and the best sources of information remain the various magazines and specialist journals which cover the industry from both the commercial and technical point of view. Perhaps the best recent analysis of the industry, which has filled a yawning void, is *Shipping – How it Works* by Thorsten Rinman and Rigmor Linden (Gothenburg: Rinman & Linden AB, 1979). A basic introduction to how the industry works may be obtained from *Elements of Shipping* by Alan E. Branch (London: Chapman & Hall, 1978). As far as the technical developments in cargo-handling are concerned, MacGregor Publications (Hounslow) have recently produced a lavishly illustrated book entitled *Ships' Cargo and Cargo Ships*, which contains essays by a selection of distinguished figures from the shipping industry around the world.

One of the foremost writers on the economics of the shipping industry is Stanley Sturmey who has produced a number of titles on this and related subjects: *British Shipping and World Competition* (London: Athlone Press, 1962); *Some Aspects of Ocean Liner Economics* (Manchester: Manchester Statistical Society, 1964); *Shipping Economics*, a collection of papers published by Macmillan (London) in 1975. Stanley Sturmey is currently based in the Ivory Coast establishing a maritime training centre for Francophone African countries. Before that he was the deputy director of the shipping division of UNCTAD.

A wide range of studies has been published on the tanker market, but the best personal view of how the industry has developed over the last fifty years is provided by Erling D. Naess in his *Autobiography of a Shipping Man* (Colchester: Seatrade Publications, 1977). The same author has also written what is widely regarded as the definitive work on flags of convenience, *The Great PanLibHon Controversy – the Fight over the Flags of Shipping* (Farnborough: Gower Press, 1972). Other studies on flags of convenience include *The Economics of Tramp Shipping* by Dr B. N. Metaxas (New Jersey: Humanities Press, 1971); *Ships Flying Flags of Convenience* (Stockholm: University of Stockholm, 1972); *The Impact of Flags of Convenience* by Professor R. S. Doganis and Dr B. N. Metaxas, published in 1976, sponsored by the UK Social Science Research Council and available from the Polytechnic of Central London NW1; and *Flags of Convenience – the EEC Shipping Policy and Opinion* published by the EEC, Brussels, 1979.

Finally a certain amount of literature exists on the psychology of the seafarer. One book worth looking at on this subject is *The Human Element in Shipping* by David H. Moreby (Colchester: Seatrade Publications, 1975).

1 A lucid analysis of the rationale for developing countries' involvement in shipping was given by Sven H. Salen, chairman of Saleninvest AB, in the Reginald Grout Lecture *Protection and Development – Cross-currents in Shipping* delivered in March 1979, and published in the *Journal of the Chartered Institute of Transport* (July 1979).
2 See the speech delivered by Henry O. Karsten, director of Overseas Containers Ltd, 'Development of codes of conduct for conferences', at the Seatrade Conference, Towards a Shipping Policy for the EEC, held in Brussels in September 1978.
3 See 'Arab shipping 1979', *Seatrade Guide* (Colchester: Seatrade Publications, February 1979).
4 See the speech delivered by Dr Abdulhady H. Taher, governor of Petromin and chairman of the Arab Maritime Petroleum Transport Company, 'Energy transportation in the Arab world', at the Seatrade Conference on Energy, Trade and Shipping, held in Kuwait in January 1979.
5 See the speech delivered by Sheikh Yamani, Saudi Arabian Minister of Petroleum and Mineral Resources, 'Energy: a view of the year 2000', at the Shipping 2000 Conference held in London in June 1979.
6 See *Red Flag Versus Red Ensign* (London: General Council of British Shipping, 1975).

Chapter 7

The Contemporary Use of Maritime Power

PETER NAILOR

DOCTRINE AND FUNCTIONS

The need for a body of general doctrine about maritime power began to
be positively necessary when the technological basis of sea warfare
began to shift, as it did from the middle of the nineteenth century. It was
then that the capacity of ships and weapons began to alter radically and
the potentialities of scientific and engineering research began to
dominate naval thinking. There are a number of general points to make
about this development. Most of the major analyses come from states
which already possess 'sea power', and make assumptions which are
more often implicit rather than explicit about its necessity and its utility.
They also usually define its utility in terms of the ability it may confer to
obtain success in war: there has not been very much written about sea
power by those to whom it is not a necessity either as a basic attribute or
as an instrument of power, nor very much about the disadvantages that
could arise from an absence of sea power. Richmond put it this way:
'The causes which impelled or compelled states in the past to develop sea
power may be very broadly divided into two categories. In the one there
are those nations for whom the development of sea power was the result
of natural or spontaneous economic or social movements ... In the other
case are those nations who, themselves not dependent upon trade or
territory but desiring it for the added wealth and strength and influence
which it would confer, strove to acquire that which others had
established.'[1] This accounts, in part, for the rather strained theorising in
France and Germany at the end of the nineteenth century; and also for
the complacent way in which the British received the works of Mahan,
missing the point that he was using history to urge a particular line of
policy upon his own country, which became for a time a dangerous and
successful competitor. It also accounts, in part, for the explanations
about the advantages of sea power which Admiral Gorshkov has now
produced, to give a theoretical underpinning to the military development of the Soviet Navy.

Most of the major writers explain what they believe the components of sea power to be. Mahan and Richmond both identify three basic elements: a fighting fleet, a trading fleet and bases. Brodie widens this last one to 'geographical circumstances', and Rosinski emphasises a financial and economic element. Richmond and others add the element of political will, and Richmond also identifies what he calls 'other elements of a moral nature: aptitudes, character and courage – these are outside the powers of the statesman'.[2]

The functions which maritime forces can perform are less clearly a matter of agreement, although this is partly due to the way in which individual writers have structured their analyses. Some of the most distinctive are as follows. *Strategic deterrence* is not a new mission, in one sense; the defence of the homeland from attack was a function attributed to battlefleets before it was transferred to seaborne nuclear forces. But the more general use of maritime force, and of ballistic missile nuclear-powered submarines in particular, to deter war, as well as to safeguard the national territory, is a new and extended function that relies upon the relative invulnerability of the submarines to retain the power to retaliate, even after an otherwise disarming first strike. *Formal combat at sea* can, of course, be undertaken by fleets, or by squadrons, or by single ships; and although the common element is that combat signifies that open hostilities have begun, it is still more often the case than not that combat at sea, as in the Arab-Israeli or Indo-Pakistan wars of recent years, is a component part of a more general war rather than an isolated activity. *The projection of power ashore* is often seen as another category of function, and although it is very often identified with amphibious landings (as at Suez in 1956 or Imchon in 1950), it also includes bombardment by sea or seaborne aircraft and, now, missile strikes: and, as such, it is part of the function of combat. *The control of the use of the sea* can be attempted either to secure the safety of one's own resources or to prevent the enemy from having that advantage. This is a very broad function, which obviously includes, for example, convoy protection and anti-submarine patrols in war; but it also includes protective or demonstrative activities at times when war has not yet occurred, as well as occasions when what is being protected, or contested, is the claim to proprietorial rights. The United States' 'quarantine' of Cuba in 1962, the international patrols in the Mediterranean during the Spanish Civil War, the seizure of the *Pueblo* by North Korea, the recapture of the *Mayaguez* from Cambodia by the United States in 1975, and the Canadian patrols to demonstrate sovereignty in the Arctic Seas are all past examples, and we are likely to see more patrolling done in the future as states seek to enforce international recognition of new sea regimes in EEZs or new territorial zones. There is another broad function which, rather loosely, can be called *the support of diplomatic objectives*. The usage is loose because the majority of all uses of maritime force belong to the field of external policy and security;

but it is a convenient term to describe ship visits (which can be either friendly, to demonstrate interest or support, or minatory, like the visit of the *Agadir* to Morocco in 1911), the establishment of support facilities in friendly states, humanitarian relief and even assistance in repairing war damage (as in the Suez Canal clearances). The precise value to be put upon this function is open to argument; it is certainly the case that the value is sometimes greater in the eye of the provider than of the recipient. But when the activity becomes in any way competitive, and the naval forces of a rival state intervene with similar activities (as the Soviet Navy began to do in the Mediterranean and Indian Ocean from the mid 1960s), any intrinsic value in the activity is quickly overlaid by wider foreign policy concerns. *Surveillance and intelligence-gathering* can be performed either as a specialist function or in the course of carrying out other duties; indeed one of the analytical problems of identifying particular functions is that most of them are not mutually exclusive or intrinsically separate. Ships may inherently be able to perform several functions; it depends almost as much upon where they are, and what they are ordered to do, as it does upon whether they are big or small.[3]

Now the orthodox pattern of argument that derives from all this can be summarised quite briefly – though necessarily rather arbitrarily.

Sea power confers a range of advantages on those who possess it and can apply it. It enables them to obtain, or to contest, the control of sea areas that are of importance to them. Their power has to be overwhelming for such control to be anything more than local or transitory. It confers advantages of mobility and flexibility, and enables, even without the projection of force ashore, pressures to be exerted upon an adversary and support to be given to allies. In this respect, it is generally held to be slow-acting: it may be important but it has seldom been decisive. But how slow-acting it would be if such pressures were applied to states that are heavily dependent upon external supplies has not been as well explained: and the experience of the two World Wars can be held to show that such states, like the United Kingdom and Japan, are in fact extremely vulnerable, and have to devote very large proportions of their resources to combat such pressure. It is also conceded that the advantages of sea power are most evident when the balance of forces is asymmetrical, that is, when the possessor of sea power does not have to concentrate his forces upon a constant defence of his objectives. Even so, sea power then has to be joined to land power to procure a decisive outcome to a major conflict. This is the problem which, as Michael Howard points out in his Ford Lectures, led the United Kingdom to assume a continental commitment.[4] One final point can be made about the standard analyses of maritime power. They are, in general, couched in general terms and do not often go into detail about the sort of problems we would now call size and shape arguments about what sort of forces to provide; discussions about battle tactics and the need for different levels of force are often included, but they are, of necessity, *post hoc* discussions. And in today's world, when the technical revolution of the last twenty years or so is quite as significant as Jacky Fisher's *Dreadnought* revolution, it is not altogether surprising to find that the public discussion of size and shape problems is rather tentative. These are not analyses so much as prescriptions, usually for specific cases or circumstances.

TECHNICAL CHANGES

The pace of technological change has extensively affected the strategic environment in which maritime military forces operate, as well as the instruments upon which these forces are commonly based. Leaving aside for the moment the quantitative consideration that there are more states than there used to be which possess navies of a wide variety of capabilities, the ability of governments to communicate rapidly, and with a relatively high level of reliability, with their naval forces spread over wide areas is now much more highly developed; and a number of the more important maritime states have a range of intelligence acquisition systems which enables them to turn the power to communicate quickly into a power to direct and control, in a very much more specific and effective way than ever before. Not only satellite-derived information, but radar, sonar and other electronically based data collection devices can provide a range (and a quality) of information that turns one of the oldest problems that have beset military commanders on its head. The 'fog of war' used to be a mixture derived from inadequate and out of date information; but, from now on, the problem will be to select what is relevant and important from a mass of specifics that builds up – perhaps – so remorselessly that the selection of what items are crucial to decisions that have to be made quickly may not be able to be made consistently. It is now entirely feasible to suppose that a number of governments will be able to order even minor tactical moves in distant critical situations, and that the central government controllers will know even more about what is happening – as it happens – than 'the man on the spot' to whom, historically, it has been common practice to defer. This is not to assume that the reactions and the perceptions of the central government controllers will be the same as those of the tactical commander, whose sense of urgency and danger may be more pointed; and it certainly will not mean that tension between headquarters and the local command will be eliminated. It might even be, as a general phenomenon, that such tension will be more intense, at least in so far that one of the attributes that is currently expected of experienced commanders is that they will take individual initiatives when local predicaments seem to require urgent reaction. But, in the future, when governments are playing for high stakes, which they may not have had time fully to explain to the man on the spot, initiative may not be so highly prized as a virtue.

This problem, however, may be a relatively unusual and therefore untypical example, likely to affect only a small number of states; although it may become quite typical, in a confrontation between a major state and a minor one, that the major state's forces are relatively at a tactical disadvantage because of the disparities in the values, and in the sense of urgency, that impel the responses that both sides want to make. The relatively isolated, and relatively irrational, force commander of the weaker antagonist may be playing a different and perhaps confusing game and may therefore have the tactical edge; and a much wider range of states can now deploy military forces at sea in ways which – although they may seem relatively primitive by comparison with what is attainable by the most advanced states – might nevertheless be quite significant and effective in particular situations.[5]

'Sea power' now, of course, means not only surface ships, but sea-based aircraft (fixed wing and rotary wing), shore-based aircraft, submarines, hovercraft and hydrofoils, shore-based surveillance systems, fixed surveillance systems on the sea bottom and, much more rarely, satellite surveillance systems. And the weapon systems that are now generally available include surface-to-surface, surface-to-air and air-to-surface missiles, some of which have sophisticated guidance or target acquisition capabilities and many of which can be shore-based. Cruise missiles and subsurface missiles are, as yet, still rather exotic; torpedoes are, as yet, still rather primitive, in relation to the money that has been spent on their development over the years. Mines are much more effective and difficult to counter than they used to be: and guns, though less common than they once were, are still highly effective weapon systems for many purposes. Target acquisition and control systems, both on board ships and in aircraft, are much less bulky and more reliable with each succeeding mark or variant.

Ship propulsion systems have become more varied. Nuclear propulsion has transformed the capabilities of advanced submarine designs to perform a wide range of tasks unattainable even by the most elegant, and quiet, conventional designs and has conferred impressive endurance capabilities upon some surface ships. It is however extremely expensive in its training demands, as well as in financial and engineering terms, and is still restricted to a small handful of navies. Conventional propulsion machinery is now much more efficient than only a few years ago, and is supplemented by the use of gas turbine machinery, which in some ships has now become the prime propulsive unit. New ranges of materials, metallic and non-metallic, are now used for hull and component construction: and, altogether, warship design and construction tasks are now substantially different from, and generally more sophisticated than, what most merchant shipbuilding yards are equipped to deal with. This is not true across the board, because in roles such as fishery protection or coastal patrol it is still possible for civilian designs to be adapted; but it is the case that, for major naval units, specialised and inevitably expensive facilities are necessary which have to be backed up by scientific and engineering research facilities. This requirement means that a relatively large number of navies depend upon foreign assistance to obtain, and perhaps maintain, modern and advanced ships; and that even the most advanced navies depend upon a relatively small number of specialist building and repair yards. Another consequence is that there is probably a wide disparity between the efficiency levels which different navies are able to maintain, even though they may apparently be equipped with ships of comparable designs. Unit efficiency depends on crew training, as well as upon the intrinsic capability of the equipment, and there are likely to be wide variations in the standards that are actually achieved. A difference in skills, in speed of reaction and in the ability to turn orders into efficient execution are still important, not least in the sense that they both impart a confidence that suffuses the morale of a force, and may make a crucial difference in combat.

In one important way, however, the maritime environment has not changed. It may seem a trite point to make, but it is so often not said that it is too often forgotten: the sea is a hostile, infinitely variable environment in which to work. It presents a constant challenge, and sometimes requires extreme exertion in order merely to survive. Storms, currents, hazards that are natural or accidental as well as man-made, all combine to provide a spatial choreography that is intrinsically dangerous, and may for long periods of time be inherently debilitating.

THE EFFECTS OF CHANGE

The general trend of technical progress has produced a number of changes in the expectations that we should have about the utility of naval forces. Among the most important is the greater lethal capability of weapons. Target acquisition and reconnaissance equipments are as significant in this respect as longer ranges and higher accuracy. Until relatively recently, the chances of finding and then hitting a moving target with a salvo of gunfire or even an air-delivered bomb or rocket were sufficiently low to seem to call for either a superiority in numbers or a lengthy attack pattern: the prospects of a first-shot hit were statistically very low. We must now expect that, even in single ship exchanges, there is a highly significant probability that – if the full range of weapon capabilities is efficiently exploited – the first shot will kill. 'Kill' in this context does not necessarily mean that the opposing force is sunk; it is enough if their ability to respond is broken, or significantly impaired. Higher lethal capability means that surface ships in particular are now more vulnerable than they used to be, and the question of how dangerous it would be to maintain squadrons of prestigious ships – like, for example, large aircraft carriers – in tactically exposed locations is now a cause for concern, and indeed for extensive professional debate within the major navies.

It may be the case that if such ships can be covered by defensive weaponry, including efficient electronic counter-measures that can interfere with guidance or homing mechanisms, their vulnerability can be diminished; but the nature of the general proposition, on which the debates are based, calls into doubt some of the expectations that were commonplace only a few years ago, that conflict at sea was likely to be rather slower than war on land would be to develop politically significant levels of damage, that might set in train an escalation of the intensity, or the extent, of the conflict. It still might be possible for governments to affect to ignore the loss of a small unit, in order to retain a rational control of other events; but the loss of a major unit, which embodies a self-attributed importance, would be very much more difficult to ignore. It is still possible to argue that 'a shooting war' would be slower to develop at sea than on land, once hostilities had become open; but it is more likely to be so now because major units are held back than because their importance is, artificially, downgraded. And if this is the case, it might also affect the willingness of states to use naval forces in exposed, or 'provocative', circumstances short of war.

The debate, about what war at sea might be like in the future, has important general implications. It is relatively easy to decide what weapon system specifics should be; the size, the range and the operational characteristics of a particular weapon can be identified by analysis against a set of parameters that will exemplify a typical role or tactical function. But one of the historic attributes of naval forces has been that they have been used in a variety of missions, in the execution of which particular ship roles or specialised weapon characteristics have been transformed, as it were, into components of a larger and rather diffierent whole. A ship that is primarily designed as an anti-submarine frigate becomes part of a squadron or task force which collectively can perform a wide range of duties of which anti-submarine warfare may be a small, or even a non-existent, component. Some of these duties may be political in character as much as they are military: to demonstrate some policy intention by 'showing the flag' in port visits, or in patrolling some sensitive area. But the military issue that is perhaps most important to the shape of future navies is whether the continuing rate of technical change is going to force so great a concentration upon specific role characteristics that even major navies will become unbalanced. What this means in effect is that navies would be able to continue to perform particular tasks, but they would be less well equipped to cope with that general function which used to be summed up as 'command of the sea' but is now sometimes referred to, in its major aspects, as 'sea control' and 'sea denial'. All of these terms are shorthand descriptions of sets of arguments which have many ramifications, but the link between them is that they all imply that navies have – and ought to have – a general capacity to carry out protracted conflict at tactically varying levels of intensity. The concept of 'a balanced fleet' has been the way in which the intention to maintain such a capability has been expressed; and it implies, of course, that a navy will contain a range of vessels and capabilities that will enable it to defend itself while it carries out a range of tasks to achieve the ends of state policy. At the technical level of argument, the central problem is that the scope of the attacks against which such defence must be successful has become much wider and more dangerous; but at the politico-strategic level of argument, the navies of the major maritime states have also had to contend with the perception (or, rather, the current orthodoxy) that general war in the nuclear age will be short and cataclysmic, that protracted war at sea is unlikely to occur and that, therefore, the need for a balanced fleet, in the relatively traditional mode, is very much diminished.

The response to this argument, in the West, has been the contention that unless a general, and fairly extensive, set of conventional forces is maintained, to deal with challenges short of nuclear aggression, the apocalyptic vision of a brief and nuclear war will become a self-fulfilling prophecy. On land and in the air, as well as at sea, a range of flexible responses is necessary; and this is what the Atlantic Alliance agreed to use as a basis for planning, in 1967. But there is no general agreement on what a protracted conflict would call for; and the technical analysis about what an appropriately balanced fleet should look like, and what it would cost, still continues, and is now being developed in an environment in which the growth and the geographical reach of the Soviet Navy cast a lengthening shadow.

CONTINUING PROBLEMS

There is, in fact, a good deal of difficulty in providing an analytical framework that enables us to identify the roles of maritime power with sufficient clarity to devise ideal solutions. At a relatively detailed level, it is possible to identify necessary weapon system characteristics: range, rate of fire, explosive effect, and so on. At a very general level of abstraction, it is equally possible to make sensible deductions about the useful place of maritime power in the range of factors that determine a state's ability to prosper, or to influence its neighbours, in the international system. But, in the middle, the use of formal analysis, and even of historical extrapolation, does not seem to be sufficiently precise to meet the needs of policy planners in government at least: although it may still be useful to scholars and outside observers. Michael MccGwire has reminded us that maritime strategy is wholly about the *use of the sea* and only partially about navies: while we can identify what is predominantly military in character, there are many commercial activities which have implicit military utility.[6] The shipment of metallic ores, or oil, or the extraction of oil from beneath the sea, quite clearly are matters of strategic importance, and one could give many other examples where the continuation of orderly trade promotes that prosperity which is a core security value to most states.

But on the military side of the argument there are some difficulties too. A number of roles are indisputably military, but with the extensions to the use of the sea which have recently developed – and which have precipitated the United Nations Conference amongst other political phenomena – changes and additions have also developed which may (or may not) be appropriate to navies. The surveillance and enforcement of EEZ regulations, and the keeping of order in constricted navigational zones, are functions which require organised control activities: but need they be military organisations? In some particularly crowded areas, like for example the North Sea, need they be *national* military organisations? The protection of oil installations from unlawful or accidental hazards is another example: does the Royal Navy (in the British case) need to assume a function which – historically – would be intrusive and unusual, or should it remain as a force upon which the civil power (in this case the Grampian Police) can call *in extremis*? The substantive issue which underpins these matters is that, with the developing use of the sea, functions are emerging that do not necessarily fit neatly into our existing organisational stereotypes. There is a requirement, perhaps, to reorder our thoughts and our institutions: but there is also a need, which in some cases will be a fairly urgent need, to provide an instrument which adequately covers the function, however untidily or incrementally. There are two structural influences in this predicament which may cause naval forces to be used in a prominent way. The first is that national military forces are used to doing what they are told by their governments to do, and generally have a good record of responding willingly and creditably. It does them no harm institutionally and may sometimes enhance their position in the competition for budgetary resources: it may also extend their 'public image'. The second factor is that both nationally and internationally it may be easier for governments to use their military forces in ways that do not fit neatly into the established framework, but have a basic compatibility with what the forces – the navies, in this case – already do. In an area like north-west Europe, for example, where there is already a habit of inter-governmental co-operation in various ways, in NATO and in the EEC, it may, structurally, simply be easier to extend the co-operative role of an existing and efficient institution than to negotiate a new role for a new trans-departmental or trans-governmental body whose responsibilities would not add to overlap and confusion.

In the event, however, it probably makes better sense to grasp the nettle more firmly and to determine at the beginning what the fundamental problems seem to be. One of the fundamentals for navies is that there may be incompatibilities that attend any wide extension of their mission. The first is that the sorts of vehicles and systems that are necessary to cover the extended responsibilities may not mould with what they already have. If too many 'role-specific' warships are devised, the ability to interchange units, and benefit from the limited flexibility that the sea confers, may be diminished; and the combat capacity of the navy as a whole may be restricted. The second is that a 'role-specific' navy may come to be thought of as a 'resources-specific' navy, that will give a certain output for a measured input. The econometric basis of much policy analysis will tend to create such an expectation. But, to the extent that *any* navy ultimately has to justify itself by its ability to perform satisfactorily in war – even in an age of deterrence – the output that ought to be measured is the wartime capacity to be successful, under the stress of combat: and this probably means building into the fleet's resources a degree of overlap and a margin of redundancy that, econometrically, do not look as if they are 'value for money'.

The number of states that depend upon extensive analysis to assist policy decisions is not, however, very large; and most navies, in the near future, will be provided within the limits of less precise or detailed considerations. Most states still do not plan very far ahead; they have neither the resources nor the range of policy interests that confer such caution. They will buy what they think they need as and when they can: they will be less concerned than major states are about technical obsolescence or intrinsic military capability. They will hope for help, on preferential terms. And they may be more ready to use what forces they have, because they do not have to worry as much as the major states do about the consequences of escalation. Their concerns are more likely to be related to taking advantage from whatever chances to happen: and in these circumstances, still, navies are useful things to have around.

NOTES AND REFERENCES

There are a number of major works on the nature of maritime power which are still well worth reading, although they predate the era of nuclear weapons and long-range communications; the books by Admiral Mahan and Admiral Richmond referred to in notes 1 and 2 of this chapter fall into this category. So do *Some Principles of Maritime Strategy* by Sir Julian Corbett, which was republished in 1972, with an introduction by Professor B. McL. Ranft (London: Conway Maritime Press, 1972), and *Theories Stratégiques* by Admiral Castex (Paris: Société d'Editions Géographiques, Maritime et Coloniales, 1937).

Among more modern analyses, it is impossible not to single out the work of Bernard Brodie (see note 2), whose range of scholarship is always most impressive. Professor Laurence Martin's book on *The Sea in Modern Strategy* (see note 3) occasioned some controversy when it was first published, but is a succinct, valuable and stimulating analysis. Sir James Cable's account of *Gunboat Diplomacy*, in the same series, is elegant and scholarly, and it is to be hoped that he will produce a continuation of a valuable piece of specific analysis: Kenneth Booth is perhaps the most original scholar working in the field today, in the United Kingdom at least, and *Navies and Foreign Policy*, while not as easy to read, is a valuable contribution (see note 3). Admiral S. G. Gorshkov has produced a number of contributions to the literature which would be important if only because of his position as the professional head of the Soviet Navy for well over twenty years; but his most recent publication is a major work in its own right: *The Sea Power of the State* (Oxford: Pergamon, 1979).

The studies published by the International Institute for Strategic Studies in their series of *Adelphi Papers* offer a convenient, cheap and periodic way of keeping in touch with changing problems and perspectives. In particular, the three papers which contain the major contributions to their 1976 annual conference are very well worth looking at (Adelphi Papers Nos. 122–4, *Power at Sea*, see note 3), not least because they provide an introduction to the viewpoints advanced by a number of distinguished protagonists in the debate about the future significance of maritime power. In the same series, Admiral W. H. Bagley, of the United States Navy, has written on *Sea Power and Western Security: The Next Decade* (Adelphi Paper No. 139, 1977) and Barry Buzan has contributed a fascinating analysis in *Sea of Troubles? Sources of Dispute in the New Ocean Regime* (Adelphi Paper No. 143, 1978).

Recently there have been a number of studies published in the United States about the need to ensure a strong and well-equipped United States Navy in the face of the growing strength of the Soviet Navy, and against a concern to make good technical choices at a time when the cost of technical innovation has been growing very fast. An early study, which is a good introductory analysis to the general problems of policy that are involved, is *Sea Power in the 1970s*, edited by George H. Quester (London: Dunellen, 1975). A couple of more detailed studies, of which the first provides a comprehensive account of the existing pattern of forces, are *Securing the Seas: The Soviet Naval Challenge and Western Alliance Options*, edited by Paul H. Nitze and Leonard Sullivan Jun. (Boulder, Co.: Westview Press, 1979), published for the Atlantic Council of the United States; and *Problems of Sea Power As We Approach the Twenty-First Century*, edited by James L. George (Washington, DC: American Enterprise Institute for Public Policy Research, 1978).

There are, in addition, a large number of professional journals that are concerned with naval questions: for example, *Navy International, U.S. Navy Institute Proceedings* and, for members only and by subscription, *The Naval Review*.

1 Sir Herbert Richmond, *Sea Power in the Modern World* (London: Bell, 1934), p. 17.
2 A. T. Mahan, *The Influence of Seapower Upon History* (Boston, Mass.: Little, Brown, 1890), ch. 1; Sir Herbert Richmond, *Statesmen and Sea Power* (London: Oxford University Press, 1946), pp. ix–x; Bernard Brodie, *A Guide to Naval Strategy*, 5th edn (New York: Praeger, 1965), ch. 1; Herbert Rosinski, *The Development of Naval Thought*, ed. B. Mitchell Simpson III (Newport, RI: Naval War College Press, 1977), ch. 7.
3 There are interesting and useful discussions of roles and missions in L. W. Martin, *The Sea in Modern Strategy* (London: Chatto & Windus, 1967), K. Booth, *Navies and Foreign Policy* (London: Croom Helm, 1977) and in *Power at Sea*, three pamphlets in the Adelphi Paper series published by the International Institute for Strategic Studies (*Power at Sea*, Adelphi Papers Nos. 122–4, London: IISS, 1976), especially *Super-Powers and Navies* Adelphi Paper No. 123. The standard reference book on the principles and the precedents of the use of limited naval force is *Gunboat Diplomacy* by Sir James Cable (London: Chatto & Windus, 1971). In the Appendix there is a chronology of incidents which gives brief details of many of the examples referred to, up to and including the *Pueblo* incident of 1968. See also *Soviet Naval Diplomacy*,

edited by B. Dismukes and J. M. McConnell (New York and Oxford: Pergamon, 1979), for a discussion of developing Soviet practices.

4   M. E. Howard, *The Continental Commitment* (London: Temple Smith, 1972).

5   There are now more than sixty states which possess navies with sea-going ships in quantity with modern weapons systems equipments; and a dozen or so more with a range of patrol craft that in theory, at least, could cause significant damage to an attacking force. *Jane's Fighting Ships* remains the standard annual authority.

6   M. MccGwire, 'Maritime strategy and the super-powers', in *Super-Powers and Navies*, Adelphi Paper No. 123, op. cit.

Chapter 8

The Law of the Sea Conference: The Search for New Regimes

R. P. BARSTON

INTRODUCTION

The Law of the Sea Conference is the most ambitious and complex of contemporary attempts at multilateral diplomacy. Since the Caracas session in 1974 the conference has become in effect a standing international institution, having been periodically in session by 1979 for over sixty weeks. Alternating between Geneva and New York, the conference resembles a large-scale production with over 1,100 delegates; it has become a UN industry not only involving UN conference time but large numbers of supportive personnel and vast documentary output. For many of the delegates too, particularly those associated with the early stages of the conference, UNCLOS is a unique club.

Progress in revising the law of the sea has been slow, in part because of the large number of states accredited to the conference (149), which has resulted in frequent and lengthy 'clearing' meetings of bloc, regional and special interest groups, bloc statements of position rather than negotiation and the tendency to reopen issues upon which 'conditional' consensus had been reached. The technical range of issues before the conference – the revised informal composite negotiating text (ICNT)[1] has 304 articles and seven annexes – has without doubt added to the difficulties of achieving consensus. Nevertheless, those current sections of the ICNT covering the living and non-living resource regimes within the exclusive economic zone (Second Committee) and the regime for protecting the marine environment (Third Committee) command a fairly wide degree of support. This, together with the fact that although a formal treaty has not yet been adopted a number of provisions dealing with the EEZ regime have been incorporated in a variety of forms into state practice, makes UNCLOS the most successful of UN multilateral conferences.

MULTILATERAL CONFERENCE DIPLOMACY

The Framework of the Conference
The main work of the conference has been conducted formally at least

within and through three committees, set up to deal with the deep seabed (First Committee), the exclusive economic zone and a wide range of other issues (Second Committee) and marine scientific research (Third Committee). Apart from the negotiations in these committees, the business of the conference has been conducted through less formal groups, bloc or group consultations during the sessions of the conference, and, of course, intensive intersessional negotiations. During the earlier stages of the conference, the three committees tended to operate in a somewhat self-contained manner, and indeed produced separate documents. It was not until in fact the publication of the ICNT in 1977 that overlap between the work of the three committees was reduced and texts were reordered and combined in a single document forming the basis for a draft treaty. The chairmen of each of the main committees, Paul Engo (Cameroon, First Committee), Andrés Aguilar (Venezuela, Second Committee) and Alexander Yankov (Bulgaria, Third Committee), along with the president of the conference (Shirley Amersinghe, Sri Lanka), are collectively responsible for any revision of the negotiating text. An interesting and remarkable feature of the conference has been the absence of formal voting on substantive proposals throughout the history of the conference to date. Under the so-called 'gentleman's agreement',[2] which forms part of the 1974 rules of procedure, states participating in the conference have accepted that differences should be resolved on the basis of consensus and that formal voting should be avoided until the negotiating process has been completed.

At the seventh session of the conference in April 1978 an attempt was made to break the impasse by defining the remaining hard core issues. Seven negotiating groups were as a result established on the following:[3]

(i) the system of exploration, exploitation and (deep seabed) resource policy,
(ii) financial arrangements relating to the International Seabed Authority,
(iii) the institutional machinery of the Authority,
(iv) access to the resources of the economic zone for landlocked, 'geographically disadvantaged' and certain developing coastal states,
(v) settlement of disputes arising from the exercise of sovereign rights by coastal states in the exclusive economic zone,
(vi) the definition of the outer limits of the continental shelf and revenue sharing of profits from offshore operations between the outer limit of the EEZ and the continental margin,
(vii) delimitation of maritime boundaries between adjacent and opposite states and dispute settlement.

At the eighth session of the conference in 1978 work was halted in the three new negotiating groups set up to deal with seabed questions and a

Working Group of 21[4] instead was established. This move, coming at a time when many delegations considered that outstanding issues should now be rapidly resolved, was an important procedural innovation; unlike previous formal groups, membership was restricted, and drawn from ten developed industrialised states, including the United States, United Kingdom, France, Federal Republic of Germany, Canada, Australia and the Soviet Union, and ten developing countries represented for example by Brazil, Peru, Mexico, plus the People's Republic of China. In practice, however, the membership of the group tended to expand through the presence of alternates and observers.

Multilateral Negotiations
The highly politicised nature of the negotiating process is a key distinguishing feature of UNCLOS. Unlike the First and Second Law of the Sea Conferences, negotiating texts have been prepared in the three main committees and other forums rather than initially drawn up in a legal drafting committee prior to general debate. The language used in the ICNT is as a result often ambiguous and loosely drafted to allow for political negotiation and differing interpretations. Obligations are frequently qualified to allow for a state's level of development. Thus the requirement to establish international rules and practices to prevent pollution of the marine environment from land-based sources is made dependent on 'the economic capacity of developing states and their need for development'.

Yet unlike other multilateral negotiations, such as those within UNCTAD before the Manila Conference, in which divisions of opinion have tended to be on strong north–south lines, UNCLOS negotiations have involved many types of cross-cutting alignments. Negotiations have been characterised by changing and shifting groupings around both limited or specialist interests such as the regime for straits or the outer limit of the continental margin, as well as the formation of 'strategic' groups to agree and promote negotiated 'packages' on, for example, the general regime for the exclusive economic zone. A variety of negotiating, discussion and contact groups have in fact been established. Some are limited in the composition and basis of membership such as the five major powers group, the Soviet and Eastern European group and the Arab group. Others span both Western and Eastern European states such as the Group of 17,[5] which included the Soviet Union, several socialist states, the United States, Japan, Norway, Finland and the United Kingdom which was formed to discuss particularly Third Committee questions. The so-called Evensen group, for example, chaired by a Norwegian minister, Jens Evensen, was set up before the Geneva session in 1975 to bring together representatives of the main interest groups, especially the major maritime powers and key members of the Group of 77, at the level of heads of delegation and legal experts. During 1975–6 the Evensen group concentrated on Second Committee questions, whilst at the sixth session it dealt with the International Seabed Authority.

The variety of interest groups is indicative of a second feature of the UNCLOS negotiating process: the diffusion of political power. Both the Soviet Union and the United States, finding much in common in the need to defend global maritime interests, have similarly found it difficult to wield influence in the conference. That difficulty stems partly from the different maritime perspectives of the great powers (the Soviet position, for example, on the International Seabed regime was for a long time closer to the West than to the Group of 77), and partly from the very diverse range of interest groups, each seeking to promote, secure or 'trade off' its particular set of interests. The process of interest aggregation during which consensus is built up is one in which a varied range of states can wield influence. For some that influence may last only as long as the special interest remains unresolved; others, perhaps because of wider sets of interests, deadlock on an issue or chairmanship of a negotiating group, manage to play a consistently more important role. Under these conditions the minor power is able to achieve a degree of importance within the framework of the conference which is generally higher than its ranking and international role in non law of the sea questions would suggest (for example, Malta, Fiji, Cameroon, Bulgaria).

The process of building consensus upon a complex range of issues illustrates a third characteristic of the conference – the highly personalised nature of the political process. Individual representatives of minor and small powers do play highly active roles, with the capacity to block, delay or facilitate compromise, like others, yet with the advantage of far fewer constraints than might be imposed by a large and divided delegation, a domestic constituency or the need to appear frequently constructive. The personalised nature of the diplomacy is underlined by the number of minor states which have retained the same representatives from the outset of the conference, consequently both gaining expertise and in some cases obtaining important positions in the formal and informal machinery of the conference. Indeed some small states have even gone to the extent of hiring foreign nationals to act as spokesmen. Conversely the smaller actors who have regularly changed delegations have found it more difficult to make effective contributions.

The proceedings of the conference have, fourthly, become protracted because of the concept of negotiating until consensus is reached. Considerable time, for example, has been spent on procedural questions: a plenary debate can have anything up to eighty or more speakers which has tended to discourage the holding of such sessions. Perhaps one of the most potentially damaging procedural issues before UNCLOS has been the issue of the presidency. During the first three weeks of the seventh session in 1978 the conference grappled with whether the president, Shirley Amerasinghe, who had been the Sri Lankan representative when elected to the post of conference president but was subsequently not retained as a delegate by the Sri Lankan government, could hold the presidency of UNCLOS for the remaining sessions as a private person. Intensive debate followed on this and related questions as to whether the matter was one of procedure or substance and whether it ought to be solved by voting or consensus. Eventually, after some considerable bitterness, the issue was resolved by vote in a closed session on the night of 5–6 April 1978 with 75 states in favour of the resolution put forward by Nepal on behalf of the Asian group for Amerasinghe continuing as president, 18 against, 13 abstentions and 21 stating they were not participating in the vote.[6] In the subsequent open debates, several states including Peru, Uruguay, Venezuela, Chile, Ecuador, Nicaragua and Argentina, expressed reservations on the decision, indicating that in their view the presidency could not be held legally by an individual not representing a state. The conference subsequently turned in the following weeks to discuss how the work of what was to become an extended session should proceed. The eventual outcome was the establishment, as we have noted earlier, of seven negotiating groups on core issues.

This was only, however, after lengthy procedural debate on the content of the agenda for the rest of the conference. It was after several hours of position statements, many of which addressed themselves to narrow interests rather than to the broader issues connected with the direction of the conference, that the Uruguayan delegate made a simple but elegantly expressed plea: 'Let's start'.

The pace of the negotiations has been shaped not only by the diversity of issues but the size of negotiating groups. The practice of allowing membership of official conference negotiating groups to be open to all states – open-ended negotiation – has inevitably led to delay and complicated the process of negotiation. Attempts to limit their membership have until the eighth session consistently met with opposition, particularly from the smaller members of the conference.

SECOND COMMITTEE: TERRITORIAL SEA, ECONOMIC ZONE, HIGH SEAS AND OTHER ISSUES

The work of the Second Committee since the Caracas session has focused on three main areas: the regime for the 12 mile territorial sea; the delimitation of the EEZ; and the nature and scope of states' rights and obligations within the zone. The protracted discussions on Second Committee questions at the Geneva and New York sessions (1975–6), especially on the innocent passage regime through the territorial sea and passage through straits, reflected the divergent interests of the major maritime powers on the one hand, and several groups of states on the other which aimed to enhance and extend the rights of coastal states in the EEZ. The major maritime states, including the United States, Soviet Union and United Kingdom, have been concerned to retain, on commercial and security grounds, maximum freedom for navigation and to secure uniform international standards and regulations within the territorial sea and EEZ. Thus the maritime states' position has been influenced in part by the likely effect of a multiplicity of state regulations and practices within EEZs. A second major implication of extended jurisdiction of concern to the maritime states was the issue of the right of unimpeded passage through straits, since the prospect was over a hundred straits, formerly including an area of high seas passage within them, would be enclosed by extended territorial waters. However, by the sixth session of the conference considerable progress has been made on the Second Committee questions through the intersessional negotiations during 1975–6 in the Evensen group.

The sixth session of the conference focused in particular on the third of the issues mentioned above – the legal status of the economic zone.[7] Undoubtedly this has proved to be one of the more difficult questions before the conference. Discussion within the Second Committee centred on the question of residual rights[8] within the EEZ (that is, the traditional high seas freedoms of navigation, visiting ports in passage, cable-laying, overflight, fishing and marine scientific research). On this issue the United States, Soviet Union, United Kingdom and Japan along with other maritime states argued that the EEZ should be regarded as high seas except for those rights provided for by the convention. The maritime states were opposed by the members of the Group of 77, such as Ecuador, Brazil and India, who considered that the EEZ was distinct from high seas and that the coastal state had the exclusive prerogative to make regulations and enforce standards.

Three further subsidiary issues in the Second Committee are worth noting as illustrations of both the role of special interest groups and the complexity of issues before the conference. Apart from the question of the legal status of the EEZ, the renewed demands of the landlocked and geographically disadvantaged group (LLGDS) which is made up of some forty-nine states, including Austria, Switzerland, Nepal and Afghanistan, for access to the resources of neighbouring EEZs, also resulted in extensive debate. A 'group of 21' (ten LLGDS, ten coastal states and a chairman) was formed to bridge the gap between the two main groups. Discussion in the group centred on the 'right' of participation and whether the 'right' of access applied to surplus fisheries which the coastal state was unable to harvest, or whether it should also apply to cases where there is no surplus.

The issue of the extent of the outer limit of the continental shelf was a source of continued disagreement and of particular concern to those states with 'wide' margins such as the United Kingdom, New Zealand, Australia and India. Whilst it was generally accepted that the coastal state would have rights within the 200 mile EEZ over resources in the zone including the continental shelf, the precise extent of coastal state jurisdiction beyond 200 miles remained undecided. Opposition to the definition of the outer limit of the continental shelf as the edge of the continental margin came, predictably, from, amongst others, the landlocked and geographically disadvantaged states, who would neither gain economically nor be able to extend their limits. Although no precise formula was included in the ICNT, the Irish formula,[9] introduced in April 1976, whereby the outer edge of the shelf would be determined by distance criterion from the foot of the continental slope, or by a depth of sediment test, received broad support. Further progress on this question was linked to the related issue of revenue-sharing. The ICNT provides for a revenue-sharing regime (article 82) under which, after the fifth year of operating an offshore site between the outer limit of the EEZ and continental margin, 1 per cent of the value or volume of production would be paid to the International Seabed Authority. The rate of payment would increase by 1 per cent per annum until the tenth year and subsequently remain at 5 per cent, which was increased to the twelfth year and 7 per cent respectively in the compromise package on the shelf limit and revenue-sharing put forward by Second Committee chairman Aguilar during the first part of the eighth session in 1979.[10]

A third subsidiary area of intensive discussion in the Second Committee was the choice of baselines for the delineation of the limits of archipelagic states and the regime for passage through archipelagic waters – which was of particular importance to Indonesia and the Philippines. On the latter question the ICNT in article 53 provides for a new concept of archipelagic sealanes passage, analogous to the right of transit passage through straits (article 38) for routes across an archipelago.

The question of the legal status of the 200 mile economic zone was substantially resolved by the close of the sixth session. In the final stages of the session a high level group was formed on 2 July 1977 under Casteneda of Mexico, which produced a compromise package around the existing articles concerned with rights and obligations in the EEZ and high seas freedoms. The framework of the regime is set out in articles 55–8 and is based on the distinction drawn in article 56 between the *sovereign rights* and *jurisdiction* of the coastal state. The former extend *inter alia* to 'exploring and exploiting, conserving and managing the natural resources, whether living or non-living, of the seabed and subsoil and the superadjacent waters', whilst other coastal state powers are limited to jurisdiction over artificial islands, installations and structures, marine scientific research and the preservation of the marine environment.

THIRD COMMITTEE: PRESERVATION OF THE MARINE ENVIRONMENT AND
MARINE SCIENTIFIC RESEARCH

The Third Committee section of the text (Part XII) contains *inter alia* provisions on states' obligations to protect the marine environment, regional co-operation and land-based sources of pollution. However, the bulk of this part of the ICNT (articles 212–38) is devoted to measures aimed at controlling vessel-source pollution.[11] As such, the text reflects the dissatisfaction of a number of developing coastal states with the existing flag state regime. The traditional regime is modified consequently in a number of respects including new provisions on qualified coastal state enforcement rights in the EEZ. In addition the text provides for a type of universal port state jurisdiction,[12] in which the port state under certain conditions may initiate investigations and subsequently commence proceedings for pollution offences committed outside its own internal waters, territorial sea and economic zone. These and other changes to the traditional regime, which we discuss in Chapter 5, including innocent passage (article 212, para. 3), are subject to a number of safeguards such as release of a vessel on bonding, which the major maritime powers have sought in order to protect their worldwide shipping interests.

The concern of those states vulnerable to pollution because of their location on important shipping routes or whose sea areas are vulnerable for ecological and oceanographic reasons finds expression in a lengthy draft article which gives the coastal state regulatory powers to designate special areas within the EEZ, subject to international approval of such areas by the competent international organisation; this provision, in fact, would complement the Annex II regulations of the 1973 IMCO Convention. In addition, the text contains a provision, again largely at Canadian insistence (article 235), which allows coastal states to establish non-discriminatory regulations within the EEZ in order to reduce the likelihood of major pollution damage in certain ecologically vulnerable ice-covered areas such as may be found in the Arctic.

The revised regime for maritime scientific research (MSR), which draws substantially on the draft articles submitted by Columbia, El Salvador, Mexico and Nigeria in May 1975,[13] modifies the traditional regime (that is, high seas freedom for research, subject to the 1958 Geneva Continental Shelf Convention) in three respects. First, the coastal state is given jurisdiction with regard to MSR within the EEZ, including the water column of the zone. A consent regime (articles 247–53) is provided for and although it is qualified in two ways – the coastal state in normal circumstances may not withhold its consent for 'pure' scientific research projects, and the researching organisation has the right to proceed with a project six months after notification if no request for further information or objection has been received – it is likely that the regime would in practical terms become one of full consent for all marine scientific research projects within the EEZ. The coastal state moreover has the right to halt research if it considers that the project is at variance with the initial description of it or with the conditions for approving the research. Secondly, while states have the right to conduct MSR in the water column beyond the EEZ in conformity with the convention, under the ICNT the International Seabed Authority would harmonise and co-ordinate MSR concerning the International Seabed Area. A third change to the traditional regime envisages a role in marine research projects in neighbouring EEZs for landlocked and geographically disadvantaged states. In the International Area all states, irrespective of their geographical location, have equal right to conduct MSR, subject to Part XI of the convention.

INTERNATIONAL SEABED REGIME

The major outstanding issue at UNCLOS has been the deep seabed mining regime. By the fifth session the conference had seemingly become deadlocked over the issue, with the technologically advanced Western states and the Group of 77 deeply divided. In order to achieve a breakthrough, the first three weeks of the sixth session were devoted to seabed mining questions, including the basic system of exploitation, resource policy and financing the Enterprise, under the First Committee chairman's special representative Jens Evensen. After the close of the sixth session a substantially modified text was issued by First Committee chairman Paul Engo, which was incorporated into the ICNT.

In general, the Engo text goes further than previous documents in extending the powers of the Authority (which is made up of the Assembly, Council and the Secretariat) over all stages of exploration and exploitation of deep seabed minerals.[14] Under article 158 of the ICNT the Assembly is designated the supreme organ of the Authority, with powers of establishing general policies; substantive decisions of the Assembly, in which each state party has one vote, require a two-thirds majority. Amongst the other powers of the Assembly are those of electing the Council, assessment of contributions from member states until the Authority has sufficient income (article 158) and reviewing every five years the progress of the deep seabed regime, as well as responsibility for the major review of the regime twenty years after the entry into force of the convention (articles 152 and 153). The Council itself – the executive organ of the Authority with responsibility for specific policies within the framework laid down by the Assembly – is made up of thirty-six members (article 159), of whom half would be elected on the basis of equitable geographical distribution, whilst the remainder would represent special interests (for example, major researching states or developing country mineral importers).

Under the ICNT the International Seabed Authority, which could have its headquarters in Jamaica, although Malta and Fiji have also put in bids, is given an extensive range of powers both over seabed mining and other activities within the International Area, including scientific research and technology transfer.[15] On resource policy, the exploration regime provides for both independent operations by the Enterprise (the operational arm of the Authority) and joint ventures, production-sharing or service contracts between contractors and the Authority. In the latter cases the contract areas must be sufficiently large to enable the Enterprise to mine one-half (the so-called 'reserved areas') independently or in conjunction with developing countries. Provisions on the transfer of technology have been strengthened in the text so as to provide for discussion of this issue, as well as the participation of developing countries, at the contract stage of negotiations rather than after mining operations have commenced. Two further provisions strengthen the position of the Authority on resource policy. For the first five years[16] of the interim period of production control the Authority is empowered to limit the production of minerals from nodules in the Area to the projected cumulative growth segment of world nickel demand. Subsequently the production level is limited to a percentage of the growth of nickel demand in any one year. Secondly, in order to protect developing countries from any adverse effects on their economies caused by seabed mineral production, the Authority is empowered to participate in any commodity conferences dealing with the categories of minerals produced in the Area and become a party to commodity agreements. If the agreements become ineffective the Authority would resume the power to limit seabed mineral production.

The publication of the ICNT provisions on the International Seabed regime after the close of the session immediately caused further controversy and led to a major review of US involvement in UNCLOS. The text, issued against the background of US deep seabed mining legislation, served to sharpen the substantive differences between the core members of the Group of 77 and the technologically advanced Western maritime states which had been evident during the Evensen discussions. The text was also criticised by US Ambassador Elliot Richardson on procedural grounds in that it had not been discussed widely within the conference framework nor did it take into account sufficiently the detailed discussions which had taken place within the framework of the Evensen meetings.[17]

Apart from the procedural issue, three questions of substance divide the Group of 77 and the advanced Western states:[18] the conditions of access to the International Area, production levels and the balance of political power within the various organs of the Authority. As a result of the sixth session the major Western maritime powers – including the United States, United Kingdom, West Germany and Japan – have been concerned to obtain a clear right of access for states and companies, and to prevent the parallel system from reverting to a 'unitary' one organised exclusively by the Authority at the end of the review period. A second related issue concerns the regulatory powers of the Authority over production and price-setting. The developing countries have sought to retain the prime role of the Authority and ensure adequate initial finance for the Enterprise. In particular the developing copper and nickel producers – Chile, Peru, Zaïre, Indonesia and Cuba, supported by Canada – have insisted on limiting seabed nickel output to 60 per cent of the cumulative growth of the nickel market. The third issue which has divided the conference centres on the institutional arrangements for managing Seabed operations. The technologically advanced Western states have, in particular, opposed the provisions in the ICNT on voting procedure, the powers of the Assembly and the composition of the Council. The preference of the maritime powers for weighted voting and changes in the composition of the Council reflects their concern that the states with special interests, particularly those with large investments in seabed mining, could be in a permanent minority.[19]

THE SEVENTH AND EIGHTH SESSIONS OF UNCLOS

The first part of the seventh session (28 March – 19 May 1978) was dominated, as discussed earlier, by the issue of the presidency. The remainder of the session concentrated on the 'hard core' issues in seven negotiating groups set up after the confirmation of Amerasinghe as president. Substantial progress was made, however, in only one of the groups – Group 6 – chaired by Constantine Stavropoulos (Greece) on the settlement of disputes relating to coastal states' fisheries rights. The Second Committee had been divided on this question between those states which favoured compulsory dispute settlement and those preferring some form of conciliation procedure. In revised article 296 a conditional consensus – dependent on the overall package deal for the convention – was built around the concept of compulsory conciliation for those disputes arising out of inadequate management policies or the refusal of the coastal state to allocate surplus fisheries from the EEZ. The related question of access for landlocked and geographically disadvantaged states to fisheries resources remained a source of contention until the eighth session in Geneva (19 March–27 April 1979). The chairman of Negotiating Group 4, Satya N. Nandan (Fiji), indicated that the proposals he had set out in May 1978, allowing LLGDS states access to the surplus fisheries from the EEZ, now appeared to offer a substantially improved prospect for consensus.

The achievement of broad consensus on the regime for preventing and controlling marine pollution was an important outcome of the Geneva part of the eighth session.[20] It was seen by decision-makers from a widespread group of states as largely removing yet another contentious, though not critical, issue area from the agenda of outstanding problems and therefore contributing to the incremental process of constructing an overall package. At the seventh session, which was strongly influenced, at least at the outset, by the *Amoco Cadiz* disaster, new provisions were agreed on ship routing systems and oil spill reporting but these did not alter the basic ICNT regime. Subsequent discussion at New York on outstanding proposals revealed some support for modest further extensions of coastal state enforcement powers without the balance being significantly altered between port and coastal and flag state powers. Some states, such as France and West Germany, nevertheless felt that adequate powers had not been given to the coastal state. By contrast, a number of states with extensive shipping interests such as Greece and Liberia, or located in sensitive military regimes, such as Iraq, Israel and the Republic of Korea, expressed reservations on the extension of port or coastal state powers to include information on routing and detentions in the economic zone for pollution offences.

By the final New York stage of the eighth session (19 July–24 August 1979) the major outstanding issue remained the regime for the International Seabed Authority. Two additional issues remained unresolved – the definition of the outer limit of the continental margin and boundaries between opposite and adjacent states. At the New York session, however, progress was made in a newly established smaller Working Group of 38 on the compromise formula put forward by Andrés Aguilar (Venezuela), chairman of Negotiating Group 6, on the outer limit of the continental shelf and revenue-sharing. The Aguilar formula, which draws on the revised Soviet and Irish proposals, would allow states a choice of two criteria for fixing the outer edge of the continental margin: one based on the thickness of sedimentary rocks beyond the foot of the continental slope and the other on a line 60 miles seaward of the continental slope. The outer limits for those states whose shelves extend beyond 200 miles would be set at either 350 nautical miles from the baseline from which the territorial sea is measured or 100 nautical miles from the 2,500 metre isobath.

Within the Third Committee negotiations were centred on the MSR regime. The issue had been reopened by the United States at the seventh session in Geneva, supported by a group of states which included the United Kingdom, Federal Republic of Germany, Mexico, Israel and Australia. The US proposals sought to remove some of the restrictions in the MSR regime, in particular the consent regime for MSR in the economic zone, and improve the conditions of access for research on the continental shelf beyond 200 nautical miles. Strong opposition to the US proposals came from those members of the Group of 77 favouring a full consent regime for MSR in the EEZ. In addition reservations were expressed by a number of states, which felt that substantive amendments on MSR would disturb the overall balance of the MSR regime which had been negotiated at the sixth session. Although compromise formulae were reached at New York the issue remained contentious.[22] The negotiations on MSR illustrate clearly a further feature of the UNCLOS variety of multilateral negotiations which relies on consensus as a *modus operandi* – the problem of sustaining negotiating momentum across a broad range of issues. As the MSR case, and others such as the LLGDS and fisheries dispute settlement problems illustrate, conditionally or imperfectly resolved issues can be reopened when the balance of negotiating attention and effort is switched to remaining issues over which there is deadlock and this accordingly complicates the process of achieving an overall package.

Special emphasis at the New York session was again in fact devoted to the seabed mining regime and detailed negotiations were continued on the parallel system for mining by the Enterprise and private contractors, initial finance for the Enterprise and the question of what majority should be required for taking decisions in the Council. The negotiations on the economic and financial aspects of deep seabed mining have proved to be the most technically complex of the UNCLOS proceedings so far, covering such issues as debt equity ratios of mining companies, the tax system for the Authority and the financial structure enabling the Enterprise to carry out integrated or single metal mining projects.[23] The negotiations have inevitably become protracted because of the need continually to revise financial data, modify proposals in the light of reports from technical groups and take account of the financial implications of mining and financing the Authority for differing economic systems. In view of the fact that some considerable time will elapse before the convention enters into force, the detailed provisions on seabed mining and on financing the Authority will certainly have to be renegotiated. In the meantime the completion of the convention has undoubtedly been delayed.

CONCLUSION

Since the Caracas session of UNCLOS in 1974 substantial progress has been made in revising the law of the sea. By the ninth session in 1980 the conference had succeeded in establishing, with one or two exceptions, both a general framework and detailed provisions for new regimes. Perhaps equally important, the language, ideas and concepts used and devised at UNCLOS have already begun to be incorporated into state practice. Moreover, the work of the conference has illustrated the growing importance in contemporary international politics of an international elite of specialist officials and representatives concerned with highly technical and complex policy problems.

UNCLOS has been an unusual experiment in multilateral negotiation, partly because of the adoption of consensus as an operating procedure and the building block or incremental approach to devising new regimes. The conference, too, although at times highly politicised, has benefited from being largely unaffected by outside international conflicts. This has been a reflection both of the technical nature of the negotiations and the progress the conference has made in creating modern maritime law.

NOTES AND REFERENCES

The literature on the Law of the Sea Conference and related issues has now become extensive. The proceedings of the conference have been recorded in the *Official Records* series. For example, the main draft articles (or 'L' papers) upon which the Third Committee text of the ICNT (Rev. I) is based can be found in *The United Nations Conference on the Law of the Sea, Official Records*, Vol. IV, which covers the Geneva session of 17 March–9 May 1975. Other key documents and papers are referred to in notes 7 and 21. Particularly valuable are the reports of the chairmen of the main committees and negotiating groups. The Report of the Working Group of 21, A/CONF. 62/C.1/L.26, 21 August 1979, provides a good insight into the detailed and technical nature of the negotiations on the international seabed regime. The United Nations has issued a series of bibliographical guides to literature on the sea, including *The Sea: Economic and Technical Aspects: A Select Bibliography* (New York, 1974); *The Sea: Legal and Political Aspects* (New York, 1974), and the combined series *The Sea: A Select Bibliography on the Legal, Political, Economic and Technological Aspects* (New York, 1975–9), covering the period 1974–5, 1975–6 and 1976–8.

The Law of the Sea Institute, formerly at Rhode Island, has produced a number of valuable works on the law of the sea; two of these especially provide a good introduction to the background and early sessions of UNCLOS: *Law of the Sea: The Emerging Regime of the Oceans*, ed. John King Gamble Jun. and Guilio Pontecarvo (Cambridge, Mass.: Ballinger Publishing Co., 1973), and F. T. Christy Jun. *et al.*, *Law of the Sea: Caracas and Beyond* (Cambridge, Mass.: Ballinger Publishing Co., 1975).

1   A/CONF. 62/WP.10/Rev. I, 28 April 1979.
2   Appendix to 1974 Rules of Procedure, 27 June 1974. The agreement was approved on 16 November 1973.
3   A/CONF. 62/62, 13 April 1978.
4   See for example *Report of the Working Group of 21*, A/CONF. 62/C.1/L.26, 21 August 1979.
5   There is little published information on the work of the Group of 17. Its consultations date back to the work in the Preparatory Committee which preceded the convening of the conference. A rare account is by Johannes Buhl (Danish delegation to UNCLOS) in *Iranian Review of International Relations*, nos. 11–12 (spring 1978), pp. 307–20.
6   SEA/40, 6 April 1978.
7   See Explanatory Memorandum by the president of the Law of the Sea Conference, A/CONF. 62/WP.10/Add. 1, 22 July 1977, *Official Records*, Vol. VIII, pp. 65–80.
8   For further discussion of this concept see A/CONF. 62/WP.8/Rev. I/Part II, 6 May 1976, p. 4.
9   See Piers R. R. Gardiner, 'The law of the sea', *Technology Ireland* (August 1977).
10 ICNT/Rev. I, 28 April 1979, article 82, para. 2.
11 For a summary of the work of the Third Committee prior to the sixth session see the report by the committee's chairman, Ambassador Yankov, A/CONF.62/L.18, 16 September 1976.

12 A good analysis can be found in the paper submitted by the British Branch Committee on the Law of the Sea, 'The concept of port state jurisdiction', for the 1974 Conference of the International Law Association held in New Delhi.
13 A/CONF./C.3/L.29, 6 May 1975.
14 See A/CONF. 62/WP.10/Add. 1, 22 July 1977, pp. 68–9.
15 ICNT, articles 150–192, and Annex 2.
16 The interim period was reduced from seven to five years in the ICNT (Rev. I), 28 April 1979, article 151, para. 2(a).
17 See text of Ambassador Richardson's press conference at the United Nations on 20 July 1977.
18 For the United Kingdom position see *Hansard*, 26 October 1977, cols 844–5; see also the testimony of Ambassador Richardson before the House International Relations Committee (Sub-committee on International Organisations), 23 January 1978, p. 8.
19 See Ambassador Richardson's Cincinatti address of 18 January 1978.
20 *Report by the Chairman of the Third Committee*, A/CONF. 62/L.34, 26 April 1979.
21 ICNT, Rev. I, article 76; and A/CONF. 62/C.2/L.100, 26 April 1979.
22 *Report by the Chairman of the Third Committee*, A/CONF. 62/L.41, 23 August 1979.
23 See section II, and Annexes A–D of A/CONF. 62/C.1/L.26.

Chapter 9

Contemporary Maritime Legal Problems

P. W. BIRNIE

Chapter 1 examined the problems existing in the law of the sea at the time of the first United Nations Conferences and drew attention to those arising from the four conventions adopted by UNCLOS I. It is apparent that the law of the sea is, as it always has been, in a state of flux. The UNCLOS III has served to focus, as never before, the attention of the whole international community on this fact and has accelerated changes. The problem now facing legal advisers is to predict the direction the law is taking and to evaluate the extent to which, even before UNCLOS adopts a treaty, if it ever does, its texts (or parts thereof) have become part of customary law as states introduce them into their practices. The law is more likely to develop uniformly if there is a treaty but, as the period following the Geneva Conferences showed, this is not necessarily so as there will be an interim period of several years before any treaty enters into force. The Geneva Conventions took six to eight years to do so. Article 299 of ICNT (Rev. I) proposes that the treaty requires ratification and article 301 adds that it will not enter into force until an as yet unspecified time, following a certain number of ratifications or accessions. Even then a treaty (according to the Vienna Convention on Treaties) will bind only the states party to it, some of whom may make reservations the status of which will be doubtful since the customary law on the subject is contentious.

The ICNT (Rev. I)[1] is silent on this problem. The consensus approach of UNCLOS should ensure wider ratification than the Geneva Conventions achieved, however, and parts of the treaty may bind other states if they become customary law; it can, for example, be argued that provisions concerning 200 mile fisheries zones have done so, as described in Chapter 2, and perhaps that articles concerning the rights of states bordering international straits to require that transiting vessels observe internationally approved sealanes (following IMCO's recent approval of the Malacca Straits scheme) have also. There remain many issues in the ICNT, however, which are unlikely to secure the approval of one or more groups of states.

The prevailing uncertainty concerning the law of the sea is thus likely to continue for some years and in the interim state practice based on claims and counter-claims, the forcefulness and determination with which these are asserted and the extent to which they are accepted or acquiesced in by others will develop the law. It is inevitable that this process will continue to generate the kind of conflicts and problems that have occurred in recent years. International law is derived, however, not only from treaties and legal customs but also from general principles of law and secondary sources such as judicial decisions. International organisations, both global and regional, are increasingly playing a part in developing the norms upon which new law can be based. There are many such concerned in ocean affairs, and states have increasingly resorted to them and established new regional bodies to manage particular maritime problems by providing a forum for the resolution of political and legal disputes by negotiation with Commissions to administer and develop rules of conduct. Decisions of such bodies bind only the states party but the proliferation of Commissions concerned with, for example, prevention of marine pollution is bound to establish norms for the behaviour of states outside them and to provide models for the institution of similar bodies in other areas.

UNCLOS III, as we shall see, has contributed to this trend. As any treaty or practice based on ICNT (Rev. I) is likely to reflect the many verbal ambiguities which enable the compromises necessary to secure consensus, international organisations will increasingly play a major role. Their present functions are likely to be affected in two ways: first, by the many extensions of coastal state jurisdiction to which they will have to adapt their functions and policies, and secondly, by assuming the new tasks laid upon them, directly or indirectly, by the ICNT (Rev. I). There are numerous references therein to the need for 'competent international organisations' as well as 'general diplomatic conferences' to develop international rules and standards, as for example in articles 201–12 relating to pollution prevention. Organisations such as the IMCO, ILO, FAO, and more recently UNEP, have already been fulfilling this role and their large membership indicates that states perceive the need for such international forums to negotiate the rules and avoid if possible unilateral actions which might provoke open conflicts.

We must now look at the kind of legal problems which have caused friction in recent years, the nature of the solutions adopted by states and the means by which they arrived at them, before we can reach conclusions concerning the handling of future problems that have a maritime dimension.

CONTENTIOUS ISSUES IN THE LAW OF THE SEA

Many uses of the sea that have recently given rise to disputes are those that have done so for hundreds of years and will no doubt continue so to do for as many more. Others are new, arising from modern technological developments. Traditional problems are those concerning fishing and navigation and the limits of coastal state jurisdiction over these activities. It is still these issues that provoke most conflicts between states, but with a new dimension since they too have been exacerbated by current technology.

Navigation

The unsettled limits of the territorial sea and the uncertain rights of innocent passage for foreign vessels, especially military vessels, navigating them have given rise to serious incidents. The most notable involved United States vessels and typify the confusions that can arise when there is no uniformity of limits.

CASP

The Pueblo Incident[2]

The first concerned a United States naval vessel, the *Pueblo*, which in 1968 was seized by North Korea about 15 miles off the nearest coast, a Korean island, situated seaward of the closing line of a mainland bay. Both or either of these points could legally be used as the territorial sea baseline. North Korea claimed that the *Pueblo* was spying within her 12 mile territorial sea. The US at that date recognised only a 3 mile limit. It seems likely, on subsequent evidence, that the *Pueblo* did enter the disputed 12 mile limit and that its activities therein infringed the innocence of its passage according to customary criteria. The ICNT's proposals for a 12 mile limit and its twelve specific criteria of non-innocent passage would obviate such a dispute in the future. It is possible, however, that the proposal that the coastal state should have jurisdiction over scientific research in the 200 mile exclusive economic zone would result in some clashes over intelligence-gathering operations. The *Pueblo's* crew were eventually released by diplomatic negotiation between the US and North Korea in which the United States suffered a considerable diplomatic defeat. *5* FOOTNOTE,

The Mayaguez Incident[3]

A similar incident occurred more recently; this time it concerned a US merchant vessel, the *Mayaguez*, which was arrested by Cambodia in the Gulf of Thailand in 1975, when *en route* about 60 miles from the Cambodian mainland and 6½ miles off the Cambodian Pulo Wai Islands. As in the previous case the US still maintained a 3 mile limit whereas Cambodia claimed 12 miles. The US, no doubt recalling the international humiliation it had suffered during the *Pueblo* negotiations, and the recent defeat in Vietnam, this time released the crew of the *Mayaguez* from Cambodia by the use of force, justifying its action by reference to the international law of reprisals. As this law requires that the state against which reprisals are taken must have, *inter alia*, committed an illegal act, and as the law concerning the limits of the territorial sea were so unclear, it must be doubted whether the Cambodian limit was *internationally* illegal and therefore whether the US action was lawful.

The Passage of the Kiev[4]

Another interesting incident concerned passage through an international strait and related to the voyage of the Soviet aircraft carrier *Kiev* through the Turkish Straits in 1976. These straits are regulated by the 1936 Montreux Convention which allows only 'capital' ships of Black Sea states to transit the Bosphorus, the Sea of Marmara and the Dardanelles which make up these straits, and defines these to include cruisers but specifically excludes aircraft carriers. This led to the absurdity that for political reasons the Turkish authorities permitted the *Kiev* to transit the straits, accepting the Soviet designation of the vessel as an 'anti-submarine cruiser' although it had a large flight deck, helicopters and other aircraft of board. A strict interpretation of the convention would clearly require passage to be refused but the political difficulties of renegotiating the convention to accommodate aircraft carriers are so great that the states concerned would rather accommodate the passage by stretching the existing terms of the convention.

Hot Pursuit: The Taiyo Maru Incident[5]

Another problem arising from the ambiguities of the Geneva Convention on the Territorial Sea and Contiguous Zone and from customary law concerns the application of the doctrine of hot pursuit to fisheries zones. It will be remembered that the convention permitted it from these two zones restricting it in the latter case to violations of the zonal regulations, the zone retaining its status as high seas. In 1974 the US by unilateral legislation – the Bartlett and the Contiguous Fisheries Zone Acts – prohibited fishing by foreign vessels in its then 3 mile territorial sea plus a 9 mile fisheries zone and extended its enforcement powers to the whole 12 mile belt. A Japanese fishing vessel, the *Taiyo Maru*, violated the fisheries zone and the United States Coast Guard engaged it in hot pursuit on to the high seas and arrested it. A United States court accepted that the fisheries zone was not a contiguous zone within the Geneva Convention, to which the US is a party, and that hot pursuit did not therefore *prima facie* apply to it. However, the court controversially also held that the convention's Article 24 was permissive, not restrictive and that the US could establish a contiguous zone for fisheries purposes and that hot pursuit could commence therefrom. One commentator considered this to be 'an assault on the Freedom of the Seas', later compounded by the US extension of its fishery zone to 200 miles in 1976. Since hot pursuit is a useful, probably essential, enforcement tool it seems likely that the sixty-eight to seventy states with extended fishery zones would now endorse the US action. In a recent parliamentary inquiry into the UK fishing industry, the Captain of the Royal Naval Fishery Protection Service stated in evidence that the UK would hotly pursue violators of its zone on to the high seas but not into a foreign fishing zone, although the latter retains the status of high seas. The fact that the UK relies mainly on its navy for enforcement purposes and not a Coast Guard may have influenced its decision.

FISHERIES

Traditional fisheries problems have been given complex new dimensions additional to that of hot pursuit, since the widespread claims to 200 mile fisheries zones seriously undermine the effectivity of existing Fishery Commissions. In the past, as outlined in Chapters 1 and 2, disputes arose from the concern of states with distant water fleets to limit coastal states' exclusive rights to a narrow band of territorial sea. The Anglo-Icelandic fisheries dispute was at first related to this issue.

The Anglo-Icelandic 'Cod War'[6]
Following the failure of UNCLOS I and II to establish either uniform limits or fishery zones, Iceland first asserted a 12 mile fishery limit in 1958 and extended it to 50 miles in 1972. The UK forcefully resisted Iceland's efforts to exclude its fishermen from first one, then the other limit.

The first so-called 'Cod War' was settled by an Exchange of Notes in 1961 following negotiations. The UK withdrew its objection to Iceland's 12 mile limit and agreed to phase out its fishermen from it within three years. The Notes recorded that Iceland would continue to 'work for' a 50 mile limit but that she would give the UK six months' notice of such extension and that disputes relating thereto would be referred, at the request of either party, to the ICJ. Iceland announced in 1971 that a 50 mile limit would be imposed in September 1971. The UK opposed this as illegal but endeavoured to negotiate on the basis of catch limitation. Negotiations failed and the UK referred the dispute to the ICJ which issued an Interim Order enjoining Iceland not to enforce the limits pending judgement.

Iceland ignored the order and in 1972 imposed the limit forcefully, alleging that the 1961 agreement had lapsed and in any case was void because it was obtained under duress. Iceland therefore contended that the ICJ did not have jurisdiction. The UK at first chartered unarmed tugs to protect its fishing vessels against the Icelandic gunboats' efforts to expel them but kept Royal Navy fishery protection vessels in the area. After several serious incidents, during which Icelandic patrol boats fired shots across the bows of UK vessels, the UK ordered the Royal Navy actively to protect its fishing vessels.

Iceland justified its extension by its exceptional economic dependence on fisheries whereas the UK was convinced that the disputed areas remained lawfully high seas. The UK claimed only a 12 mile fishery limit (6 miles exclusive, 6 miles subject to bilateral agreements with states with long-standing fishing practice therein) under the 1964 European Fishing Agreement. West Germany, which was also in dispute with Iceland, referred its case to the ICJ on similar grounds. Belgium negotiated a solution based on reduced catches.

In 1974 the ICJ, having decided that the 1961 agreement was a treaty in force and that it did therefore have jurisdiction, gave judgement. Iceland had feared that this would go against it because the court must apply existing law, not the changing law that might emerge from UNCLOS III, which was then under way. Iceland later took the view that even the first ISNT's articles concerning 200 mile fisheries zones were 'here to stay and form an indispensable part of the outcome'. The court, however, accepted that Iceland did have preferential rights to fisheries off its coast, arising from the fact that overfishing had necessitated a limitation on catches. It found, however, that this did not allow Iceland to exclude all fishing by other states. Iceland must have reasonable regard for the rights of other states which had been fishing there for a long time. International law required the parties to negotiate a solution, taking account of each other's rights. The court did not express an opinion on the amount of the total allowable catch or its distribution. It specifically followed the findings in the North Sea Continental Shelf cases that the negotiations should be based on equitable principles related to the circumstances of the case, stressing that 'it was not a matter of finding simply an equitable solution, but an equitable solution derived from the applicable law'. No doubt this judgement is having its effect in the search for a solution to the EEC fisheries dispute described below.

Iceland and the UK did reopen negotiations but the gap between the quotas sought by the UK and those offered by Iceland within the 200 mile belt proved too great for reconciliation, negotiations broke down and 'hostilities' resumed following Iceland's extension to a 200 mile limit in 1976. A temporary 'peace' resulted through the good offices of the Secretary-General of NATO, Dr Luns, after Iceland had threatened to withdraw its consent to the location of the NATO base in Keflavik, but when this short-term agreement expired in 1976 British vessels had to withdraw and a break in diplomatic relations between Iceland and the UK occurred. British vessels have never returned to Icelandic fishing grounds because it has never proved possible to negotiate mutual access on terms mutually acceptable to the EEC and to Iceland.

The EEC's Struggle to Develop a Common Fisheries Policy[7]
The UK's lack of success in attracting international support for its view that fisheries zones could not extend beyond the 12 miles agreed in the

European Fisheries Agreement led to a major change in UK policy at the first substantive session of UNCLOS III in Caracas in 1974. The UK announced that as part of a package deal treaty which must include, *inter alia*, freedom of passage through international straits, it would be prepared to consider 200 mile fisheries zones exclusive to coastal states, not, it should be noted, the EEZs favoured by African and South American states. As more states adopted the former, following their inclusion in the series of UNCLOS SNTs (the 1975 and the 1976 RSNT) the EEC announced that it too was considering recommending to its member states the adoption of such zones. The UK, which had in mind both the Icelandic débâcle and the current failure of NEAFC effectively to conserve North Sea fisheries (because of the political difficulties of restricting catches to the level required for conservation while the area remained high seas), announced in September 1976 that from 1 January 1977 it would extend its fishery limits to 200 miles, in concert with other EEC member states if possible, but unilaterally if need be. In October 1976 agreement on this course was reached at an EEC Council meeting and a few days later a Council resolution confirmed this policy for the North Sea and North Atlantic waters only of member states. The zones remain national zones (subject to the Rome Treaty requirements, however) as the EEC is not a state and cannot assert jurisdiction itself. This encouraged other states to follow suit and about ninety states have now extended their maritime jurisdiction in various forms, mostly as FZs but some asserting patrimonial or even territorial seas of 200 miles.

The EEC action, as outlined in Chapter 2, immediately subjected the new zones to the policies laid down for fisheries within member states' maritime jurisdiction in the Treaty of Rome, the Treaty of Accession (which enabled the entry of the UK, Denmark and Ireland into the EEC and permitted some derogations from the Rome Treaty requirements in the short term to protect local fishermen in some regions) and regulations made thereunder.[8] These required that a Common Fisheries Policy be adopted by 1978 for fishing in maritime waters subject to member states' sovereignty or within their jurisdiction and that the rules applied must not lead to differences in treatment of other members and in particular that equal conditions of access to, and use of, all fishing grounds in these waters must be ensured for all vessels registered in EEC member states and flying their flags.

The obligation to produce a common structural policy requires adoption of common rules and specific measures by member states to co-ordinate policies which must promote harmonious and balanced development of the fishing industry in the Community and encourage rational use of the biological resources, which necessitates that they be conserved. It has proved extremely difficult to negotiate such a policy permitting at the same time equal conditions of access. EEC regulations require the Council, on a proposal from the Commission, to adopt the measures necessary for conservation 'within the framework of economic growth and social progress and [to] ensure an equitable standard of living for the population which depends on fishing for its livelihood'. As fisheries in the area were so depleted following NEAFC's decline and as about 60 per cent of fish caught therein (formerly in a high seas area) now came within the UK's 200 mile zone the drastic reduction in TAC and stringent measures necessary for conservation, such as the closure of some traditional grounds to industrial fishing, having provoked an acrimonious dispute within the EEC.

The dispute has been exacerbated by the impact of the complete loss of the Icelandic fishing grounds on distant water fishing ports such as Fleetwood, Hull and Grimsby, the insistence of Denmark on continued industrial fishing for species such as Norway pout at the expense of fish for human consumption, and the UK's loss of opportunity, as a member of the EEC, for negotiating bilaterally for access to Norwegian and Icelandic fisheries. These problems have created acute political difficulties for both Labour and Tory governments in the UK who are caught between their legal obligations deriving from the Rome Treaty to negotiate a Common Fisheries Policy based on equal conditions of access for all member states and the forceful and persistent demands of all UK fishermen for wide exclusive belts.

The negotiations are further complicated by the case of Kramer and others,[9] a decision of the European Court of Justice, to which some Dutch fishermen took their protest against their government's imposition on them of NEAFC measures. They alleged (before the conclusion of an EEC CFP) that these could not be imposed on them since power to formulate conservation measures now lay with the Community (which had not exercised them). Kramer lost and in the course of its judgement the court held that the Community rules applied not only within member states' maritime jurisdiction but also to fishing by them on the high seas or in the waters of third countries. They also made it clear that the EEC as a Community has international personality and that member states must, under the Rome Treaty, ensure that the Community acts with a common policy in all international organisations of an economic character.

The judgement in this case encouraged the EEC's application to adhere to NEAFC as a Community. All EEC member states therefore withdrew from NEAFC (as well as the new NAFO (described later)). This caused the virtual collapse of NEAFC since the Eastern European states do not recognise the EEC as an international personality capable of ratifying the convention in its own right. The Kramer decision also implied – and member states readily acquiesced in this since a common front more easily enabled the expulsion of foreign fishermen from national zones or a reduction of their effort – that such foreign exploitation would be governed by agreements concluded by the Community (not individual member states) with these states, and that agreements for fishing opportunities in the zones of third states would also be negotiated by the Community. This creates a very different situation from that appertaining in the majority of non-EEC states with 200 mile zones which can negotiate bilateral agreements for reciprocal fishing rights, and have done so on a large scale. There has been public outcry in the UK at its inability to negotiate directly with Norway or Iceland for such rights. The EEC after 1 January 1977 did conclude short-term agreements with Eastern bloc and other states to fish in the EEC area. Failure to negotiate adequate reciprocal fishing rights in the USSR zone after it declared a 200 mile zone on a provisional basis (the USSR originally opposed 200 mile zones to protect its huge distant water fleets but accepted them once it recognised the trend) led, however, to the withdrawal of all Soviet and Eastern bloc vessels from the EEC zones. Some now, however, engage in 'klondyking', that is, transshipment from UK to foreign vessels which is not specifically prohibited under the UK fisheries legislation; they moor in UK waters and buy fish, such as mackerel in Falmouth, direct from UK vessels and process it into meal on board in UK waters. This has resulted in considerable local nuisance and problems with harbour and planning authorities which are now taking legal steps, amending their by-laws and other powers.

The EEC has concluded 'framework' agreements with some third states such as Norway and the Faroes (Denmark) but the failure to agree on a CFP held up final agreements. Because the EEC has had difficulty in establishing a TAC and quotas for its member states internally there was uncertainty concerning the amount surplus to EEC requirements which can be made available to third states. This has further disturbed UK fishermen who now find themselves drastically restricted when fishing in Norwegian waters, on their traditional grounds. The ICNT article 62 requires only that the surplus to the coastal states' harvesting capacity as determined by it be made available, on the basis of priorities laid down by the ICNT, a provision which conflicts with the Community's policy of internal free access for its members. The EEC hopes at UNCLOS to negotiate additions to the ICNT articles to permit regional preference schemes and to enable the EEC to adhere to any UNCLOS treaty as a Community. Meanwhile its member states have been endeavouring to harmonise their policies at UNCLOS, but because of the many conflicts of interests they have not been entirely successful: Belgium, for example, much preferred a regional approach to fisheries than adoption of 200 mile zones since her potential zone was much smaller than this and it has therefore still not declared one. Luxembourg, as a landlocked state, and West Germany, as a shelflocked and therefore geographically disadvantaged state, also have other interests.

Although other states, even Ireland (which originally resisted the Commission's proposals but withdrew its objections on receiving promises of specific concessions), have accepted the TACs suggested by the Commission and the criteria on which they were based, the UK still rejects them since it considers that, *inter alia*, the fact that the major part of the catch in Community zones is taken from the UK zone entitles it to a preferential share and that states which have in the past built up large industrial fisheries, which may be more ecologically harmful, should bear the brunt of the cuts in catch necessary to prevent over-exploitation. The UK asserts that it is more desirable to take fish for human consumption as the UK itself does.

In these circumstances it is not at all surprising that the Community has not been able to formalise a CFP though the Treaty of Accession required that this be done at the latest by 1978. The EEC has surmounted this difficulty by resorting to the fiction of 'stopping the clock'; for Community purposes the CFP negotiations are treated as though they were still taking place within that period. The treaty also requires, however, that by December 1982 the Commission must review and report on fisheries policy since the derogations to protect local fishermen which were permitted in the Accession Treaty expire in 1982 if not renegotiated. This would mean that member states would have equal access to each others' maritime waters, including the territorial sea and possibly internal waters, although it is not entirely clear whether the term 'maritime waters', which has no legal meaning, includes the latter. The Commission is desperately seeking a formula which will accommodate the UK demands and at the same time meet the interests of other member states without resorting to the NEAFC policy of fixing the TAC higher than the scientists advise that the stocks will bear if optimum yield is to be maintained. It is currently proposing allocations of non-traditional stocks, such as blue whiting, and allowing coastal state preferences based not on the variable exclusive belts of up to 50 miles which the UK demanded, but on vessel steaming time, which would favour local vessels without excluding, or unfairly discriminating against, vessels of other states, and which could be combined with the forwarding for approval by the Commission of the fishing plans of all vessels.

Meanwhile the UK, having insisted in 1976, when agreeing on concerted EEC 200 mile zones, that, pending a CFP, in cases of urgency member states should be permitted to enforce unilateral conservation measures, on certain conditions, has imposed a number of measures, such as preventing fishing for Norwegian pout (an industrial fishery) and use of certain mesh sizes, which the Commission does not accept as necessary for conservation. The matter has consequently now been referred to the European Court of Justice.

The EEC policies have created a major dispute of serious consequence primarily for its member states but which has drastic effects on third states also, such as the reduced allocation of quotas to them, their exclusion from many former grounds and the improved enforcement that national fisheries zones have enabled compared to the former NEAFC Joint Enforcement Scheme, under which vessels could only be reported to their flag state. The UK in 1977 boarded 1,546 foreign fishing vessels including those of EEC members, and prosecuted forty-two; by October 1978, 11,136 had been boarded and twenty prosecuted. The heavy fines imposed, often accompanied by confiscation of catch or gear or both, have provoked little protest since other states now have an interest in similar policies to deter over-exploitation. Intensive surveillance by ships and aircraft has been necessary to acquire the above figures, and it must be doubted whether developing countries will have the technical and financial resources properly to enforce their zonal regulations at the same level. The EEC has so far not pursued joint enforcement although the European Parliament has suggested that a European Coast Guard to enforce fisheries, pollution and other laws should be instituted. Regional bodies such as the EEC could also improve enforcement by co-ordinating inspection of landings in port and market checks; it seems likely that the rising cost of military methods, as fuel becomes scarce and dearer, may force this solution. Developing countries might follow this model. The EEC's regional solutions could become a model generally for enclosed or semi-enclosed seas if a CFP can be negotiated and made to work.

THE FUTURE OF FISHERIES COMMISSIONS[10]

Extensions of 200 mile fisheries zones have affected a large number of existing Commissions which, like NEAFC, are now seeking to adapt to the new situation which require constitutional and institutional changes, with a new approach to regulation and enforcement based on the consensus which has crystallised round the relevant parts of the UNCLOS SNTs. Commissions are, however, still needed, as NEAFC has concluded, for co-operation in collection of statistical information and its analysis; monitoring of environmental factors such as pollution; for stocks which traverse two or more national zones; for stocks which cross from the high seas to national zones; for stocks which remain exclusively in the high seas. The new North Atlantic Fisheries Organisation (NAFO) (replacing ICNAF) includes the giving of advice, on request, to member states concerning management of stocks within their zones. Scientific knowledge of the principles of fisheries management is still inadequate but has advanced and scientists are proposing that a more ecological approach is needed with more allowance for error arising from the inter-relationships between species, food chains and the marine environment generally.

The International Whaling Commission[11]
The policies of the IWC have been a source of major controversy in this respect but recently the IWC adopted New Management Procedures for assessing and protecting species and stocks of whales which go a long way to improve conservation, though they are subject to severe criticism from some cetologists, and the USA, in particular, is seeking to revise them. The IWC also strengthened its Secretariat and budget to cope with its new policies. More states, for example, the USA and Australia, are acting unilaterally, by means of their national legislation, to impose higher standards and are now banning whaling completely in their 200 mile zones in spite of Japanese protests. Two hundred mile zones create special problems for the IWC as whales migrate vast distances through many zones. There are also states whaling outside the Commission and thus not subject to its regulations; three (Chile, Ecuador and Peru, the originators of the 200 mile zones) belonged to a rival body until 1979 when Chile and Peru joined the IWC; the others were unregulated and remain so except for Spain and South Korea which joined the IWC in 1979. Portugal, China and North Korea amongst others remain outside. Even nationals of member states of the IWC whale without regulation by registering vessels under flags of convenience, such as Somalia and Cyprus. The activities of MV *Sierra* with a Norwegian captain and South African and Japanese crew are notorious in this respect. The IWC endeavours by recommendations and resolutions to persuade these states to join it; other non-binding resolutions urge member states not to trade in whale products and equipment with non-member states, and not to aid them by transferring equipment or personnel or providing advice and know-how. A new Convention on Trade in Endangered Species (CITES) lists these and requires states parties to follow similar tactics. At its 1979 meeting it controversially listed all cetaceans in one or other of its annexes. In June 1979 a Convention on Migratory Species of Wild Animals listing some whales as requiring international protection was concluded. It is likely to have a wider membership than the IWC. Economic sanctions are however difficult to enforce and evasions are frequent. The IWC is considering extending its unique International Observer Scheme to more species and areas but this will improve enforcement only at sea and at land stations; it will not cover national imports and exports in contravention of CITES. Outside pressures from national and international legislation are, however, having a considerable impact on the whaling members of the IWC and at the 31st meeting in July 1979, not only did six new members (four whaling and two non-whaling states, Sweden and Seychelles) join it, bringing the membership to its highest ever (twenty-three), but a moratorium on pelagic whaling was accepted, except for minke whales taken by Japan. The USSR's operations in the Antarctic will be ended. At the Seychelles initiative the Indian Ocean was declared a whale sanctuary.

The Northwest Atlantic Fisheries Organisation[12]

The USA, in its Fishery Conservation and Management Act, required that states seeking access to the part of the catch in its 200 mile zone surplus to US requirements enter into bilateral agreements, enforced by US national means. Bilateral agreements have proliferated following the declaration of so many 200 mile zones.[13] This and similar Canadian legislation led to the International Commission for Northwest Atlantic Fisheries being replaced by NAFO. As most of the area covered by the new agreement is within the Canadian 200 mile zone, Canada was able, by making access to fisheries within its zone contingent on participating in NAFO, to ensure the speedy ratification of NAFO's constituent treaty and it entered into force in January 1979. Since the naming of the states party has been avoided it has proved possible for both the USSR and the EEC to become parties to it and the new NEAFC.

NAFO is more limited in scope than ICNAF in that quotas are set nationally, but it establishes a Fishery Commission, backed by a General Council of all states party; and a Scientific Council which will advise on optimum yield taking account of ecological factors, act as a forum for consultation, co-operation, compilation of statistics, dissemination of reports, and so on, on fisheries, and, at the request of coastal states or the Commission, provide scientific advice on management inside and outside the coastal states' zones respectively. The Commission can formulate proposals for joint actions by parties to achieve optimum utilisation of fisheries, taking into account the coastal states' management measures within their jurisdiction and the inter-relationship of stocks. NAFO, however, retains the objections procedure which undermined previous bodies – it should be less objectionable now that the major part of the area is not subject to high seas freedom of fishing. NAFO provides for negotiation of a joint enforcement scheme. It introduces innovatory financial arrangements: contributions are based, and graded, on a combination of several criteria – coastal state catches, all state catches, equal shares. It may well become a model for renegotiated fisheries bodies.

Sedentary Species

The problems to which the Continental Shelf Convention gave rise because of its ambiguous definition of these species and its inclusion of them within the resources of the continental shelf (as described in Chapter 1) have been removed by the adoption of 200 mile fishery zones since these give the coastal state sovereign rights to exploit both the living and non-living resources and the previous arbitrary distinction becomes irrelevant. There will remain some, but very few, sedentary species which fall under the continental shelf doctrine where the continental margin extends beyond 200 miles but the former disputes concerning lobsters and crabs should not recur.

REGIONAL ARRANGEMENTS AND EXCLUSIVE ECONOMIC ZONES[14]
The growing number of uses of the sea and the overlapping of extended
jurisdictions in some areas resulting from claims to a 12 mile territorial
sea, in the 200 mile fisheries or exclusive economic zones, are leading
some states to seek regional solutions to their problems but this is not
such a simple option as it sounds. There are many preliminary problems,
the most important or which is defining the region concerned as there are
no criteria for this laid down by international law. A dictionary
definition is '*any* area or district, especially one characterized in some
way'. Such regional agreements concerning maritime problems as do
exist have a wide variety of characteristics. They include the EEC, the
primary objective of which is economic protection which includes protection of fisheries and the marine environment, and NATO, a defence
organisation, which through its Committee on the Challenges of
Modern Society has extended its interest to protection of the marine
environment. Some bodies relate to a particular area, such as the Baltic
Commission, or to particular functions (the London Convention on
Ocean Dumping), or both (the Oslo Convention on Dumping in the
North Atlantic; the Paris Convention for Prevention of Land-based
Sources of Pollution in the same area). The Fisheries Commissions have
already been referred to: they too vary – their terms of reference may be
geographical (the North Atlantic Fisheries Organisation), species
specific (International Pacific Halibut Convention) or functional (Convention for the Regulation of Whaling). Other regional organisations
are based on proximity and wide common interests (the Nordic
Council).

The UNCLOS text particularly, which generates many new roles for
regional bodies, urges in ICNT article 123 that 'states bordering
enclosed or semi-enclosed seas should co-operate with each other in
their exercise of the rights and duties' under any convention and that
they should try to do this directly or through 'an appropriate regional
organization'. This may give rise to considerable dispute given the
choice of organisations that the variety of criteria on which they are
based gives rise to, as illustrated above. The North Sea, for example, has
at least a dozen organisations whose activities impinge on these
objectives and in almost all of them (membership of which is disparate)
the states party are in dispute whether the issues concern prevention of
pollution or fisheries because of the political, economic and social
implications of these issues. None the less, states are increasingly
endeavouring to co-operate through such bodies whilst retaining
ultimate national control over policy decisions.

Exclusive economic zones, where adopted (and in the North Sea
region only marginal states such as Norway and France have formulated their extension of 200 mile jurisdiction in this form), will give
states the opportunity to co-ordinate their national maritime policies

more effectively than before but they also encourage chauvinism and a tendency to regard, wrongly, the new area as part of the state territory to be defended against all foreign intrusion. About half the approximately ninety states claiming 200 mile jurisdiction at the present time do so in the form of an EEZ, most others claim only fisheries jurisdiction (as does the UK), but some South American states have claimed a 200 mile territorial sea, for example, Ecuador, Brazil and Argentina. The latent jurisdictional ambiguities in these zones are highly likely to cause conflict unless regional solutions are arrived at.

One advantage of EEZs, however, even if limited to fisheries jurisdiction, is that they resolve the former dispute concerning whether some species are resources of the continental shelf and therefore exclusive to the coastal state, or of the high seas above and therefore open to free access. In the late 1960s major disputes occurred over this question between France and Brazil over lobsters, and between the USA and Japan, and the USSR and Japan concerning the status of Alaskan king crabs. Under the extended EEZ or fisheries zones, virtually all these species (since few of them exist beyond 200 miles from the coast) would clearly be subject to coastal state control.

DELIMITATION OF THE CONTINENTAL SHELF

The Outer Limit: The Rockall Dispute[15]
The problems arising from the Continental Shelf Convention's definition of the outer limit in terms of depth and exploitability beyond 200 metres have been described in Chapters 3 and 4, as have the ICNT proposals, following the North Sea Continental Shelf cases, that the shelf includes the whole of the coastal state's 'natural prolongation' to the edge of the continental margin and that 'islands which cannot sustain human habitation or economic life of their own' should attract neither continental shelf nor EEZ rights, although the Geneva Conventions accepted that islands (defined as areas of land above water) did have shelf rights. ICNT (Rev. I) proposes that the margin's limit be fixed by a choice of formulae based on the so-called Russian formula, ultimately limiting it to 350 miles from the territorial sea baselines, or the Irish formula, relating it to the depth of sediment on the continental rise. These proposals remain *de lege ferenda* and a dispute has arisen between Ireland and the UK concerning the delimitation of the UK shelf west of the mainland of Scotland, off the Hebridean Islands and Rockall Islet. The dispute centres on the question of whether Rockall, a tiny uninhabitable rocklet 180 miles west of Barra, can, since islands are not defined in the Geneva Conventions to exclude such rocks, be used as a basepoint. Ireland, unlike the UK, has not ratified the Geneva Conventions and the ICJ found in the North Sea cases that West Germany was not (in the circumstances of that case) bound by the Conventions' delimitation provisions.

The UK and Ireland have agreed to refer the dispute, not to the ICJ, but to arbitration, following Irish protests after Britain designated under the UK Continental Shelf Act areas off the Rockall Bank which Ireland considered fell within her sector. The court's decision is likely to be influenced not only by the North Sea cases but by the 1977 and 1978 decisions in the UK-French Channel and South Western Approaches Arbitration, since it will not only raise questions concerning the outer limit of the shelf but, as in that case, delimitation between both opposite and adjacent states, as the UK and Ireland face both situations because of the geography and geology of the disputed areas.

Delimitation between Opposite and Adjacent States: the UK–French Case[16]

The North Sea cases had concerned delimitation between adjacent states, one of which had not ratified the Geneva Convention, and the ICJ found that the Convention's article 6 (which laid down that in the absence of agreement (on another line), and if there are no special circumstances, between opposite states a median line equidistant from the baselines of the territorial sea should be drawn, and for adjacent states, subject to the same qualifications, a line of equidistance) had not become a rule of customary law binding non-parties. The UK–French Channel case of 1977–8 was the first in which both disputants were parties to the convention. The court found however that in practice there was little difference between the equitable principles applied in the North Sea cases and the effect of taking into consideration 'special circumstances' under the convention, where these existed, as they did in the present case. It decided that they should be used for the purpose of mitigating the inequity that would be produced by them if a line of strict equidistance was used and the parties were on the same shelf – as in this case. The court, somewhat arbitrarily in the view of the UK, decided that equity required that the Channel Islands (UK islands, some situated as close as 6.6 nautical miles to the French coast) should therefore be accorded only a 12 mile continental shelf, so that France could have shelf rights beyond them to mid-Channel, and that the distortion south-westwards resulting from an equidistance line drawn from a baseline based on the Scilly Islands required that its angle be so bisected that it be given only a half effect – thus giving France a larger sector to the south and west.

This decision is likely to have considerable effect on future delimitations throughout the world, especially the dispute referred to below, and other disputes concerning islands.

The Graeco–Turkish Dispute in the Aegean Sea[17]

Oil was found under the Greek island of Thassos in 1972. It was indicated that the deposits spread thinly but widely in the Aegean Sea. In

1973 Turkey published a claim to twenty-seven areas in the Aegean, which Greece promptly objected to on the grounds that these were part of her continental shelf.

There are about a thousand isles and islets in the Aegean; many of these, which are under Greek sovereignty, are close to the Turkish coast, the nearest only about a mile away. If each island is claimed to generate its own continental shelf, the Turkish shelf would be very restricted. Turkey, stating that it 'would never allow the Aegean to become a Greek lake', ignored the presence of the Greek islands, many of which are uninhabited, in asserting its claims in 1973 which it based on a median line drawn from the mainland baselines of the two states.

Greece, which had ratified the Geneva Convention (Turkey had not), claimed that all islands attracted shelf rights; Turkey responded that as they were on her geological shelf they were part of the natural prolongation of her land territory.

There have been several abortive attempts at negotiation and the case was referred to the International Court of Justice in 1977. There are many special circumstances in this case which are likely to be taken account of in any judgement, as they were in the Channel case.[18]

ISLANDS

In addition to the kind of delimitation disputes generated by the uncertain status of islands in effecting division of submarine areas, because of their non-definition in the Continental Shelf Convention, and very brief definition in the separate Convention on the Territorial Sea (bearing in mind that parties to the latter are necessarily parties to the former and vice versa, and that some states are party to neither), islands have given rise to other kinds of disputes. Because of their value as basepoints for claims to contiguous submarine areas, title to some groups of islands has been forcefully disputed.

Disputes Concerning Offshore Islands in South-east Asia[19]
For example, Kampuchea's claimed continental shelf boundaries pass through islands belonging to Thailand and Vietnam in the Gulf of Siam and are disputed by them. The dispute centres on the historical basis of the claims to various small islands. Various attempts at negotiation have failed.

A more serious dispute is that between the People's Republic of China (whose position is supported by the Republic of China (Taiwan) on this issue), Vietnam and the Philippines concerning the title to the Parrcel Islands in the South China Seas. This led to an outbreak of violence between the PRC and South Vietnam in 1974 which resulted in the PRC's forceful seizure of these islands.

In the East China Seas both the PRC and Taiwan dispute Japan's claim to the Senkaku (Tiao-yu-Tlai) Islands. They also, in the South China Seas, contests the Philippines' claim to various of the Spratley Islands, ninety-six small islands scattered over an area of about 180,000 square kilometres. Six of the islands were occupied and garrisoned by the Philippines in 1971, Vietnam garrisoned three islands in 1974, Taiwan has been in possession of a single island since the Second World War, the PRC vociferously asserts a claim to the islands but so far has not sent troops. The Philippines has been the most active in asserting its claim, which is based partly on the islands' closeness to its territory, their location on its continental shelf (although some are 250 miles away and separated by a trough in the shelf), and partly on the contention that the islands are derelict and open to occupation. Oil exploration is taking place under licence from the Philippines but the strategic importance of the islands to China, since they command the southern entrance to the South China Sea, makes it unlikely that it will abandon its claim.

THE 'BOAT PEOPLE'

It was pointed out in Chapter 1 that the Geneva Convention on the High Seas (article 12(i)), which purports to codify the customary international law, obliges every state to order the masters of its flag ships, with certain exceptions in favour of the safety of the vessel and its crew, to render assistance 'to any person found at sea in danger of being lost' and to rescue speedily 'persons in distress, if informed of their need of assistance, as far as this can reasonably be expected'.

The language of the convention is broad but vague. It does not specifically require masters to take these people on board, it does not lay down the criteria for assessing the danger concerned or the degree of need of help, but none the less there is a clear duty not to refuse any kind of help in the kind of desperate situation that many of the boat people have found themselves on the high seas. A ship, however, is not equated with territory so that taking refugees on board does not confer the nationality of the flag state upon them. Most states moreover have specific legal requirements for granting their citizenship, and there are also different views on the law of asylum; some states grant asylum only if the refugee's life is urgently threatened by political persecution. The 'boat people's' motives for leaving Vietnam may not be considered by many states to meet their criteria for asylum, hence the disputes that have arisen concerning their admission into harbour. Their continuous passage through the territorial sea, however, should not be impeded; it is clearly innocent, within both the treaty and customary law, and should be unimpeded. The international community seems to be realising that an international solution must be found to provision of ultimate resting places for these maritime nomads.

CONCLUSION

Although states pursue their national interest in the uses they make of the oceans, and although conflicts do arise, they have on the whole sought to resolve these disputes by peaceful means using traditional methods such as negotiation, both bilateral and multilateral, treaties, international organisations, global and regional, and have recently, as their uses of the sea have intensified and proliferated, established new bodies to harmonise their management policies. These are, of course, imperfect and fraught with political and economic problems but they are a dynamic contribution to rationalisation of interstate relations with a maritime dimension.

States have resorted to unilateral action only when there are gaps in the law, new activities or new factors (including the emergence of new developing states). The Truman Proclamation, the Canadian Arctic Waters Pollution Act and the Patrimonial Sea Declarations evidence such initiatives. States have subsequently sought to legitimate these interests by international negotiations – using bodies such as the UN, IMCO and diplomatic conferences such as UNCLOS. They have negotiated compromises with some success; the 200 mile fishery zone has almost certainly become part of customary law as a result of the UNCLOS negotiations.

Bi- and trilateral disputes concerning continental shelf delimitation have been referred to the international court, as in the North Sea case, but this is exceptional; there is a marked preference for resort to arbitration, as in the UK–French case, which enables the parties to the dispute to choose their own judges, which they perceive as a better safeguard of their interests. It is in respect of dispute settlement machinery that the most noticeable gap in the new regimes appears. In spite of the trend to regional organisations it has not been accompanied by establishment of regional dispute settlement machinery (though NATO was used in the Icelandic fisheries dispute), apart from the bilateral Frigg Field Agreement. The EEC's Court of Justice is limited to disputes concerning the Rome Treaty. An UNCLOS treaty might, therefore, with its innovatory maritime dispute settlement proposals, fulfil a useful role. That treaty is, however, being delayed by the biggest current problem of all – the institution of a legal regime for the exploitation of the seabed areas beyond national jurisdiction, which is detailed in Chapters 3 and 8.

The most notable features of the past decade have undoubtedly been the trend to 200 mile jurisdiction and to regional organisations for a variety of purposes, and the interactions between these two new factors. It is to be hoped that the latter will be more effective in providing, in the context of this new jurisdiction, forums for the resolution of political and economic difficulties than were the earlier Fisheries Commissions whose failures (which were, of course, the failures of their member states to compromise their national interests instead of those of the fish) initiated the trend to extended coastal state jurisdiction. Extended national jurisdiction does provide the means for improved enforcement, the weakness of which also contributed to the failures of many Fisheries Commissions, but, as fuel prices rise, the cost to states, especially developing states, of maintaining the necessary aerial and maritime surveillance may become more than they can bear, and it is likely that we shall eventually see a trend to joint enforcement schemes for regional and functional purposes.

The trend to regional organisations is reinforced by the requirements of the ICNT (Rev. I) which makes many references to the need to develop standards and so on by means of 'competent international organisations'. A law of the sea treaty, or customs based on ICNT, would require such tasks either to be voluntarily assumed by or to be allocated to existing bodies. A recent study of the ICNT's implications[20] concluded that there is no case for the creation of a new global international organisation within the UN system to deal with ocean affairs, though new regional bodies may be needed. There is certainly a need for organisations to take stock of their existing programmes and to assess the directions and emphasis of their activities in the light of the emergence of a regime such as that under consideration at UNCLOS. There is a need to minimise overlap and improve communications between existing bodies at the regional and international level. Internationally this can be done by improving the UN's ACC (Administrative Committee for Co-ordination); regionally new bodies may be needed; there is, for example, no overview body in the North Sea though there are Commissions for the Baltic and Mediterranean. An evaluation of the proliferation of regional bodies indicates the need to rationalise their activities and to consider the definition of 'region' for this purpose. It is possible that more joint use could be made of existing Secretariats, as is done by the OSPARCOM. This could overcome some of the problems described whilst minimising the growth of international bureaucracy.

The objective of the law of the sea is to create order and avoid conflicts. International organisations have a role to play in this but the changing law and the additional requirements that it imposes on such bodies raises new problems of possible conflicts between them, for which new regulatory mechanisms must be found.

NOTES AND REFERENCES

1   ICNT (Rev. I) A/CONF. 62/WP.10/Rev. I, 28 April 1979.
2   A. Akinsanya, 'The Pueblo affair and international law', *Indian Law Journal*, vol. 15 (1975), pp. 485–505.
3   R. E. Ward, 'The Mayaguez: the right of innocent passage and the legality of reprisal', *San Diego Law Review*, vol. 13 (1976), pp. 765–73.

4   F. D. Froman, 'Kiev and the Montreux Convention: the aircraft carrier that became a
     cruiser to squeeze through the Turkish Straits', *San Diego Law Review*, vol. 14 (1977),
     pp. 681–717.
5   E. A. Sisco, 'Hot pursuit from a contiguous fisheries zone – an assault on the freedom
     of the high seas', ibid., pp. 656–80.
6   *Fisheries Dispute between the United Kingdom and Iceland 14 July 1972 to 19 May
     1973*, Cmnd 5341; Fisheries Jurisdiction Case, UK v Iceland (Merits) 1974, *ICJ
     Report*, p. 31.
7   'The fishing industry', *5th Report from Expenditure Committee 1977–78, Trade and
     Industry Sub-Committee (TISC)*, Vol. II, Evidence Taken to 18 May 1977, pp. 93–4,
     qus 385–8.
8   *TISC Report*, op. cit., Vol. I, Report and Appendix I to Minutes of Evidence,
     Appendix I, P. W. Birmie, 'The history of the EEC Common Fisheries Policy',
     pp. 92–118, E. D. Brown, 'Sea use planning and the North Sea; law of the sea:
     neglected issues, *Proceedings of the Law of the Sea Institute's 12th Annual Conference,
     October 23–26, 1978* (The Hague, Netherlands), pp. 436–80'
9   *Kramer and others, European Court of Justice, Joined Cases*, nos. 3/76, 4/76, 6/76, July
     1976.
10 FAO, 'Progress and problems of regional fisheries bodies', COFI/77/10, March 1977.
11 J. Scarff, 'The international management of whales, dolphins and porpoises: an
     interdisciplinary assessment', *Ecology Law Quarterly*, vol. 6 (1977) pp. 323–638.
12 'New Convention on North West Atlantic Fisheries signed', *Canada Weekly*, vol. 6,
     no. 45 (8 November 1978), p. 6; the convention was signed on 24 October 1978.
13 J. E. Carroz and M. J. Savini, 'The new international law of fisheries emerging from
     bilateral agreements, *Marine Policy*, vol. 3 (1979), pp. 79–98.
14 P. Birnie, 'The North Sea: a challenge of disorganised opportunities?', in *Europe and
     the Sea: The Case For and Against a New International Regime and its Approaches*,
     proceedings of Greenwich Forum Conference (V), 2–4 May 1979, publication
     forthcoming.
15 E. D. Brown, 'Rockall and the limits of national jurisdiction of the UK – Part I,
     Marine Policy, vol. 2, no. 3 (July 1978), pp. 181–211; Part II, ibid., no. 4 (October
     1978), pp. 275–303.
16 E. D. Brown, 'The Anglo–French Continental Shelf case', *San Diego Law Review*,
     vol. 16, no. 3 (1979), pp. 461–530.
17 L. Gross, 'The dispute between Greece and Turkey concerning the continental shelf in
     the Aegean', *AJIL*, vol. 71 (1977), pp. 31–59.
18 D. E. Karl, 'Islands and the delimitation of the continental shelf: a framework for
     analysis' *AJIL*, vol. 71 (1977), pp. 642–73.
19 La Yong Leng, 'Offshore boundary disputes in southeast Asia', *Journal of Southeast
     Asian Studies* (1978), pp. 175–89.
20 J. D. Kingham and D. M. McRae, 'Competent international organisations and the
     law of the sea', *Marine Policy*, vol. 3 (1979), pp. 106–32, at pp. 127–32.

Index

Adair Red 120
Aegean 2, 184–5, 189 n.17
Aguilar, Andrés 160, 165
Amerasinghe, H. Shirley 155, 158
Amoco Cadiz 108, 117, 118, 122, 127 n. 22–3, 165
Anchoveta 31
Arab Group 156
Arab, tanker fleet 136
Arbitration 23–4, 183–4
Arctic 2, 25, 60; and Canadian Pollution Act 187
Argentina 46, 158, 183; shipping policy of 133
Asian Group 158
Australia: attitude to deep seabed mining 71, 160; fisheries management policies 39; involvement in seabed mining 67

Baltic Conventions 7 n. 6
Barcelona Convention 114
Barents Sea 1, 43, 47, 59
Base line: for measuring territorial sea 15–16; and archipelagic areas 61, 160; and continental shelf 61–3; and delimitation 184–5; and exclusive economic zone 58–60
Belgium,174; attitude to fisheries regimes 177
Blue whale, as unit of measurement 40–1
Bonn Agreement 116, 125
Boundary, types of maritime 10–11, 12–13, 16, 21–4, 44–7, 58–63, 155, 158–60, 174, 182–6
Bowett, D. 26 n. 14
Brazil 102; attitude to Exclusive Economic Zone 159, and deep seabed mining 71
Britain, approach to maritime limits: 9, 174, 178, 184; and fishing limits 19, 21; and liability for oil pollution damage from off-shore installations 116; and pollution control 113–14, 120; changes policy on fishery limits 175; conflict with EEC over Common Fisheries Policy 174–9; and exacerbated by cod war 176; continental shelf dispute with France 23, 184; dispute with Ireland over Rockall 183–4; importance of UK EEZ fish stock 176; involvement in deep seabed mining 66–7; membership of EEC prevents bilateral fisheries arrangements 176–7;

policy at UNCLOS on marine scientific research 165–6; and marine environment 167 n. 5; and seabed mining 162–3, 168 n. 18; North Sea oil reserves 83–4, 87–93; and boundary agreements 85–7; and development of reserves 109; and policy on American involvement 102; opposition to Latin American concept of EEZ 175; role at UNCLOS 156, 167 n. 5; scope for fish farming 33; under appreciation of North Sea oil 78
Bulgaria 155, 157

Cabotage 133
Cameroon 157
Canada 41, 64, 80; attitude to seabed mining régime 70–1, 164; concern over pollution in Arctic waters 2, 161; role in establishing new NAFO 46
Capelin 29
Cargo sharing 135–6
Caribbean Sea 59
Caspian Sea 59
Castaneda, J. 160
Celebes Sea 59
Challenger, expedition 55
Chile 12–13, 41, 158, 164; proclamation of 200 mile zone 13
Civil Liability Convention 125
Cobalt 69–70
Command of the sea 148–9
Common Fisheries Policy: origin 48; and criteria for management 49–50; political difficulties over 174–9
Common Heritage of Mankind, concept of 5–6
Contiguous zone 16, 60, 172
Continental margin 63–4, and wide margin states 63
Continental shelf: definition of 12, 21, 58, 61–3; delimitation disputes 181, 183–5, 187, 189 n. 16–19; extent of 79; jurisdiction over 23–4, 59
Continental Shelf Convention 12 n. 14, 21–22, 26 n. 27, 181
Conventions 126 n. 5, 39–44; areas covered 115, 119; limited coordination 98, 110, 115–16; poor enforcement, 117; problem of entry into force 116–17

Danish North Sea Fishery 29